RELENTLESS

Thirty Years of Sepultura

JASON KOROLENKO

Dave,
Thanks for the years of killer drumming and killer riffs. Frontliner for life!

[signature]

188

First published in the United Kingdom in 2014 by
Essential Works Limited

ISBN: 9781906615925

10 9 8 7 6 5 4 3 2 1

rocket88books.com

CONTENTS

FOREWORD

Brazil.

1983.

Nothing, absolutely nothing happened in our music scene that was truly worthy of emphasis, but in the Belo Horizonte area, state of Minas Gerais, something was about to appear that would change the status quo forever.

In São Paulo everything was beautiful and wonderful, we had a scene full of metal heads enjoying the various heavy metal bands from other countries who were starting to become legends here, bands like Iron Maiden, Judas Priest, Saxon, and Black Sabbath who reigned at the time. Bands from the United States were also beginning to arrive at full throttle: Metallica, Anthrax, Slayer, Exodus, and many others. But nothing happened here. We had only a few bands that wanted to have fun playing their own songs mixed in with a few bad covers of their favorite bands' numbers.

Record executives at Brazilian companies began to recognize this emerging musical niche though, and some compilations began to emerge that highlighted the scene in São Paulo. Very soon there followed collections from Rio do Janeiro and Minas Gerais, focusing their attention on local bands.

The compilations that would gain most prominence amongst metal heads were the now famous *Metal SP 1* and *Metal SP 2*. Both included great bands, but few of them had earned a place in the top league of heavy/thrash metal at the time. Among them Korzus and Virus would be the most popular, but still nothing glorious had come out of Brazil.

1984.

In the Belo Horizonte area things were starting to happen. Two bands were gaining ground with the long-suffering Brazilian Bangers. From Rio de Janeiro came Dorsal Atlântica, and from Belo Horizonte some kids who looked like crazy guys arrived with full force: Sepultura. The name itself drew attention simply for being bizarre. *Sepultura!? Fuck, that name is different*, we thought. *Who knows if the sound will be, too?*

In the late 70s, early 80s, headbangers from Brazil had to have cassette tapes. It was a mandatory item for anyone who wanted to stay updated on the heavy metal scene. Too few people could buy vinyl. We listened to everything metal on tapes that were swapped among us, looking for something that sounded really brutal and rotten. Many bands tred to please us, but with no luck: we were too demanding!

And then we found a record company—Cogumelo Records— which released a split album that would changemetal history forever.

The two bands featured would provide the definitive article for everyone here who yearned for change. One side was by Overdose, who were similar to the international bands that already existed at the time, but the other side had Sepultura, who–finally– offered us the sound we wanted. Soon all of Brazil knew about these 'crazy looking' kids. The split album had to be re-pressed several times. Finally, it seemed, things were changing for the better. In a short time more and more copies sold out in specialty shops, including the most famous, the historical Woodstock store in the downtown of our beloved Sampa. Sepultura soon became the main topic of conversation in bars, and then they could be seen and heard on stage in Brazil, blasting everything to pieces!

From 1985 to 1987, Sepultura did not stop. They played in several cities and venues with zero structure, but their will to play was so gigantic that they overcame difficulties with incredible courage, creating a mystical aura by playing legendary, over-whelming shows. The release of *Morbid Visions* (1986) and *Schizophrenia* (1987) brought them greater opportunities to tour the country, and they played in places where it had previously seemed that metal had never been heard before, in the most remote areas of Brazil. Sepultura had to be where the fans were. It has always been that way, and it remains so to this day.

After overwhelming their homeland Sepultura became a global success and that is the story told in this book.

The Sepultura Official Brazilian fan club was founded in 1990. In those days, our glorious Sepultura were surrounded by many friends. But we didn't see anyone offering themselves up to work, to support the band in Brazil and abroad, so we decided to talk with Max and Igor, and later Paulo and Andreas about our ideas. Thus, after several years of dedication to the band, we felt that it was time to do what many had not even thought about. With great honor, pride, and respect, we hoisted the Sepultura flag on our headquarters located in São Paulo's downtown, to show our admiration and to guide fans from all over the world!

After that we started to help to promote the band. Over time, we built a shield to capture all the positive and negative energies that were directed toward the band. We faced many disagreements, and things that I can't even begin to tell you. Sepultura were both loved and hated by many people for trivial and personal reasons. Many people aimed their anger at us fans, those who decided out of pure pride to have a headquarters to highlight the band's art. Several times we had to withstand the bad vibes that envious people mercilessly sent for the band, and that's why, for many years, we were an essential link between Sepultura and their fans.

Although everything appeared to the outside world to be wonderful at the time, during all those years we faced many obstacles, fighting for the band, doing the right things for Sepultura, to keep their work always in evidence. This has always been our purpose, to fight for the band, to defend it. When Sepultura were eliminated from the lineup of the Hollywood Rock Festival, we immediately began a campaign for them to be added back into the schedule, and we got it done through the dedication that all fans had for the band.

We were tireless! For many years, myself, Sergio Caffe, and Airton Soares did everything to keep the Sepultura flame alive.

The SOBFC always had support from many families, friends, and fans of Sepultura, and I will name a few of the club members and legends here: Vânia Cavalera, Sr. Simão Bass (RIP), the Bass family, Alberto Turco Loco and the Hiar family, Sr. Paulo (RIP), Dna. Odete, the Xisto and Pinto families, Sr. Mario, Dna. Olga and the Perissinotto family, Sr. Siegfried, Dna. Anna Maria, the Kisser family, Djalma Thrashão, Tom, Cição, André Sapo, Tuka Quinelli, Japoneis, Kazu Nishimori, Gil Cubas, Fabricio from Hell, Billy Waldo and Pancho, among others from this gigantic Sepulnation who helped out on several occasions.

Such victories as have been achieved are due to our belief in a band that always does the most honest thing. Sepultura always remain honest and true to their several generations of fans, and always have done from the very beginning until today.

SO, KEEP MOVING AHEAD, SEPULNATION!

Have a good read

ANTONIO VICENTE COELHO (TONINHO)
Founder and President of the Sepultura Official Brazilian Fan Club

PREFACE

Sepultura enjoyed a very good year in 1996.

Or did they?

The popularity of heavy music comes in waves, and when it's not "cool" to like this visceral, aggressive style of music, it goes largely underground. Many devotees would argue that this is where it belongs. In the early 80s, for example, bands like Metallica and Slayer weren't even a blip on the mainstream radar. These long haired, pissed off teenagers recruited their fans one by bloody one, inciting violent mosh pits in the smallest, most decrepit venues, and trading tapes with kids all over the world who hungered for something more *real* than the shit MTV passed off as "metal" at the time.

In the first half of the 90s, the grunge movement invaded the music scene, spawning an army of clones dressed in flannel. By 1996, depression was cool. Doc Marten boots were cool.

Metal was not cool.

But a few bands had broken out and risen into a sort of "mainstream" of metal. Metallica were, of course, the first, leading the way for the other three of the 'Big Four'; Megadeth, and to a lesser extent, Anthrax and Slayer. Pantera did it too, and without compromising an ounce of brutality in their music.

February of '96 saw the release of Sepultura's groundbreaking *Roots*, an album that heavily integrated the music and rhythms of the band's native Brazil. Their sound had evolved through black metal and death metal and straight-razor thrash of earlier material into something slower and sludgier, down-tuned, with a groove that made your hips swing as much as your head bang. On *Roots* they collaborated with such stars as Brazilian percussionist Carlinhos Brown, Korn's Jonathan Davis, and Mike Patton of Faith No More. Even the Xavante indian tribe from northern Brazil made appearances.

The album debuted at number twenty-seven on the Billboard charts in the US, an incredible feat for such a band in those days, and went on to sell over 2 million copies internationally. It topped "Best of the Year" charts around the world. It received rave reviews from *The New York Times* and *The Los Angeles Times*, two of the influential newspapers in the United States. The innovative mix of metal and Brazilian rhythms prompted MTV (at a time when the M in the channel's name still stood for Music) to consider them "perhaps the most important heavy metal band of the 90s."

Not bad for a group of Brazilian youngsters who—though forming in 1984—hadn't played a show outside of their own country until 1989.

Sepultura toured relentlessly throughout the US, returned to South America for a triumphant series of hometown dates, played massive stadium gigs at festivals all over Europe, even soldiered through a set at Castle Donington in the United Kingdom as a three-piece after vocalist and co-founder Max Cavalera was forced home to Phoenix for the funeral of his stepson.

They were no longer solely a Brazilian phenomenon, but a worldwide phenomenon, having brought a slice of their homeland to almost every corner of the globe.

Yet, while everything seemed fine from the outsider's point of view, 1996 on the whole was the most miserable year of the band's storied career. And ten short months after the release of *Roots*, at the absolute peak of their popularity—and to everyone's surprise—Max left the band he had founded with his brother twelve years prior.

Suddenly, there was a very real possibility that Sepultura's career was finished, just as they were on the verge of breaking through to an unbelievable level of success.

ONE

MORBID BRAZILIAN DEVASTATION

We are products of environment, molded through family traditions and the lessons of those who came before us, our behaviors and personalities shaped by our languages and our cultures. Nature and nurture at not at war; instead, they collaborate, experiment, and work to develop the most important part of a person's structure; the ideals, beliefs, and morals that run much deeper than this tenuous organ we call skin.

To understand people, we must seek to understand the complex environments in which they were cultured. To understand Sepultura, as a band, and many of the individuals who populate their story, we must first seek to understand the political and economic climates of Brazil during a period of devastating change—the military dictatorship that lasted from 1964 to 1985—for it was against this backdrop that most of the band's members grew up.

It is also worth noting that Sepultura's first recording, the raw and visceral *Bestial Devastation*, hit the streets in 1985, the same year as Brazil's return to democracy. But before exploring that connection in detail, we must delve a little further back into the nation's history.

The seeds of the dictatorship can be traced back to as far as 1889, when the military first realized its power by overthrowing Dom Pedro II, and fostering the transition of Brazil from an empire into a republic. After 40 years of waning support, even while acting as the republic's checks and balance system, they would again exercise their strength during the Revolution of 1930.

In 1929, a global depression caused the collapse of even the strongest economies. Brazil's most lucrative export, coffee, suffered a severe decrease in demand, with then-President Washington Luís fighting to stabilize prices rather than cheapen them, and otherwise refusing to either change existing policies, or create new ones, to battle the depression. As a result, the national debt grew to absurd proportions.

The Revolution of 1930 was, in part, a reaction to this *laissez-faire* attitude, but it was also a response to the government's growing neglect of the military. Perhaps just as crucial were the events that took place after that year's election. Julio Prestes, the government's official candidate to replace President Luís, won the election easily over his opponent Getúlio Vargas. But Vargas had the support of the military on his side, which served a greater purpose when his running mate, João Pessoa, was assassinated before Prestes could even take office. The rebels mobilized, forcing Luís to step down, and installing Vargas as Provisional President.

That "provisional" rule lasted 18 years.

The outspoken Vargas established a new constitution in 1937 that initiated the era of *Estado Novo*—the New State. He ushered in the age of populism, siding with the people rather than the political elite, and shifted Brazil's focus from agriculture to industry.

To some, Vargas was a dictator and a fascist. To others, he was The Father of the People. He fought for workers' rights, as well as those of the existing native Indian tribes. Regardless, the core tenets of his constitution, which were modeled after Mussolini's in Italy and Franco's in Spain, did indeed promote industrial growth, but at great expense.

During the *Estado Novo*, Vargas alerted the nation to a communist plot that intended to overthrow his regime, which allowed him to further lock down his rule over the country. In response to this "threat," he eliminated all political parties and modified the constitution to give himself explicit, authoritarian control.

In truth, Vargas had staged the whole thing.

World War II pulled the traditionally passive Brazil into its clutches with the sinking of merchant ships by German and Italian subs. But the nation's involvement in the conflict was short-lived, and at the end of the war, Getúlio Vargas was ousted by his own establishment. In an attempt at redemocratization, the *people* would legitimately elect him president only a few years later when Brazil was again on the precipice of an economic crisis.

The pressure was too great. Facing unimaginable foreign debts and international pressure regarding his increasingly nationalistic views, Vargas killed himself in 1954.

In the wake of Vargas' suicide, and the transfer of the nation's capitol from coastal Rio to the interior city of Brasília, the volume of money in circulation rose suddenly and drastically in an effort to salvage failing industries. The result was an unplanned, unexpected financial collapse. Foreign debts doubled and the cost of living tripled.

At the onset of the 60s, Brazil was ruled by two opposing factions: President Jânio Quadros, of the democratic party, and his polar opposite, the pro-Vargas Vice President João Goulart. But Quadros didn't stand a chance; the majority of congress was still in love with Getúlio Vargas, and thus supported Goulart by default. With Quadros ignoring the economic and inflation issues, and making what appeared to be communist connections in his international relations, he was eventually driven to resignation.

The military attempted to prevent the impending presidency of João Goulart, once head of the Brazilian Labor Party, and a man they feared to be too radical and too liberal to lead the nation. Tensions between congress and the conservative right rose, and eventually, Goulart became president despite an attempt by both sides to compromise and give Goulart diminished powers.

Military forces stood at the ready.

Once in office, Goulart's primary concern was to rebuild the working class through a system of reforms. He supported the establishment of labor unions and wage increases for peasant farmers in the northeast, but these peasant revolutions infuriated the landowners, most of whom sided with the conservative right. Goulart's attempts at economic reconstruction did nothing to limit inflation, and in fact, they had the opposite effect, plunging the nation into its worst recession yet.

It all came to a head in 1964.

Fearing some sort of drastic retaliation by the military leaderships, Goulart appealed first to congress and then directly to the people to expand his powers. But appealing to the people may have been the single greatest misstep of Goulart's presidency. Already with the support of the United States, who were in the midst of their own "red fever" in a Cold War with the Soviet Union, the Brazilian military accused the president and his congress of communism. They rose up and forced Goulart into exile, thus beginning a fifteen-year reign that would impact the country in unimaginable ways.

Among the first line of business for Castelo Branco, the newly installed military president, was to round up those he considered to be communists, political dissidents who spoke out against his system, and make them disappear either through arrest or exile. He stripped the pro-Goulart administration of their political rights, replacing them all. He directed his police to find—and confiscate—communist literature, propaganda, or anything else he considered subversive. Student libraries were ransacked, leftist militant homes were invaded, labor unions were driven underground if not dissolved completely.

What followed was a revolving door of authoritarian leaders who first rewrote the constitution to allow their despotic rule, and then created their own legislation. The implementation of the 5th Institutional Act (AI-5) in 1968 brought about the most dramatic change. Among other sweeping permissions, it gave the regime the legal right to arrest and imprison political dissidents without allowing *habeas corpus*—the right to a fair trial—and it outlined a strict code of censorship for any and all means of mass communication.

When considering the history of art and music culture in Brazil, it is practically impossible to understate the effects of AI-5. For nearly ten years, the Public Entertainment Censorship Department (DCDP) fought to eliminate or heavily censor all forms of protest—even *suggested* protest—in movies, plays, television programs, and music. Musicians, for example, were required to submit their songs to the DCDP for approval before release. If found to be critical of the regime in any way, the songs were denied release and their writers were exiled.

This strict attention to musical forms of protest drove artists underground, and gave rise to a particular type of songwriting. Shrouded in metaphor, and sung to the nationalistic beats of samba and bossa nova, these "protest songs" appealed to the people on multiple levels. Some of the metaphors were decoded by the DCDP, and national treasures such as Gilberto Gil and Caetano Veloso were banished for their thinly veiled critiques. The songs that survived helped give rise to the MPB—Brazilian Pop Music.

In more than a handful of extreme cases, under the guise of military president Médici's "Security and Development" plan, those political dissidents who weren't exiled were arrested and tortured, sometimes outright killed.

Had Sepultura been around then, writing openly scathing and politically critical songs like "Dictatorshit" and "Refuse/Resist," they would have been exiled at best, arrested and tortured at worst.

At the height of Médici's repression, Massimiliano Antonio Cavalera (known as Massi or the English equivalent Max) and his brother Igor Graziano were born; Max on August 4, 1969, and

Igor on September 4 of the following year. Their parents, Graziano and Vânia, lived in the Higienópolis neighborhood of São Paulo, where Graziano's salary as an employee of the Italian consulate was more than sufficient to keep the Cavaleras from wanting. Still, Vânia traveled back to her hometown of Belo Horizonte to birth each boy, as both her mother and the longtime family doctor worked in the hospital there. A few days after the boys were born, mother and child would return home to São Paulo.

Life in the Cavalera household was calm then, with Vânia— who had left home at a young age to model in Rio and São Paulo— exceedingly supportive of her boys in everything they chose to do. And Graziano, with his passion for music of all types, from MPB and traditional Italian opera to Black Sabbath and Led Zeppelin, ensured the apartment was always filled with the sounds of music.

Though still under strict military repression at the time, the country was somewhat of a dichotomy then, and in the midst of experiencing a "Brazilian Miracle." The near fascist nationalism promoted by Gétulio Vargas had transformed into a sort of patriotic pride following the national soccer team's triumph in the World Cup of 1970. Led by legends Pelé and Carlos Alberto, the club reclaimed their title after a disappointing first-round elimination in England four years earlier, and became the first nation to win three titles.

The economy, as well, was flourishing for the first time in years, thanks in large part to a massive state-driven impetus known as Post Import Substitution Industrialization. Vehicles proudly sported bumper stickers with the motto *Brazil: Love It or Leave It*. There was a sense of hope and change in the air, even while, paradoxically, the dictatorship tightened its grasp over control.

With samba and Afro-diasporic rhythms running through the veins of Brazilian music, Igor began taking interest in the drums at age 6. The snare drum was his first love, and whenever Graziano brought the boys to Palestra Italia in support of Palmeiras, the Cavalera "family team," Igor was sure to bring his snare so he could pound away with the torcida.

Not yet a fan of rock music, the youngster spent hours playing samba with his friends, intoxicated by rhythms that throbbed like a racing pulse. As his desire to learn more about the instrument grew, Igor asked his father to enroll him in a drum school. The boy didn't last long, uninspired and turned off by the structure and rigidity of the training.

The Cavalera brothers were always together as children, though fights were commonplace. In a particularly memorable incident, Igor broke one of Max's teeth after Max squirted lemon juice in his younger sibling's eyes. But boys will be boys, as the saying goes, and childhood offenses between brothers disappeared as quickly as they occurred.

In 1979, the Cavaleras were poised to move to Italy. Graziano's post had been transferred to Rome, and living arrangements were already being made when he suffered a sudden, fatal heart attack. The boys—Max at ten years old and Igor at nine—as well as their younger sister Kira, were in the car with him when he died.

Vânia, devastated and in shock, continued steadfastly working at the consulate for a couple of years afterward. She refused to allow time for suffering, understanding that her boys needed her now more than ever. The financial toll of losing Graziano's salary eventually caught up with the family, and they were forced to return to the fairly impoverished Santa Teresa area of Belo Horizonte where they moved in with Vânia's mother.

But not before Max and Igor attended a concert in São Paulo that would change their lives forever.

AI-5 had been redacted a few years before Graziano's death, which saw many of the exiled songwriters returning to their homeland, and the influx of more and more international acts adding cities like São Paulo and Rio de Janeiro to their itineraries. One of these was Queen, who played two consecutive nights at Morumbi Stadium in 1981 while touring for their album *The Game*.

Attending with a cousin, the Cavalera brothers were blown away by the spectacle. Igor saw and heard Roger Taylor and immediately knew what he wanted to do with his life. This event, more so than any other, turned young Igor from a samba specialist into a rock drummer. And Max, who had also been a fan of music, though not as intensely as his brother, got a glimpse into his future as a musician.

He discovered in a closet an old acoustic guitar—his father's—on which the elder Cavalera used to play old traditional Italian songs. Max immediately began goofing around, teaching himself riffs even though he didn't know how to tune the instrument, inspired by his father's deep love of music. As an impressionable young fan himself, after learning that KISS's Paul Stanley played a guitar that looked like a shattered mirror, Max had to create a similar effect with his acoustic. As legend has it, he broke a mirror, and glued pieces of it onto the guitar's body. It didn't quite work out as well as he had planned.

In 1982, a band from Pará called Stress released their self-titled debut. The significance of this album cannot be understated, as it was—and still is—considered by most to the very first Brazilian metal album. Sung entirely in Portuguese, many of the original lyrics had to be changed because even though AI-5 no longer existed, censorship still did. Sounding like a mix between early Iron Maiden, Judas Priest, and Motorhead, *Stress* was a huge hit among the young Brazilian fans fed up with MPB, samba, and bossa nova. These kids were angry, pissed off with the state of the nation, and they hungered for music that reflected that anger.

Max and Igor were getting into heavier sounds, growing out their hair, wearing dark sunglasses and black t-shirts, adopting the aesthetic of the scene. A preoccupation with Motorhead, Sex Pistols, and Black Sabbath soon worked like a gateway drug, opening the boys' ears to even more brutal music. But in those days, it was hard to get a hold of records in Belo Horizonte. From a trip to São Paulo and the historic Woodstock record store, Max returned with three vinyl albums that would change the Cavaleras' young lives; one a classic by Iron Maiden, and one each from a pair of new American bands called Slayer and Metallica.

In 1983, the brothers' interest in playing music was limited mainly to talk around school. Max had shown an early interest in pounding on the drums, but by then, Igor was much better, so Max changed his focus back to the guitar. There was no band as such, however, until the following year when the brothers settled on a name after learning that their original choice, Tropa de Choque, was already taken.

That name was Sepultura, famously translated from the Motorhead track "Dancing On Your Grave."

The brothers spent most of their time together, writing primitive songs on primitive gear. Max's first real guitar, purchased from a pawnshop, was nicknamed Podreira because it was old and rotten and the fretboard gave him splinters in his fingers. Igor's drums consisted only of a snare, a floor tom, and a cymbal that had to be held up with a broomstick. They soon added a neighbor, Cássio, on guitar to form the first unofficial and incomplete lineup of Sepultura.

Cássio didn't last long. He was, in fact, a temporary fill simply because Max couldn't play guitar very well at the time.

After Cássio moved on, the brothers recruited a schoolmate named Wagner Lamounier who wanted to be a singer. More than sing, though, the vocalist had to scream to be heard over the music because no one could afford a microphone. The limitation would inspire the development of a visceral, screeching style that became a signature of the extreme metal Sepultura played in those early days.

Roberto UFO (so nicknamed because of his obsession with British rockers UFO) and Roberto "Gato" Raffan, on guitar and bass respectively, rounded out the first *complete* lineup of Sepultura.

The kids practiced in earnest at Gato's house, whose father was a Methodist preacher. The home was owned by the church and would serve as an ironic location for rehearsals, especially as the boys' musical tastes began swaying closer to black metal bands like Venom, Hellhammer, and Celtic Frost, and their own lyrics adopted "evil" themes. Wagner even took on the nickname "Antichrist."

"The whole Satanic thing we took as a joke," Igor later explained. "We've never been serious about it. It was a way to freak people out."

And freak people out, they did.

For these 14- and 15-year-old boys who were no longer children but not quite yet adults, black metal (as coined by Venom on their classic album of the same name) may have been the perfect aesthetic identifier. Enrolled in a military school with strict rules and nationalist ideals, Sepultura tended toward rebellion. One is reminded of the classic Brando in *The Wild Ones* exchange, *What are you rebelling against?* followed by the brash, hormonal and too-dramatic response, *What have you got?*

Every choice the boys made then—playing loud, heavy music instead of Brazilian Popular Music, singing about Satan, even the eventual decision to change their lyrics from Portuguese into English—was based in rebellion. But it is important to remember the environment in which they had been raised. Barely teenagers, they were afraid of the police and the government, and their fear inspired a sort of escapism through music.

However, by all accounts they were very respectful and polite, Max and Igor especially. They had their mother, Vanîa, to thank for that.

Their discontent came out only through music.

Musically, black metal also worked for the boys. The style was fast, noisy, and sloppy, and Sepultura's inexperience gave their music a naturally raw sound.

Further inspiring this black metal idolatry was a band based out of Rio de Janeiro. Dorsal Atlântica slathered their faces with "corpsepaint"—black and white makeup in a style similar to that of KISS or King Diamond, wore outfits adorned with inverted crosses and belts made of rifle bullets, and wrote songs about the devil. Max, in particular, was inspired by Dorsal Atlântica and their image. If they could do it, (and in a country such as Brazil where Catholicism was rigorously adhered to), then Sepultura could do it, too.

The face paint and crosses were easy enough. When Igor saw a picture of Destruction wearing bullet belts, he was forced to be more creative, so they'd tape batteries to their belts for photo shoots. From a distance, the boys thought, no one would even be able to tell. Even Vanîa assisted the boys in the creation of Sepultura's image, helping to rip their pants in all the right places, and adding metal studs to their jackets.

Gato was the first casualty of this lineup, splitting after a fight with Wagner. His departure dealt a double-blow to the band; not only did they lose a bass player, but they also lost a place to rehearse.

They soon found both in a Mineiro with big black hair like Paul Stanley, and nicknamed in kind as Paulinho KISS.

Born on April 30, 1969, Paulo Xisto Pinto Júnior, the son of a lawyer, lived in the Horto neighborhood of Belo Horizonte with his two brothers and a sister. Paulo's younger days weren't typical; he didn't spend hours hanging out at the mall, and like most kids in less than well-to-do families, received his rock music education through bootlegged copies of the albums everyone was listening to. Quite understandably then, his early influences were no different than those of his friends: Black Sabbath, Iron Maiden, and KISS among them.

Thankfully, Paulo discovered music early on in life. Had he not, the junior would likely have followed in the footsteps of his father and become a lawyer.

A steadfast supporter of the Galo—Atlético Mineiro, his chosen soccer team—Xisto grew to be a lover of laughter, beer, and good times, and though he harbored a passion for music, his abilities on the bass guitar were practically nonexistent when he met Max and Igor.

Paulo had recently been kicked out of his previous band, the aptly named AI-5, because he, admittedly, couldn't play very well. He was introduced to the Cavaleras through a mutual school friend, and they immediately accepted him into the band when they found out he had a brand new Giannini Stratosonic bass. Paulo's family even allowed Sepultura to transform the shed in front of the Pinto home into a rehearsal space. The boys went straight to work plastering the walls with heavy metal posters and album covers. That little shed became the band's home base for nearly five years.

Paulinho KISS's skills as a bass player weren't even a consideration.

They spent much time rehearsing with their poor equipment, breaking up the sessions by waging blueberry and banana wars under the trees outside. But still, none of the kids had money for equipment, and they had to scrape by in desperate measures. At a local show by another group, Igor jumped up on stage and stuffed a microphone down his pants, diving back into the crowd before anyone noticed.

And they were rehearsing for a real purpose; just before accepting Paulo into the fold, Sepultura had booked their very first concert to take place on December 4, 1984, in the Borroca neighborhood, with Overdose and Tropa de Choque.

Sepultura played—badly—as a trio that night. Roberto UFO's mother wouldn't permit him to be out so late, and the guitarist was kicked out of the band as a result. Paulo's absence, however, was understood. He had departed earlier on school holiday to Montes Claros with his family, a vacation that had been planned before the show was scheduled.

Max, Igor, and Wagner raged on stage with passion, if not grand musical excellence. For Igor, donning an army helmet, a wig, and black makeup around his eyes, it was a success simply because he got to use a full drum kit, courtesy of Overdose drummer Helinho, who shared his equipment that night.

Sepultura didn't make many new fans at that concert, but the pure, youthful innocence of their entry into the local scene would make the coming years' successes that much more inspirational.

1985 was a groundbreaking year, not only for Sepultura, but for Brazil in general. The military dictatorship stood on its last legs, having been slowly dissolving for some time. In early January, the first Rock In Rio festival was held that brought international bands from every genre to the Marvelous City, but the most important for our purposes were Iron Maiden, Queen, AC/DC, and Ozzy Osbourne. A couple of months later, the dictatorship fell completely, and plans for Brazil's first democratic election were laid.

The underground metal scene was becoming very strong between three key cities: Belo Horizonte, Rio de Janeiro, and São Paulo, and Brazilian metal of all kinds enjoyed a boon of exposure. Dorsal Atlântica released their long-awaited debut EP *Ultimatum*. Record label Baratos Afins in São Paulo unleashed *SP Metal I*, a compilation of the extreme Sampa bands Vírus, Avenger, Centúrias, Salário Minimo, and Cabeça Metal. *SP Metal* was, in a sense, the Brazilian equivalent of the American *Metal Massacre* releases that introduced Metallica, Slayer, Overkill, Hellhammer, Possessed, and many of the other bands that influenced the Brazilian scene.

And a record store in Belo Horizonte called Cogumelo, where the local metalheads passed their days, branched out and became a record *label*. Their very first release would reunite two of the

The old guard in the old school, Caverna, Rio de Janeiro.

bands that had played in together in Belo at the tail end of 1984: on one side of the record was Overdose's *Século xx*, and on the other, Sepultura's *Bestial Devastation*.

But before the recording could happen, some drastic changes came to the band. The Metal BH festival in March marked both Paulo's first performance with Sepultura and Wagner's last. Depending on who you ask, the vocalist either left or was booted out as disagreements over the music escalated and personal relationships devolved. Lamounier would almost immediately take over rivals Sarcófago, a black metal band that had also performed at the Metal BH fest. Wagner (who was joined, for a time, by Roberto UFO), used every press opportunity to trash talk Sepultura, vocally deriding his former band mates as fake and willing to do anything for money. Sarcófago was, in his words, the only *true* black metal band in Brazil.

Whether by accident or design, Max took over the vocal duties, but his guitar skills were still rather unpolished. They could not survive as a trio. Sepultura needed a lead guitarist.

Enter Jairo Guedz, a local musician brought into the world on November 25, 1968, whose talents would tie together the sometimes disparate threads in Sepultura.

When Jairo met Max, Igor, and Paulo in Savassi, outside of Sabor & Arte on Rua Rio Grande do Norte, he was already familiar with Sepultura. The boys were making a name for themselves through their name and image, if not so much their music, which was still very crude and unrefined. But Jairo was immediately attracted to their hunger, their determination, and knew he wanted to be a part of this exciting new scene.

Almost immediately, the guitarist brought a semblance of order to the group, teaching Max chords and tricks and convincing them all that they needed to rehearse more.

Jairo's addition to the group was just what Sepultura needed at the time to step up to another level. While the music was still chaotic, with his input it grew to a sort of controlled chaos. Song structures made more sense, even though the overall style of the music was derivative of the many death metal and black metal bands they worshipped at the time.

Still, there was an indefinable quality that set them apart from their peers. Fans could sense it. The other bands sensed it. Sepultura themselves knew it, so much so that they gradually began to abandon some of the imagery staples like corpsepaint,

Max and Jairo in Belo Horizonte

leather, and spikes, to set their band further apart from the rest. In tropical Brazil, it made more sense to perform without the physical burden of those things anyway. And with their decision to sing in English, perhaps as further proof of their "rebellion" against everything Brazilian, the band played tribute to their musical heroes while carving out a niche entirely their own.

Bestial Devastation was recorded and mixed in two days during August of 1985, and features what many consider to be the first *real* lineup of Sepultura: Max "Possessed" Cavalera on rhythm guitar and vocals, Jairo "Tormentor" Guedz on lead guitar, Igor "Skullcrusher" Cavalera on drums/percussion, and Paulo "Destructor" Jr. on bass. It would be released December 1, 1985, almost a year to the day after their first "concert." They proudly tagged their side of the insert for *Bestial Devastation* with the death metal label, despite the sound leaning closer to a variant of black metal.

Following a spoken word, Halloween-style intro—"The Curse"—that toes the line between scary and silly, "Bestial Devastation" comes screaming out of the speakers with speed and atmosphere. Even though the band members were young, still teenagers, the song's arrangement shows maturity beyond their ages, alternating tempos to emphasize certain aspects of the track. Already, these boys knew what they were doing.

"Antichrist," a remnant from earlier days with lyrics penned by Wagner Lamounier, continues in the same vein. It comes replete with a catchy chorus, even, begging to be shouted along with Max. The first song they'd ever recorded as a band, "Necromancer," opens with a slow, doomy riff—perhaps the best on the album— that the band wisely revisits during the track's chorus. "Warriors of Death," an uncompromising number easing back on the gas pedal only for the breakdown and Jairo's finger-tapped solo, completes the EP too soon, leaving fans thirsty for more. In the echoing wake of the last cymbal crash and the final guitar chord strike, it is clear that Sepultura is in a league of their own.

After such violent slamming on their guitars during the first day of recording, the instruments were out of tune on day two. No one could afford a tuner, much less higher quality equipment, the best of which was usually imported. None of their families were financially well off, though none were anywhere near as destitute as those in the favelas. The reality in those days was that a non-Brazilian guitar carried import taxes much higher than the cost of the actual instrument. Max, Igor, Paulo, and Jairo didn't really care anyway. They preferred how rough and raw those sessions sounded.

And the fans preferred it, too.

Cogumelo released the *Bestial Devastation/Século XX* split EP on December 1, 1985, to an immediately accepting base of headbangers that largely favored Sepultura's side of the record over Overdose's, despite the cartoonish cover depiction of a hand drawn demon (which was lifted from the painting "In The Underworld" by Peruvian artist Boris Vallejo) looming over a cathedral. Its popularity was boosted in part by the madness of Sepultura's live performances with Jairo, some of which were recorded and cassettes of which spread through the underground like a virus.

In April of 1986, they again teamed up with Overdose for a number of shows, this time to promote the EP. When not rehearsing, the band was already beginning to plan for the future, mailing tapes to fanzines across the world and also to record labels in the US. Functioning out of the Cavalera household on Rua Dores do Indaia, they would sometimes receive rejections months later, long after they'd forgotten a tape had been sent.

With all their local popularity came the demand for a full-length Sepultura album, and the boys continued writing, working toward this next goal. When Jairo met Max for lunch one day, and brought with him a song called "Troops of Doom," it was on. This simple tune based around chromatic riffs would go on to become the band's first "hit."

Merchandise order form in Igor's handwriting.

And even though they weren't playing more than a couple of shows every few weeks (with months sometimes passing between gigs), Sepultura were already beginning to creep their way to the top of the list of underground bands. But at the time, within the scene, the members of Mutilator or Vulcano or even Sepultura never recognized any sort of hierarchy. They were simply friends helping friends, loaning each other instruments and places to stay, helping to carry gear, and organizing festival shows in which all of them could participate, in one way or another.

One such show was the Festival da Morte in August, held at Camisa 10 in Belo Horizonte. Mutilator vocalist Silvio SDN (aka Silvio Gomes) organized the event, booking Vulcano from Santos, as well as Belo Horizonte's Chakal, and a side project of his own named Guerrilha. But since he was not only working the event, but also performing with Mutilator that night, Silvio handed over Guerrilha's vocal duties to a friend named Gentil Bastos Netto.

Also in Guerrilha's ranks were Max Cavalera on guitar, his brother Igor on drums, and Jairo Guedz on bass. Among the songs they played—frenzied originals like "Bla," "Chaos," and

"Figueiredo"—the short-lived project threw in a cover of Death's "Infernal Death" for good measure. (Video footage of the festival, with backstage interviews and shenanigans hosted by Jairo, was eventually acquired by Cogumelo, who included some of the live clips in the 2008 re-release of Vulcano's classic *Bloody Vengeance*.)

The day after the Festival da Morte, Sepultura set out for Estudio Vice Versa, where they'd begin studio work on their own new songs.

As with its predecessor, *Morbid Visions* was recorded fast, in just seven days, and its production values aren't much better than those on *Bestial Devastation*. But therein lies much of the record's charm. Early pressings opened with an extensive section from the Carl Orff opera *Carmina Burana*, that was removed after copyright concerns. The album didn't need the piece to set the proper tone, though; it seemed more appropriate to blast right into the first riff of the title track than to employ an oft-used heavy metal staple as a prelude.

Flyer promoting Morbid Visions release party shows.

On the whole, *Morbid Visions* sounds much like an extension of the EP, intended to satiate the fans' hunger for more music and to give the band more original material to play in concert. Lyrics, at this point, were still being written in Portuguese and translated into English, lending themselves to interpretations that are sometimes confusing and often humorous. Max's staccato barking in tracks like "Mayhem" and "War" render his words mostly unintelligible, but Brazilian fans either didn't understand the translated words or weren't at all bothered by them. What mattered was that Max's heavily reverbed vocals made him sound demonic, as if he were some creature howling in a dark cave.

The prevalent themes continue to be Satan, speed, and extremity in sound, but that doesn't necessarily mean the music is one-dimensional. "Crucifixion" utilizes hanging chords, pinch harmonics, and slow, grinding passages to offset the blistering pace in the song's verses. "Show Me The Wrath" begins with a heavy, slow burn; a deliberately picked melody made up of single notes that develops into a similar chordal pattern. Featuring some of the group's most complex guitar work and time changes yet, "Show Me the Wrath" sits slightly apart from the rest of the album as a highpoint.

While "Funeral Rites" is similar enough in tone and arrangement to "Troops of Doom," especially its first minute or so, it bleeds nicely into "Empire of the Damned," a journey into thrash metal that would be explored even further on the next record.

The crudly drawn demon from *Bestial Devastation*'s cover makes a repeat appearance on that of *Morbid Visions*, but the standout feature is the refined Sepultura logo, looking sharp and shiny like a blade ready for battle.

Little by little, the band was working toward professionalism.

An influx of concerts led up to the release of the album on November 10, each seemingly more brutal than the one that came before. Tuka Quinelli, a native of São Bernardo do Campo who attended the same high school as Pestilence guitarist Andreas Kisser, recalled, "I went to Americana, São Paulo countryside, to see some bands at Slaughter Festival, and there I met Max and Igor for the first time. Sepultura were still small and they walked through the crowd naturally. Igor gave me his address in Belo Horizonte and invited me to go there. I went at the first opportunity. Then I went back to see them opening for Venom. I stayed at their house and made friends with their mother, Vânia, who is a wonderful person, very strong, modern, and always supported them."

Opening for Venom (and special guests Exciter) for two dates on the English group's Brazilian tour represented one of the first great triumphs for Sepultura. Though no one within the inner circle of local bands openly spoke of the previously mentioned hierarchy, the fact that Sepultura—not Sarcófago, not Vulcano, not even Dorsal Atlântica—opened for Venom spoke volumes.

By the beginning of the following year, even though *Morbid Visions* was only recently released, Sepultura already had a reputation outside of Brazil based almost entirely on their reputation within Brazil. Like any underground metal band worth its salt in the pre-Internet age, they devoured fanzines in search of the newest, most extreme music. With the help of Cabrito, a neighbor who spoke and wrote English, the boys corresponded with key members of the Florida death metal scene, such as Morbid Angel and Death. In fact, it was on the latter's *Scream Bloody Gore* album that Max's name first appeared on a real record outside of Brazil, in 1987, when Chuck Schuldiner thanked him and Sepultura in the album credits.

In Norway, a musician by the name of Gylve Nagell, also known as Fenriz, sent letters to Max asking for copies of Sepultura's tapes because the deeply underground metal fans in Europe had been hearing stories about these insane Brazilians. Fenriz's own group, Black Death, would eventually transform into Darkthrone, one of the more notorious of Norway's first wave of black metal bands. Infamous Oslo groups Mayhem, Thorns, and others would later praise this era of Sepultura (and Sarcófago, as well) as a prime influence on the Norwegian black metal scene that would rise to prominence in the early 90s.

One of Jairo's last shows with the band.

For Max, Igor, Paulo, and Jairo, their world was suddenly becoming bigger. For Jairo, a personal highlight came in the form of a tour around São Paulo's interior, with Dorsal Atlântica and Vulcano, that drew the band closer together in both trust and friendship.

But, strangely, these would also be Jairo's last days in the band.

TWO

THE OTHER SIDE OF THE MIRROR

As writing for the next album commenced, Jairo became less and less motivated to continue the routine Sepultura had fallen into. In a number of early interviews, Max would claim Jairo was tired of playing death metal and preferred music like Poison or Motley Crue, though this may have been little more than media posturing. Whatever the reasons for the guitarist's departure, it's clear the situation was complicated and Jairo has remained silent on the topic in the years since..

When Jairo made his departure official, the remaining three members were understandably disappointed, but they knew immediately who should replace him. In fact, they had jammed with him already.

The ABC region of São Paulo consists of three municipalities on the outskirts of the capitol: Santo André, São Bernardo do Campo, and São Caetano do Sul. An industrial hub known mainly for its manufacturing plants and automobile factories, the ABC was an

Jairo out, Andreas in.

Esfinge at the Tenis Clube, Santo André.

ideal locale for the creation of Brazil's first Workers' Party, a coalition of people (one of whom—Luiz Inácia Lula da Silva—would later go on to become president) who stood up to the military dictatorship and fought for workers' rights.

It was also the birthplace of Andreas Rudolf Kisser.

Born in São Bernardo on August 24, 1968 to a Slovenian mother and a first-generation Brazilian father who worked as an engineer at the Mercedes Benz factory, Andreas was surrounded by art, music, and culture from a young age.

Growing up in the Rudge Ramos neighborhood, Kisser's home was filled with the sounds of Sertanejo and samba, The Beatles and the Bee Gees, caipira music, acts like Tonico and Tonico, and Sérgio Reis. His father's parents, who were German by birth, preferred classical music. In fact, Andreas's first guitar was an acoustic given to him by his maternal grandmother, who was a singer in her younger days in Slovenia. He took to the instrument right away, practicing without prejudice MPB and whatever music was playing around the house. Caetano Veloso. Guilherme Arantes.

But his first love was soccer.

An avid follower of São Paulo Futebol Clube, young Andreas went with his father to watch matches at Morumbi Stadium whenever he could, and when he couldn't, he'd play in the streets with his friends. Soccer was his passion then, and still is today, and were it not for two bands in particular, Andreas may have pursued a career as an athlete rather than a musician.

These two "firsts"—his first album and his first concert—changed Kisser's life. His first album, Queen's *A Night at the Opera*, and his first concert, KISS, as bombastic as ever. *Creatures of the Night* was the tour, their last before removing the face paint, and the year was 1983. At just 14 years old, Andreas had successfully talked his mother into letting him attend the concert with a friend.

From there, his preferred tastes in music grew to include heavier rock in the form of Deep Purple, Led Zeppelin, Black Sabbath, and Iron Maiden. Randy Rhoads, the virtuosic guitarist on Ozzy Osbourne's *Blizzard of Ozz* and *Diary of a Madman*, became an early idol particularly because of his creative blend of classical and heavy metal guitar styles.

While attending Colégio São José, Andreas's routine was fairly straightforward; school in the morning, soccer in the afternoon, with music as the soundtrack all day long. Shortly after that KISS concert, he joined up with like-minded friends to play cover songs at school functions, everything from the glam rock of Twisted Sister and Whitesnake to the self-proclaimed black metal of Venom. Andreas, as guitarist and vocalist, initially, was so shy he had to stand on the far side of the stage and hide away from the audience when he sang.

With more time in front of an audience, his confidence grew. "Once he and his friends did a show in the school," Tuka Quinelli said, "and set fire to a poster of Menudo. The nuns were strained at the time..."

By 1985, the lineup of Kisser's first real band had rounded out with Julinho Cassettari on vocals, Andreas on guitar, Fabio Bonatelli on bass, and Osvaldo Ferreira Junior on drums. Named Esfinge (Sphinx) because of Kisser's fascination with Egyptian history, they recorded a demo tape and expanded their performance areas to include friends' parties, small bars, car washes after closing time, and even a Festa Junina—Brazil's version of the European Quermesse festival.

Inspired by their heroes in bands outside of Brazil, Esfinge soon decided to try singing in English rather than Portuguese, and changed their name to Pestilence.

They gathered a small but dedicated following in the ABC before an innocent jam session in 1987 changed everything.

"We were very united in the underground scene," Andreas explained. "People who listened to the same bands, and people

Andreas and João Gordo (Ratos de Porão) get married.

who had their own bands. Between São Paulo, Rio, and Belo Horizonte were many bands, and the scene was very strong. So we knew each other very well, not only Sepultura, but all the bands. It was a lot of people. You felt part of a family, a tribe."

Shortly before Sepultura announced Jairo's departure, Andreas and a friend named Paulinho traveled to Belo Horizonte to party and meet girls, and it was there Kisser first encountered the band. "We went to Sepultura's practice," he said, "and I met them, and I jammed with them."

The meeting was fortuitous. That same week, at a concert with Ratos de Porão, the band played as a trio since Jairo was already planning to quit and, in fact, hadn't shown up to rehearsal for a few weeks.

Kisser stayed with Guedz during that vacation, using the equipment of Alexander "Magoo," whose guitar was shared between Holocausto, Sepultura, and Magoo's own band Mutilator. Jairo didn't want to leave on bad terms. He at least wanted to give the guys enough time to find a suitable replacement.

"We jammed Kreator, Slayer, we jammed Destruction," Andreas said. "We spent a week or two weeks there just blasting and having a good time. And then Sepultura had this gig in São Paulo [state]."

The bands traveled 400 miles together on a commuter bus from Belo Horizonte to Santa Isabel, a small town an hour east of downtown São Paulo, where Sepultura would perform (*with* Jairo this time) at the Holocaust Festival on January 18, 1987.

Speaking of Kisser's introduction to the band, Max has famously quipped, "He was my guitar roadie." Although the "roadie" definition may have been lost in translation.

"I was never a roadie," Andreas said. "I didn't even know that name existed. It was a big festival. Of course I was together with them, and I helped, but more as a friend because it was very common for friends to help everybody around. We were very united. I was just there helping out everybody. Paulo. Max. But I didn't carry fucking stacks of amps, I didn't put the show together and stuff. And, coincidentally, Max's guitar string broke and I went on stage to pick up the guitar to try to change the string or whatever, to help him out, and there's a video of that," he said, laughing. "Of course, that moment. And the legend was born."

Still laughing, Andreas added, "I guess I fixed the string and he could go on and play, so ... I was a good roadie."

A couple of months later, the switch became official.

"We had a long holiday, Easter," Tuka Quinelli said, "and I decided to go to Belo Horizonte to visit my friends. It was a very important period because Jairo was leaving and Andreas was coming in. I went to the rehearsal at Paulo's home and there I took the first picture of Andreas in Sepultura."

By all accounts, it was both a sad and exciting day in the band's history; sad because Jairo's departure was not the result of a fight or an argument, and exciting because of the new spark that

Andreas' first rehearsal with Sepultura. Belo Horizonte, April 1987.

Max and Paulo practicing in Belo Horizonte.

Andreas brought to Sepultura, a spark they had all felt since their first jam sessions prior to the Holocaust Festival.

"When I met them," Andreas said, "the connection was there. It was done. We felt great playing together, especially me and Igor. Max couldn't really play all those fast and difficult riffs, but me and Igor could play the stuff pretty fucking well. It seemed like we knew each other for so long. It really clicked. I think from the first practice, we knew.

"And I was looking for a band, really, because I had my school friends that started Esfinge and then Pestilence, and they all left. They were working with their dads, the family businesses, and they didn't have the same commitment. They didn't want to follow a serious path in music. And then when I met Sepultura I saw that those guys were really ready for the same war I was going to fight," he said.

"[With Sepultura] we clicked right there. The ideas were the same, and the aim and the urge were the same. Musically, I think they needed someone like myself to be a little more technical, more challengeable, to do leads and riffs that were a little more difficult, that you have to think about. And I needed more of that raw stuff, to learn more about the hardcore metal and death metal, the more rude ... and *Schizophrenia* was a consequence of that."

Andreas was introduced to fans quickly and in grand fashion when, in May, he and the band traveled 48 hours by bus to embark on a mini-tour, playing Caruaru and Recife in Pernambuco, followed by Campina Grande in Paraíba. Upon return to Belo Horizonte, Sepultura got right back to work on their second full-length LP.

"When I joined they had ideas for songs like 'Rest in Pain,' 'Escape to the Void,' and 'Screams Behind the Shadows,' but they weren't ready yet. I brought lyrics to 'Escape,' talking about madness and schizophrenic thoughts, stress and despair. That's where Max took the idea to call the album *Schizophrenia*.

"And 'Escape into the Mirror' was the lyric that was turned into 'Escape to the Void,'" Andreas continued. "Musically there's nothing to do with the song 'Escape Into the Mirror' from Esfinge to the Sepultura song."

That lyric would also inspire the album cover's image of a mentally ill person looking into a mirror and seeing himself as he really is.

"And then came the concept that took Sepultura away from the

Max takes his brother's place in Rio de Janeiro.

death metal and rip-off Antichrist songs and Morbid and all that stuff they were over-repeating," Andreas said. "That gave a new [thematic] direction also, for lyrics, and to talk about our own experiences with crazy friends and drugs—a more realistic type of vibe—and be ourselves. Not trying to copy too much what's coming from outside."

So Andreas moved in with Max and Igor, and even attended their school for a while—though the Cavaleras had already quit a couple of years earlier. Vânia had sat the boys down for a serious discussion, telling them, in no uncertain terms, that if they wanted to succeed playing music, they'd have to put every ounce of time and energy into the band.

The other parents in the neighborhood thought Vânia was crazy, a bad influence, the hostess of a drug den where all the local metalheads hung out. But drugs were strictly forbidden in the Cavalera household. The only vices allowed were soda and board games. And music, of course.

In later days, long after they had become more popular than they could have dreamed, Igor praised his mother, grateful for her dedication and support from the very beginning, and credited her as one of the most important factors in their success.

Happy in Belo Horizonte.

With Kisser's influence, the remainder of the writing for *Schizophrenia* would help to sculpt a sound more refined, more technical than that of *Bestial Devastation* and *Morbid Visions*. Though the tremolo picking and breakneck pace were still evident, gone were the Satanic lyrics and imagery. Guitar riffs were more complex, the leads more thought out, melodic, and prepared. There were even acoustic, classical guitar interludes such as "The Abyss" that offset the savage speed of tracks like "Septic Schizo."

In all, it was a noticeable step away from the black/death style of earlier material, and a step toward a sound rooted more in the socially and politically aware thrash metal they would soon become known for.

Sepultura returned to João Guimarães Studio to demo a test version of the first song they'd written with Andreas, "From the Past Comes the Storms," since this would also be Kisser's premier experience in a recording studio. In August, they entered J.G. Studios again, and finished the album in slightly more time than it took to record *Morbid Visions*.

Lyrically, the songs revolved around death and insanity, though the language itself shows that the band's English, at that point, still left something to be desired. As with *Bestial Devastation* and *Morbid Visions*, in fact, the lyrics were written in Portuguese first, and translated afterward.

Sad in Belo Horizonte.

"When I first heard Iron Maiden," Andreas said, "I didn't have a clue what they were talking about. I saw the images and that was cool, and the music was great, the sound was great, but I didn't have a clue about anything that was going on, lyric-wise. I just found out how stupid KISS lyrics are, afterwards. I used to love and sing all the stuff and I didn't have any idea about it, but I still love them, regardless." Reflecting on the process of translating their own lyrics into a language the band members themselves didn't understand, he added, "When you think you're saying something, but you're saying something totally opposite, that's the danger.

"If you listen," Andreas said, "there's no sense in our English on *Schizophrenia*. It's very complicated, translations from Portuguese to English, without anybody caring too much about sentences and stuff like that. You cannot understand anything." But, he added, "That's art, man. For Max to put all those lyrics inside the songs, you have to be good to do that kind of stuff. It was a limitation that we took further and did something with it.

"Of course," he continued, "after starting to tour and living outside Brazil, in the States, you improve your English; you need less words to get the point across. Portuguese is a very different language. It's a richer language. There are more words and many situations, past and present and future, than English. English is much more compact in the way you express things. At least the English

39

we talk, not the heavy literature, of course. But Portuguese in general is more…it's one of the most difficult languages to learn. Like Russian and Chinese or something."

Lyrical content aside, the album showcases relatively sleeker production values and increased technicality over *Morbid Visions*, and musically shows the band progressing toward a more thrash oriented sound. Opening with the high-pitched screech of violins heavily reminiscent of the theme from Alfred Hitchcock's *Psycho*, and leading into the first track with the backward scream of Max—*schizophrenia*, he shouts—the album rips right out of the gate with the violent speed picking and minor key chord progression that kicks off "From the Past Comes the Storms."

The album doesn't let up, moving through the classically infused death metal of "To the Wall," the headbanging groove of "Escape to the Void," and "Inquisition Symphony." The latter track is a standout achievement for the group, a 7-minute instrumental epic complete with acoustic intro, extended lead guitar breaks (with hammer-on passages that bring Iron Maiden's "Flash of the Blade" to mind) and an incredibly complex structure. The Metallica influence here too is obvious; one wouldn't be too far off the mark to consider it "The Call of Ktulu" on steroids and methamphetamines.

"Screams Behind the Shadows" and "Septic Schizo" both have one foot firmly planted in the *Morbid Visions* style, but "The Abyss" is the album's first step toward evolution. A barely one

Igor jamming in Paulo's rehearsal space.

Max with his first BC Rich Warlock guitar. Belo Horizonte, 1988.

minute long interlude exemplifying the classical skills of Andreas, "The Abyss" shows Sepultura's hunger for growth and their understanding of dynamics. In the context of the album, the song is a calm respite in a schizophrenic mind, only intensifying the subject's eventual return to insanity with the ferocious "R.I.P. (Rest in Pain)."

The whole journey wraps up in just under forty minutes, culminating with the listener thrust into the spirit of the album cover's character, countless psychotic voices raging out of the speakers and then suddenly silenced.

Cogumelo released *Schizophrenia* two short months later, on October 30, 1987. Sepultura fans spinning the album for the first time understood immediately that the band was on another level, far above where they had been only a year earlier, and outpacing every other Brazilian metal band. Even metalheads who hadn't been fans up until that point could sense magic streaming through the grooves of the LP.

The rest of the world sensed it, too. Shark Records, a German label released it across the continent, and *Schizophrenia* was an instant success in Europe, selling thousands of copies. Shark's pressing quickly became a highly sought after collectible item. Bootleg copies appeared in the United States, and underground fanzines there reported on the album in glowing terms, many referring to the up-and-coming Brazilians as the next Slayer.

One of these fanzines, which featured Sepultura on the cover thanks to a metal writer named Borivoj Krgin, caught the attention of an A&R representative for Roadrunner Records in New York City.

In 1988, Monte Conner was still a fledgling recruit at Roadrunner, having only begun his A&R stint in December of the previous year. Besides being intrigued by the obvious hook—that the band was from Brazil instead of some small town or sprawling U.S. metropolis—Conner was blown away by the visceral mix of thrash, speed, and death metal *Schizophrenia* served up.

Krgin—a longtime friend of Conner's—corresponded with Max, telling him of the underground "buzz" about Sepultura, and persuaded him to come to New York. Neither Cogulemo nor Max, nor anyone else in the band for that matter, could afford the airline ticket.

But everyone knew this was an opportunity Max could not pass up.

So Cavalera met with a *trambiqueiro*—a scam artist—who laid out a deal. He would give Max an airline ticket in return for 100 albums. Max was to take these 100 albums to the US and sell them there, passing the money back to the *trombiquiero* when he returned. But there was a catch; on the flight, Max would have to pretend to be an employee of PanAm Airlines if he hoped to make it through customs.

Cavalera accepted the deal, and took an additional 50 albums to pass out to record companies. He borrowed a suit from a cousin (since he couldn't afford one of those either), tied his hair back into a ponytail, and hit the skies headed for New York City.

Max spent the better part of a week in NYC negotiating with Roadrunner Records, at the flagship American office of a label that had been born in the Netherlands some seven years earlier. But no deals were signed during that trip to New York.

A few months later though, back home in Belo Horizonte, Max received a phone call that would drastically alter the trajectory of Sepultura.

THREE

RISING ABOVE THE REMAINS

The tale of Max's trip to New York City has become something of a legend, earning new details and losing others, becoming more colorful throughout the years depending on who is telling it. The version included here is probably the most popular, and makes for good drama, though some of the particulars may be more fantasy than reality. No matter how embellished though, at least one fact remains: bolstered largely by their reputation and limited recorded output, Sepultura signed an international deal with Roadracer—a subsidiary of parent label Roadrunner—for seven albums, before anyone in the States had even seen them perform live.

Not bad for a bunch of Brazilian kids with an average age of twenty, who spoke little to no English. They began to take classes, however, slowly learning the language, daring to dream that they might one day be offered the opportunity to tour beyond their own borders.

But the contract wasn't all it was cracked up to be, as the band would soon find out.

The success of *Schizophrenia* within domestic territories brought with it the possibility for Sepultura to, if not yet hit international destinations, at least venture a bit more extensively

The good ol' days: Max and Paulo all smiles backstage in São Paulo.

outside of the Belo Horizonte/Rio de Janeiro/São Paulo areas. They played in Amazonas for the first time on their *Green Hell Tour*, including in the set list a song from Kisser's previous band, Pestilence, that would appear on the next album. They headed up a mini-tour with Ratos de Porão and Chakal, promoted with flyers that promised, in English, "THRASH, NOISE, AND HARD CORE PUNKS!!!"

Considering the sometimes-violent feuds between metalheads and punks in those days, seeing such a bill—as well as Max wearing a Ramones t-shirt in the advertisements—came as a surprise to many. But Sepultura had a tendency to bring together disparate crowds through their own passions. If fans caught a glimpse of Igor or Max wearing a Sisters of Mercy shirt, Paulo one of Megadeth, or Andreas sporting an R.D.P. tank top, then it was cool for them to like those bands, too.

Within a relatively short period of the time, *Schizophrenia* sold over 10,000 copies in Brazil, which was quite the feat for a band of their kind. And it happened mostly through word of mouth.

Brazilian fans had discovered something uniquely their own, and they embraced it as such, lording over Sepultura, protecting them and defending them as they would their own families. *Schizophrenia* contained everything they loved about metal—the speed, the ferocity, the riffs—and it was entirely homegrown. And with this band poised to inflict musical destruction upon the world, how much prouder could they be?

Secondary to this sense of pride, these young metal fans were encouraged by Sepultura's growing success. Paulo, Igor, Max, and Andreas—they were no different than the kids who came to their shows. They all struggled against political corruption and economic instability. They feared the police rather than trusting them. They fought for the same ideals, they fought against prejudice. Through a business, and a genre, dominated by gringos, Sepultura were beginning to show that passion, determination, and loads of hard work could make anything possible for these kids.

And they would continue to show it with increasing authority as the years went on.

For their debut on Roadrunner, the guys felt compelled to make a statement. A loud, brash, volatile statement. Rehearsing for hours on end had made them incredibly tight as a unit, and with Andreas contributing to the entire recording process this time, the band convened again at the shed outside of Paulo's house. They were ready to show the world that there was more to Brazil than just coffee, beaches, soccer, and samba.

Perhaps, if subconsciously, they even felt a certain responsibility to their peers in the underground. While Sepultura hadn't necessarily spearheaded the national heavy metal scene, they had quickly ascended to the top of the heap. Groups that had preceded them, groups they adored and felt an affinity with—Dorsal Antântica, Vulcano, Korzus, and the others—strived for so long without much notoriety outside of the tightly knit local circles. Even Wagner and Sarcófago (who damned themselves by focusing solely on being "the most extreme" of all Brazilian bands) were left in the dust. When it came to metal in Brazil during the late 80s, there was Sepultura ... and then there was everyone else.

But they were young, still had a lot to prove, and were more than up for the challenge.

There was no magic formula to the creation of this soon to be classic album, outside of the intense chemistry that existed between the four members. Most of the songs evolved out of simple jam sessions, Max and Andreas throwing riffs at each other to see what would stick. The bulk of the material was written in Paulo's shed, with the exception of "Slaves of Pain."

"We just changed the ending," Andreas said, "but basically 'Slaves of Pain' was a Pestilence song."

Besides the standards such as Bathory, Slayer, Kreator, and Vio-lence, hardcore punk rock was starting to worm its way into Sepultura's influences. Bands like Dead Kennedys, English Dogs, Trouble, Discharge, and COC, with their socially conscious and politically critical lyrics, played in heavy rotation on the their stereos. They were broadening their musical scope, becoming more well rounded not just as artists, but as fans of music in general.

Stateside, Roadrunner was running down a list of potential producers for the album ... and quickly running out of options. Quite simply, no one wanted to do it. The budget was miniscule, the paycheck even more so, and the person chosen would have to fly down to Brazil during high summer there, and work through Christmas.

The only production tag on Scott Burns' resume at that point was a courtesy credit on Obituary's *Slowly We Rot*, though he had worked as an engineer for Death, Morbid Angel, and others. Burns was, at that time, the low man on the totem pole at Morrisound Recording in Tampa, Florida, the home base of the death metal scene Max had been corresponding with only a couple of years prior. Though not intimately familiar with Sepultura, Burns knew *of* them; during the sessions for *Slowly We Rot*, another brotherly team in Obituary's Don and John Tardy would frequently spin *Schizophrenia* in the studio and gush over how unrelenting it was.

When Roadrunner contacted Burns about the gig, he jumped at the opportunity. How could he have said no? Despite the low pay and the holiday away from home, he'd get a paid trip to Brazil, a country he had never been to, and his first actual job as a producer. The experience alone, Burns reasoned, was worth it. In his excitement and enthusiasm, he even dressed the part, meeting the band at the airport wearing bermuda shorts and havaianas.

He fit in right away.

On December 15 of 1988, recording began in Rio de Janeiro at Nas Nuvens, the studio owned and operated by Liminha of Os Mutantes. (Sepultura would pay tribute to the legend by recording a cover of the track "A Hora e a Vez do Cabelo Nascer" during the sessions.) But the work didn't begin without a hitch. During Burns' first day in Brazil, his hotel room was broken into, and all the equipment he'd brought for the band, including tapes and a portable stereo to listen to rough mixes, was stolen. The locks on the room's door were unharmed, which meant only one thing; the thieves were members of the hotel staff targeting a naïve gringo.

And this was after Roadrunner had already been forced to wire more money to Burns, so he could pay off airport security just to get the equipment through customs.

But neither band nor producer was deterred. They worked at night, from eight in the evening until five in the morning since the studio was less expensive then, and slept during the brutally hot summer days.

For Sepultura—Max and Andreas, especially—Rio didn't hold the same romantic charm it did for the American. Burns appeared to be the only one enjoying his time there, hanging out on the beach, having drinks at the famous Veloso Bar, birthplace of "The Girl from Ipanema." He was determined to get the most out of the experience.

And though they were sometimes forced to communicate through translators (the band still struggled with English and

Burns' Portuguese was non-existent), everyone felt that something special was taking place in the studio. The members of Sepultura felt like a *real* band, collaborating for the first time with an actual producer on an album that would be released globally (and legally, this time, in the case of Europe). But there was some trepidation. They had produced all their own recordings up until that point, and were afraid of relinquishing control to someone "outside" of the group, someone who didn't have the same connection to the music they had.

They needn't have worried. Burns, for the most part, allowed Sepultura to do what they do best. His concentration was solely on attaining the most powerful production values he could conjure, and pulling the best performances out of each member.

They got down to business, and they got down fast because they had barely two weeks to record. For Max, Andreas, and Igor, this wasn't a problem. They had rehearsed the songs enough that playing them took almost unconscious effort. But even though he knew the songs, Paulo was unable to perform under the pressure of such a tight deadline.

Playing live and recording are two completely different procedures. For many people, the thought of walking out in front of an audience is terrifying, enough to make one freeze up or pass out. Working in a studio would be infinitely preferable to these types, where any mistake is easily patched up or recorded over.

But for some musicians, the studio is an oppressive, confining space where the stress of performing under a microscope—and on expensive time constraints—makes it impossible to play well. The stage, in these cases, is the chosen sanctum, where missed notes and mistakes are expected in the heat of battle, and often aren't even noticed by the writhing mass of bodies in the audience.

So while a depressed Paulo wasn't around much, Andreas laid down the bass tracks for the album. Even still, they ran out of time to complete the recording and Max had to fly to Florida so he could finish the vocals at Morrisound.

The acoustic introduction of "Beneath the Remains," with its ambient swells of minor key progressions, acts in a similar manner as the intro on *Schizophrenia*. It prepares the listener for the brutally paced pummeling that is to come. The band exploited Kisser's classical inclinations, working the dynamics of an oft-referenced *calm before the storm* into the album opener.

And the opening track is most definitely a storm.

Packed from wall to wall with one monstrous riff after another, *Beneath the Remains* made it obvious that Sepultura had upped their game. The title track perfectly contains everything that defined the band in those days, from Max's characteristic rapid bark and Igor's creatively Slayer-inspired drum fills to the classically infused breakdown after Kisser's guitar solo.

The biggest difference that fans will notice, however, is in the lyrics.

While *Schizophrenia* veered away from the overtly evil and Satanic stylings of *Morbid Visions* and *Bestial Devastation*, it still retained a sense of the fantastic, of the unreal. Now, with *Beneath the Remains*, Sepultura appears to be more philosophical and contemplative about world events. While not quite as reflective of Brazil, in particular, as some of their later work would be, these lyrics show Max holding court on topics closer to their reality. "Beneath the Remains" paints a dark picture of a society ravaged by war and nuclear destruction, and plants a profound hypothetical question: are there really any victors in a war of such scale? And does the fighting ever stop? The answers seem self-explanatory as the music crashes to a close with the sound of gunfire and mortar shells.

Those sounds of war lead into "Inner Self," a sort of anthem for Sepultura, that would eventually receive video treatment and become a relative hit for the band. The mid-paced verses are rather more accessible to a wider audience, but just when one wonders if their beloved Brazilians have begun to mellow out, the familiar frenetic speed returns. This back and forth between head bobbing and pure banging—inclusive of Max's spoken poetry over clean guitars and dirty riffs—is the sound of a band stretching out, exploring. Max's lyrics are more personal than ever before, exposing his feelings while walking the streets of his home and being judged by the "normal" people all around him.

"Stronger Than Hate" continues the dive into that push/pull relationship between fast and slow, and the interplay between Max and Andreas as guitarists. They're very different players; Max the crude, using only four strings on his guitars since he never needed the two high strings, and Andreas the technical of the pair. But they're becoming more closely connected here, beyond Cavalera laying the foundation of riffs beneath Kisser's leads. Similar to the breakdown in "Beneath the Remains," Andreas smoothly picks out complex melodies on top of Max's

droning chords, opening up broader dimensions i.
sound of Sepultura.

By this third song, Igor has already outshined hin
less his contemporaries. His intuition is spot on, acc
guitars when appropriate, at times making the band s
a machine grinding away at one specific rhythmic patt
he knows when to break away, too, settling into a certain
groove the band will hone over the course of their career.

"Mass Hypnosis" follows, with Max's scathing critique
"follower" mentality, and those who use their power and
ence to manipulate such people. While writing the song, mes.
around in rehearsals, Andreas stumbled onto a strange phras.
of high-pitched, dissonant notes that sounded both weird a
cool when incorporated into the opening riff. Similar atypic
lead guitar pieces would be used in many song intros through the
years, becoming a signature part of Sepultura's sound.

Another signature becomes evident in "Sarcastic Existence,"
where sliding octave chords laid over the rhythm guitars lend a
soaring, vocal quality to Andreas' work. Without putting too fine
a point on it, Kisser's mark is already found all over *Beneath the
Remains*.

The band's influences still shine through in spots, such as the
distinctly Metallica-esque tribute shortly before the vocals of
"Sarcastic Existence" kick in. Much of the song, actually, has the
epic feel of Metallica's longer tracks from their *Ride the Lightning*
and *Master of Puppets* days. Stringing together one mind numbing
guitar part after another, the track at no point devolves into a
dreaded "riff soup"—a phrase meant to describe the nonsensical
stuffing of riffs into a song with no real progression or point.

Andreas continues to carve his impression into Sepultura with
"Slaves of Pain," one of the more technically complex numbers
on the record. It is almost hard to believe he had written it long
before joining the band, considering how perfectly it fits into the
sequence. "Lobotomy" continues down this technical path with
its circular, odd time signatures, drum fills that mimic equally
percussive guitar parts, and an especially melodic solo. After the
lead break, in stop/start rhythm, Kisser introduces a riff remarkably similar to the classic in "Crazy Train," but sped up to 45 revolutions per minute. An homage to his hero Randy Rhoads.

"Lobotomy" and "Hungry" see a slight return to the lyrically
stuffed verses of *Schizophrenia*, Max's accent and limited English

nearly getting in the way. Part of the appeal, though, is in the vocals' raw imperfection. Max doesn't sing like *anyone*, and the fact that his accent was unapologetically thick leant a sense of the exotic for everyone outside of Brazil.

And the subject matter of "Hungry" appears to directly address the political corruption in the nation. The people, Max seems to lament, are starving for food, sustenance, while the rich are only hungry for money, the powerful only hungry for more power.

Even though a late addition to the album, "Primitive Future" (titled after a cult classic skate video called *Future Primitive*) is powerful enough that Sepultura would use it to open their live shows on upcoming tours. Igor deftly switches from thrashing speed to mid-paced groove while the lyrics of Max and Andreas ponder a dead world, slyly referencing their homeland with a line about waking a sleeping giant. Kisser's lead is exceedingly expressive, almost a song unto its own, and it all comes to an end with a violent crash.

Beneath the Remains is difficult to categorize, running the gamut through nearly every sub-genre of metal. Not unlike Slayer, whose classic *Reign in Blood* contains ten songs clocking in at just under a half an hour, Sepultura would achieve status as underground legends with nine tracks that run a little *over* a half an hour.

The story behind the cover for *Beneath the Remains* has become somewhat of a myth, perhaps because—like other aspects of Sepultura's history—there is more than one story. As the saying goes, when two people tell different versions of the same anecdote, the truth is often somewhere in the middle.

If we accept the word of Max Cavalera, then we accept the following: Max discovered the art of Michael Whelan on the cover of an H.P. Lovecraft collection titled *Bloodcurdling Tales of Horror and the Macabre*, and sent the book to Monte Conner, who in turn contacted the artist. Whelan agreed to license the piece, but for whatever reason, Conner offered it to Obituary for their *Cause of Death* album instead of letting Sepultura use it. Max was, quite understandably, incensed.

Donald Tardy, Obituary's drummer, shrugged off this story. He has since said that Monte Conner offered the art to both bands at the same time, and Obituary simply claimed it first.

In either case, the piece that ended up on the cover of *Beneath the Remains* could not have been more perfect. A skull tinted deeply orange, like fire, sitting off center with Sepultura's new, more readable logo emblazoned over a deep expanse of black space. Entitled *Nightmare in Red*, the art was simple and eye-catching. As heavy metal album covers went, it was much more subtle than the graphic depictions of carnage and evisceration seen on those of Slayer or Cannibal Corpse, yet it conjured up a bleak atmosphere resembling the aftereffects of war. And that's precisely what the music sounded like, too; from the clean opening strains—that pre-storm calm that lulls listeners into a false sense of security—to the sudden, apocalyptic end of "Primitive Future," *Beneath the Remains* was Armageddon in sonic form.

Sepultura, from the very beginning, was always lucky to have assistance, support, and dedication from such a passionate group of friends. One of these was Eric de Haas, a well-known Dutch photographer credited as such on the album.

"I happened to move to Brazil in November, 1988," Eric explained, "and Sepultura started to record their album shortly after that. As I was a photographer and working for most European and American rock magazines at that time, most people knew this, seeing that those magazines were available here in Brazil, too. Sepultura were the band that everyone was speaking about with high expectations, so mutual friends made sure I went to the studio where they were recording, in Rio de Janeiro, to check them out."

Max and Igor's apartment in Santa Cecilia.

The guys soon realized that opportunity in Minas Gerais was limited, and if they wanted to take a stab at the big time, they had to leave Belo Horizonte. There was no hesitation. Everyone knew where they had to go.

São Paulo.

On a solo weekend trip to the city, to surprise her boys, Vânia rented Max and Igor an apartment in Santa Cecilia. Paulo moved in with Andreas in Santo André. The quartet met daily at a rehearsal space in Pompéia not far from where the Cavaleras had grown up.

It was also quite close to where Eric de Haas lived.

"Early 1989," Eric said, "Max, Igor, [their] mother and sister all moved to São Paulo downtown, and that happened to be exactly one block from the apartment that I had rented. So we became neighbors and very soon really good friends, hanging out every day either at my place or their place, going out together nearly every night, and Max and me became inseparable party brothers then.

Though Max was far from settling down, Igor had already begun the process, in a sense, by rather seriously dating a girl he'd met three years before.

"I had this friend," Monika Bass Cavalera (back then, just Monika Bass) recalled, "and she came to me and said there's two cute guys from Belo Horizonte in São Paulo, and [she] liked this guy called Igor. We went to this girl's house and she was trying to stay with Igor and I was there with Max because it was two couples, right? And it was me and Max and I had to spend the night with him talking, and [then] I never saw him again in three years. No contact, nothing. [But] I saw Igor like once a year—he had a girlfriend, I had a boyfriend—and then on the third year we met again, and he was single and I was single, and we started dating. When I met them I was eighteen, and I started dating Igor when I was twenty-one."

Max's 21st birthday in São Paulo.

The Cavaleras' apartment quickly became known as a party house, people roaming in and out at all hours of the night. Sepultura, as individuals, were enjoying life. They were young, fun-loving musicians rapidly ascending to fame in Brazil and beyond, and about to proceed into unexpected territories with *Beneath the Remains.*

Roadrunner released the album on April 7, 1989, with cautious hope. Of course they wanted it to succeed, they hoped for it to succeed, but expectations were set low. So low, in fact, that the first pressing of the album contained no liner notes, no lyric sheet. The label was hesitant to put too much money into promotion, much less pay for the band to tour outside of their homeland, until the album proved itself.

It was a harsh reality of the music business, a vicious circle of justification. Album sales were used to finance tours, but tours were used to promote the albums. Without promotion, how could Sepultura expect the album to sell? And if the album didn't sell, how would they ever afford to promote it?

The situation sorted itself out. Worldwide recognition of *Beneath the Remains* was immediate, selling over 200,000 copies in Europe and the United States combined, and almost overnight

Max's 21st birthday in São Paulo.

there was a demand for Sepultura to bring their particular brand of South American metal to foreign lands. Having only played two or three shows per month before then, the opportunity to tour beyond their own borders was at the same time unexpected, long desired, and incredibly daunting.

A jaunt in Europe with thrash legends Sodom, originally scheduled for July, fell through due to the German group's recording delays, so Sepulture embarked on a brief Brazilian *Tour of the Remains*. At one of these shows, on July 22 with Atômica for support, they began filming a video for "Inner Self." They needed a second day to complete the video, but for continuity's sake, no one could remember what clothes they were wearing during the first day's shoot.

The clip is a landmark, juxtaposing images of the crowd's insanity with candid shots of the band offstage. As the first single from the album, and their first promotional video, "Inner Self" became an anthem for Sepultura.

Over the next couple of months, a few other international offers rolled in (most notably a European tour with Nuclear Assault and Dark Angel), but nothing concrete was established.

The guys feared they'd missed their shot. The music business, they knew, opened up brief windows of opportunity, and if artists didn't jump through when they had the chance, there might never be another.

The slot with Sodom ended up being rescheduled for September, and Sepultura dived through their window. On the twelfth of that month, the Brazilians departed São Paulo for Dusseldorf, where they took a bus to Austria and joined the *Agent Orange Tour* in Vienna on the fifteenth.

To understand how overwhelming even this level of accomplishment was, a little perspective is necessary. A year before, Sepultura mainly played at underground festivals in Brazil with several other bands because they couldn't afford to finance their own shows. A year before that, they had to share a guitar with two other bands, and not long before *that*, Igor needed a friend to hold up the broomstick he used for a cymbal stand so it wouldn't fall over when he played.

Now they were in Europe, thousands of miles away from home, not only their first time touring outside of Brazil, but their first time traveling *anywhere* outside of South America.

The band's nerves were running on high-octane fuel as they

pulled up to the venue in Austria. They had expected a legion of Sodom fans—and *only* Sodom fans—to be waiting, but were amazed to find a sea of kids wearing Sepultura shirts already queued around the building.

It was the first of many good signs.

The Brazilians took to the stage that night, hungry and ready to show Europe what they could do, opening their set with the one-two punch of "Primitive Future" and "Inner Self." They owned that crowd, stalking with blood in their eyes, as if it were their first—and last—performance.

The members of Sodom, on the other hand, were veterans, and perhaps slightly tired veterans, at that. They played with much less intensity, Igor later noted, as if it were simply a job to them. The crowds also took notice. Sepultura, fueled by the energy of the audience as well as by Sodom's perceived *lack* of energy, performed with increasing fury each night.

Touring might have been a frustrating, mind-numbing bore between sets, traveling on buses between strange grey cities where the sun didn't shine like it did back home, but nothing could dampen Sepultura's spirit. Not the manager's instructions and rules they couldn't understand, not the incredibly short amount of time they were allowed to eat during road stops. Not even the demand that Max take a shower because he smelled bad.

This was a band unified by adversity. Fuck with one of them, and you fuck with all of them. When Max decided not to shower for the rest of the tour, Igor, Andreas, and Paulo joined the pact. *None of them* would shower for the rest of the tour. But that non-confrontational plan of attack may have backfired. After a week of playing concerts in hot, dank clubs, sweat soaking into their hair and clothes, the band members couldn't stand the odor of themselves.

As the tour went on, more and more fans came solely for Sepultura, some of them leaving the venue immediately after the Brazilians finished playing. The band's standout performance came at London's legendary Marquee Club in their first UK appearance, where music journalist Dave Ling witnessed Sepultura "destroying Sodom" during a show that *Kerrang! Magazine* would list in their top ten 'greatest gigs of all time'. They could not have imagined a better start to their international career.

55

Two weeks after the final European show, Sepultura broke into the most coveted market yet, and in awe-inspiring fashion. On Halloween night—fittingly—and at the legendary Ritz Theater in New York City, they opened for one of their childhood heroes: Mercyful Fate vocalist King Diamond.

Also appearing that evening were Roadrunner label mates Sacred Reich, accompanied by their manager, Gloria Bujnowski, who had recently been asked by the label to take on Sepultura. Gloria refused despite being intrigued, as Monte Conner had been, by their reputation.

But she was overwhelmed when she saw them perform, and immediately saw the group's potential. Gloria decided then and there to manage them, but would do so only after the band either honored the rest of their existing management contract or found a way out of it.

A co-headlining tour with Faith Or Fear followed. While *Beneath the Remains* continued to sell well, audience turnout was disappointing, and less than stellar. The band received very little financial support on the road, but they were happy enough just to *be on the road*, and in the United States, no less. They again met with Gloria at the Phoenix date, her hometown, to discuss their soon-to-be partnership. The tour ended a few days later and the band returned home to Brazil excited about their prospects for the future.

But despite these successes, Max, Igor, Andreas, and Paulo weren't seeing much money coming in.

Max and Igor in Praia Grande.

Eric de Haas explained, "I did know the people at Roadrunner, and the owner Cees Wessels, very well seeing that Roadrunner is a Dutch company and I was one of the only Dutch photographers for metal magazines back then. So we knew each other for many years already before I moved to Brazil. The contract that Max had signed with Roadrunner on his trip to New York was a contract that most bands at that time got presented with by Roadrunner, and eager for them to sign with a label outside of Brazil, they accepted it the way it came.

"They were just happy to sign the album release and merchandise and future plans all together," Eric said, "but only later found out that—even after a certain time and high sales of the album and the merchandise—they still did not get any money. The contract had a clause that meant that even merchandise money could be used to cover investments in the album, meaning that every time Roadrunner had to pay them sales royalties from merchandise, for example, they took into account their investment in the band—recording studio time or another tour perhaps (before they paid royalties)."

As a result, and as was common with rock business contracts, Sepultura were constantly owing money to the record company, who were paying all their bills for them.

"The financial situation back then was quite difficult for Max, Igor, and their mom," Eric continued, "so at one point I called Cees and told him that the contract [Max] had signed was of course valid, and the band was happy with that, but could not survive without cash, so he should start getting a cash flow going to Brazil or otherwise there was a big chance the band would just stop existing because the brothers would not be able to survive without a cash flow or a normal job. Cees understood the situation and just asked for a bank account to deposit money in, and the same week, they received their first US$ 10,000."

In those days, that much money was a fortune in Brazil.

In May of 1990, Sepultura played a handful of shows with Napalm Death in Brazil before embarking on a second round of dates in Europe. Already their English had improved, mostly from traveling and talking to fans in the United States, as well as relying upon it as a mutual secondary language in European countries. The name of the tour—*Death from the Jungle*—was rather ironic. They were city boys; none of them lived anywhere even remotely near a jungle, unless one counted the concrete jungles of Belo Horizonte and São Paulo. But as a marketing ploy, it worked. Very few non-Brazilians had a clue that the Amazon was hundreds of miles away from—and starkly different than—the bustling metropolises where Sepultura had grown up. *Death from the Jungle* sparked curiosity and interest for those who hadn't yet gotten their hands on a copy of *Beneath the Remains*.

The high point of the tour was a performance at the Dynamo Festival in Holland, for 26,000 people, on June 4. This was, by far, their largest audience yet, and the band were all nervous as hell, afraid of passing out or falling down onstage. As usual though, once in the heat of the moment, Sepultura tore through their hour-long set and left the crowd begging for more.

And, once again, they had de Haas to thank.

Said Eric, "A good Dutch friend of mine, Andre Verhuysen, was the organizer of the Dynamo festival in Holland, and setting up tours throughout Europe (and also close to the people at Roadrunner), so I spoke with Andre about having Sepultura play the festival and setting up a tour for Sepultura throughout Europe since the album was getting good reviews everywhere. Andre and me spoke on the phone about all details. I then discussed everything with the band, and Andre set up their first 'own' European tour."

But as with Andreas back in the *Morbid Visions* days, Eric wasn't actually working for Sepultura, *per se*, just doing whatever he could to help. "It was more like helping out friends. In 1990, I did bring Napalm Death to Brazil to do three shows in São Paulo, for instance. Although Sepultura were the heavy metal act everybody spoke about, there was also a strong belief [among] Brazilians that anything from outside of Brazil was better than anything Brazilian. So I used the opportunity to put Sepultura as the support act for Napalm Death, but on the third day swapped them around, having Napalm Death open for Sepultura in order to show clearly that coming from Brazil was not synonymous with inferior or coming from abroad synonymous with superior. That surely made a great impact over here back then."

Dynamo marked another turning point for the band. Sacred Reich were also on the bill, which meant Gloria Bujnowski—who always accompanied her bands on the road—was there, as well. With Sepultura having (rather expensively) manoeuvered their way out of their previous management contract, Gloria agreed to work with them for one year, free of charge, on a trial basis. As hands on as she was, she understood the importance of ensuring that the personal relationships clicked.

But there's always danger involved in getting too close in business relationships, and some of those personal interactions would have certain consequences.

"Sepultura wanted to sign with a manager from outside Brazil," de Haas said, "and when Gloria first came into the picture they ended up scheduling a meeting on tour, and she even came along for a few days if I am not mistaken, in order to have time to get to know each other better. Of course, they were asking my opinion and since Andre had previously worked with Gloria and [had] good experiences, I suggested they go ahead, if possible."

In the five months between tours in 1990, the guys had already begun work on the next album. With their Roadrunner debut a largely unexpected hit in death metal circles, both the label and the band thought it best to write new music and head back into the studio as quickly as possible. They didn't want to give anyone a chance to breathe; after hitting them with a devastating album and insane live shows, they wanted to follow up with a knockout punch while people were still dizzy and weak kneed.

In August, Sepultura returned to J.G. Studios in Belo Horizonte for a couple of days, in order to rerecord a new and sonically improved version of "Troops of Doom." The track was slated to appear as a bonus on Roadrunner's US release of *Schizophrenia*, having been remixed entirely by Scott Burns.

Paulo, Igor, Max, and Andreas traveled to Florida and spent a month and a half recording the next album with Burns. The entire process took place at Morrisound this time, with Andreas again providing bass tracks. Roadrunner offered a considerably greater budget since they thought Sepultura a proven commodity now, and Burns was making a name for himself as *the* consummate death metal producer.

At the end of that year, the band returned to the United States for the *SOS Tour*, with Obituary and Sadus supporting, and Gloria at the helm. This trek far outperformed their previous run. Clubs were packed with sweaty, delirious, *ecstatic* metalheads attracted by the brutal lineup and the tagline, "Some Tours Were Meant To Stay Underground."

"Dangerous" was a fitting description of the bill. In Milwaukee, Obituary set off a flash pot that caused a rather large explosion and set Tardy's drums on fire. The final night of the tour, December

23, ended in chaos. At the Omni in Oakland, California, Sadus—the hometown boys—got all the bands drunk. Of course, parties were commonplace at every gig, but this evening went far beyond normal. Fights, vomiting, destroyed equipment, and vicious hangovers were just a few highlights of the night.

Also on that date, Sepultura received an early Christmas present when they spotted Metallica's James Hetfield and Lars Ulrich in the audience. Metallica were riding high on the massive popularity of ...*And Justice for All* at the time, idols that Sepultura had worshipped even before songs like "Welcome Home (Sanitarium)" and "One" had become hit singles in every corner of the world. The Brazilians were like little kids, giddy and in disbelief to be playing for their heroes—much less hanging out with them—on the home field of Bay Area thrash metal.

But the band had earlier received the shock of their career thus far. As the only Brazilian rockers popular enough to tour outside of their home country, they'd been confirmed to play at the following year's Rock In Rio festival.

FOUR

A BRUTAL ASCENT

If it was impossible to overstate the importance—for Brazilians and their country, in general—of the first Rock In Rio event, it was equally so for Rock In Rio II and its impact on Sepultura. Promoters scheduled them to open the day's festivities at Maracanã Stadium on January 23 of 1991, the night of which would see Megadeth, Guns n' Roses, Judas Priest, and Queensryche perform.

The band's inclusion on the bill woke people up to this little band called Sepultura. Of course many Brazilians had heard of them, but few outside of those aware of the heavy metal underground understood the group's significance on the scale of global music.

Though the new album wasn't quite finished, Scott Burns threw together a rough mix to release in limited form, and only in Brazil, to celebrate the occasion. Shortly before the festival, Max, Tuka Quinelli, Eric de Haas, and a group of friends were hanging out in Praia Grande, pleasantly engaged in the consumption of beer, batidas, and vodka, when a bunch of fans recognized Cavalera and joined the party. Before long, a small crowd had formed, and Max told the gathering that the sound coming out of their car's stereo was the new Sepultura album. Those kids were ecstatic to be hearing *Arise* firsthand with Max, and paid the Mineiro metalhead plenty of compliments. In truth, Tuka later recounted with a laugh, the music was the solo work of former Plasmatics vocalist Wendy O. Williams.

Backstage, before their set, Sepultura were looked upon as amateurs. Though members of Megadeth were friendly, meeting with the guys and asking if they'd like to join them for dinner, the promoters had forbidden Sepultura to enter the VIP tents where the foreign bands were treated like royalty. Plus they weren't offered a penny for their performance, and Roadrunner had to foot all the bills.

As could be said of big international festivals, homegrown acts were considered second-tier and of lesser importance to the occasion than internationally renowned bands. The gringo bands, the foreign bands, were the draw. Sepultura had been thrown into the mix as an obligation, an afterthought, almost.

Just before taking to the Rock In Rio stage in the scorching heat of a tropical summer sun, Igor, Andreas, Max, and Paulo were a mess of nervous energy. This was always the most anxious time, Andreas explained. Those final pre-show moments.

As soon as Max alerted the 70,000-strong crowd by shouting *"Vamos detonar, Rio!"* and Igor began the intro that led into "Primitive Future" though, the nerves melted away and adrenaline took over.

The sound was terrible, the PA system junk. Max's vocals were too loud, the guitars were so buried in the mix as to be practically non-existent, and the live television feed crossed signals from time to time, broadcasting the music of some other band.

But that half hour on stage turned their world upside down.

The promoters had expected that the early timeslot would ensure Sepultura came and went with little to no fanfare, but they were dead wrong. That was a heavy metal crowd on a heavy metal day. They were starving for Sepultura, so much so that singer/songwriter Lobão, who followed, was only able to perform a couple of songs before being forced off the stage by a hailstorm of rocks and bottles. And the songs he did play were drowned out by the audience's deafening chants of *"Sepultura! Sepultura!"*

Andreas enjoying himself in Santos.

Despite the conditions, it was an undeniably triumphant performance, their first on home territory since 1989. Suddenly, Brazil understood what everyone else had already known for a while; Sepultura were about to conquer the world of heavy music.

A couple of short months later, after a proper mix courtesy of Andy Wallace, the instant classic *Arise* hit the record store shelves. While the songs attacked straight at the jugular with a fierce mix of death and thrash metal, the astute listener caught glimpses of industrial, punk, even samba and batucada. Lyrically, more than ever, the songs reflected the violence and corruption of their homeland. The difficulties of growing up in a developing, Third World nation. Production and sound quality were both a step up from *Beneath the Remains*, due to the expanded budget and the masterful work of Andy Wallace. Max's English had continued to improve, enhancing his vocal abilities, and the lyrics were shorter, more to the point, providing greater punch and impact.

Arise foregoes all pretense, striking hard and fast within seconds after the ominous beating of drums and an air-raid siren sounding dull and muted, as if it were buried in rubble. Though Sepultura recorded a studio version of the intro they used at Rock In Rio, and would add it to future special editions of the album as a bonus track, the decision to plunge straight into the volatile "Arise" was a wise one. The song is brutal, punishing, and perfect.

Again, as with the progression from *Schizophrenia* to *Beneath the Remains*, there is a shocking improvement in lyrical depth. Max waxes philosophical here, not only posing thought-provoking ideas, but using foresight enough to phrase these ideas in such a way that will later inspire audience interaction. Kisser's leads are more frantic, more complex than ever, and Igor's drumming is both simple and extraordinarily complicated at the same time.

As the leadoff single, "Arise" gained more than its fair share of attention in part because the video was banned from MTV. The channel believed the apocalyptic and religious imagery to be controversial. The fact that it was filmed in the Mojave Desert, more specifically the area where Charles Manson and his followers spent time, only increased its infamy.

Faith No More's Billy Gould, as well as Dino Cazares from Fear Factory, accompanied the band to the video shoot. Despite its appearance and location, the clip was not filmed in scorching temperatures. In fact, it was near freezing, the crucified extras sometimes collapsing after being strung up practically naked.

The band's attention to, and awareness of, audience reaction is again explicit in "Dead Embryonic Cells," another track that received video treatment. While *Arise*, so far, shows Sepultura's music as increasingly more complicated, it is also becoming increasingly less so in all the right places. Following a smorgasbord of intricate riffing and Kisser's equally psychotic lead, "Dead Embryonic Cells" suddenly grinds to a halt, traversing into a slow groove. This rhythmic chug of a single note, an open string guitar riff that is so simple it can be played with one hand, will have audiences bouncing and headbanging for years to come. It is the deepest groove Sepultura has created yet, ensuring the track a permanent place in future set lists.

Arise enjoys its first mellow moment, as brief as it may be, with the acoustic intro to "Desperate Cry." Twenty seconds of relief later, the pummeling begins anew with only slightly dialed down intensity this time. But a reduction in intensity does not equal a reduction in heaviness. More and more, the band is learning how to restrain themselves, how to not go full bore for the entire duration of a song.

"Murder," a song Sepultura had debuted to powerful reaction while touring for *Beneath the Remains*, continues as an example of restraint. Igor slows his tempo for much of the track even while the guitars race onward. Employing slightly recognizable progressions that could qualify "Murder" as a sort of sequel to "Inner Self," Andreas and Max toy with harmonies and counterpoints. Cavalera spits fury at the constantly scrolling news of homicides and death, citing an incident in Brazil where eight inmates suffocated due to overcrowding in a prison cell.

Slayer influences move to the forefront in "Subtraction," also tipping its hat to *Killing Is My Business... And Business Is Good*-era Megadeth. Strangely, the song shreds like pure thrash, even though the listeners get a taste of hardcore—a mouthful of Dead Kennedys, maybe—about three-quarters of the way through with a highlighted bass guitar section. And the catchy, almost sing-along style chorus begs to screamed at top volume.

Igor introduces a little bit of Brazil into the intro of "Altered State" (a foreshadowing of what will come in later years), rhythms reminiscent of batucada set upon a backdrop of wind, whistles, wooded instruments, and even synthesizers. Kisser colors the song's beginning with his signature effects and octave chords, his lyrics vaguely dark and unsettling. Max' words on the following, "Under Siege (Regnum Irae)"—the latter part of the title Latin for "kingdom of anger"—are almost poetry in places. The unusual parsing of sentences and lines, spoken in a low voice reverberating like a record played backwards, allows Cavalera to contemplate in depth the battle between spirituality and humanity. Why does one tend to suffer as the other thrives?

Roadrunner would release "Under Siege (Regnum Irae)" as a

Max and Igor at Santos sound check.

single, perhaps because the song is at times the band's slowest and most accessible yet. But it is heavier than a ton of bricks. Among their many other lessons so far, Sepultura has learned that they can enhance a riff's weight just by slowing it down. This is a technique they'll experiment with greatly on coming albums.

The addictive and bouncy "Meaningless Movements" demands credit as a headbanger's delight. Riffs melt into one another, droning and dissonant notes creating an industrial vibe in the song's second half that builds into a blindingly fast verse before turning back around and ending the way it began. The album closer, "Infected Voice," is merciless all the way through, the speed of the guitars matching pace with the quickest tracks on *Schizophrenia*. It doesn't let up until the final shout, the final word, and only then can we catch our breath. On reflection, the listener realizes *Arise* hasn't let up since the moment it began.

A stomping version of Motorhead's "Orgasmatron" was recorded, but not included on the album. Instead, it would first appear as a bonus track on the "Dead Embryonic Cells" single, and much later as part of a collection of b-sides. Another song, an original titled "C.I.U. (Criminals in Uniform)," was also laid down during the *Arise* sessions. With lyrics written by former *Metal Maniacs* magazine editor Katherine Ludwig Moses (who, interestingly, has a son named Max), the track is strong, though not quite as intense as the others, and was thus understandably left off of the album.

This time around, with Michael Whelan's cover, the band got the Lovecraftian fix they were seeking for *Beneath the Remains*. Whelan's labyrinthine tower built of flesh and body parts—his vision of Yog-Sothoth, an Outer God from Lovecraft's Cthulhu Mythos—sits upon a vast, hellish backdrop, an image easily as psychotic as the music contained within the album sleeve. Roadrunner commemorated the release of *Arise* with a postcard showing the cover emblazoned with an ironic greeting:

Welcome to Brazil.

Arise debuted to unanimously rave reviews from fans and critics alike. It peaked on the US Billboard chart at 119, an unbelievable feat for such extreme music during a time when the ranks were dominated by Bryan Adams, Color Me Badd, and Mariah Carey. It went gold in Indonesia and Malaysia, and saw the band off on a promotional cycle that encompassed nearly two years' worth of shows.

Those two years were riddled with highs and lows. Among the highs were tours with Ozzy Osbourne, Ministry, and Helmet, and *Arise* eventually selling over one million copies worldwide. Among the lows was an infamous concert in São Paulo where Sepultura recorded a video clip for "Orgasmatron."

The underground metal scene in Brazil during the late eighties, as we have seen, depended on word of mouth and tape trading. This was not uncommon in other countries where extreme metal was taking its heavy baby steps. The tape trading culture was indicative of a closely-knit community in which its members were largely considered outcasts of society. They supported each other's habits, each other's addictions to music that sounded the way they felt inside. And in those underground circles, the fans and the bands were sometimes indistinguishable not only because they looked the same, with their long hair and jean jackets covered in patches, but often because they were both fans *and* musicians.

The mutual support system amongst these like-minded individuals is often glossed over. A victory for one underground band was practically a victory for all of them, and could open otherwise closed doors.

But in Brazil, more so than anywhere else, the innocent

creation of a fan club played a major role in the accomplishments of one particular band.

When dissecting the early history of Sepultura, it is virtually impossible to neglect the importance of the Official Brazilian Fan Club, fondly known as the s.o.b.f.c., which was inaugurated in 1990, and established a concrete home with the 1991 launch of the headquarters in São Paulo's Galeria do Rock.

Store number 452 became a sacred meeting place for those fans from Sampa, with others from all over Brazil—and elsewhere—making pilgrimages to the metal mecca. Covered from wall to wall in posters, album covers, stickers, emblems, flags, and everything else you can imagine emblazoned with the Sepultura logo, the headquarters frequently saw visits from the band members themselves whenever they were in town.

The idea for such a club, however, had been gestating in the mind of Antonio "Toninho" Coelho, since shortly after the release of *Schizophrenia*.

Over the years, Toninho himself has become somewhat of an icon in the Brazilian metal scene. Visible at every show worthy of note in São Paulo, always smiling and thirsty for a beer, he has been preaching the gospel of Sepultura since 1985, and pops up at several different points in the band's story.

"The first show I went was in the same year," said Toninho, "at the time they were touring together with Overdose to promote *Bestial Devastation*. The venue was a place called Heavy Metal Club in the neighborhood of Vila Carrao in São Paulo. The place was super crowded and Sepultura simply devastated everything. Overdose hadn't any chance that day! They were harassed by the audience because their clothes were like glam metal."

By 1988, Toninho recalled, Sepultura "had already conquered its space in Brazil, and the gringos were starting to notice the band's sound." So he joined forces with other fans, and printed a batch of special t-shirts that they all wore when the band returned to São Paulo to launch the *Schizophrenia* album.

It seems so ingenuous, but no other Brazilian group had ever been paid such tribute before.

Djalma "Thrashão" Agra, one of Toninho's closest compatriots, saw the band for his first time on that same tour, in Manaus, July of 1988.

He explained the atmosphere of the underground music scenes at the time, and the personal character such dedication showed. "To be a metal fan in the 80s until mid-90s in Brazil was a very dangerous adventure," he said. "There were skinheads and punk gangs always fighting each other and attacking metal fans."

On the bus headed to his first Sepultura concert at Olimpico Club, Agra was separated from his friends. Two gang members approached, yelling at him for no apparent reason. They were looking for a fight, and they got it.

Agra remembers, "My brother, who was a veteran martial arts practitioner, started a huge fight inside the bus. We literally threw the guys through the bus window and they swore vengeance."

The gang sought their revenge at the concert in Bairro Matinha. They ruled that neighborhood, it was their territory, and they had no problem finding Agra and his friends. Advancing upon them this time with a baseball bat, the gang's leader was disarmed, again humiliated by Agra's brother. Had the police not shown up shortly thereafter, the night might have ended much differently for all of them.

Sepultura also faced some difficulties that evening. Agra remembered a few technical problems, and the band felt the power of the Amazonia heat enough to pause the show a couple of times to get some air. But everyone in attendance—even the group of fans who had brought a full-sized coffin—sensed that they were witnessing history in the making.

Unfortunately, as Igor would later point out, violence was commonplace in Brazil, especially where large groups were gathered. While most came to enjoy the show and have a good time, there were always those who came for trouble or to steal things from people. These events did not go unnoticed by the sensationalist media looking for any excuse to condemn heavy metal music for being unruly and attracting undesirable audiences.

But the s.o.b.f.c. stood by Sepultura, defending their heroes—and themselves—in the face of all critics. Such devotion didn't go unnoticed, and a connection was born that grew far more intense than any typical band-to-fan relationship.

In May of 1991, Gloria worked with São Paulo's city hall and secretary of culture to arrange a special free show at Praça Charles Miller, just outside of Pacaembu Stadium where several matches had been played during the 1950 World Cup. What was planned as a fun and peaceful event to thank the s.o.b.f.c. and the homeland fans, since Sepultura had been away for so long, ended as a dark day in the band's history.

"I remember that day very well," Agra said, "because I lived nearby the Pacaembu Stadium, and since the beginning of the day I could see from my apartment window thousands of people going to the concert, most of them carrying glass bottles containing all kinds of alcohol."

When Agra arrived at Praça Charles Miller, he could easily see 15,000 fans—even though the Praça only comfortably held 10,000 people—and some police troops. The show was still a few hours away.

"The number of fans increased through the hours to more than 40,000 people," Agra said, all of them desperate to witness a rare performance before the band departed on another endless international tour.

"Being an open air and free," Toninho added, "the concert attracted people of all tribes."

"I remember too many fights around," Agra said. "The atmosphere was very heavy. There was no security. Thousands of people, most of them young, carrying alcohol, with no security around… of course fights were just a matter of time."

The crowd continued to rage out of control, more so even, while Sepultura were on stage. At one point the band stopped playing, and Igor stepped out from behind the drum kit to make an aggressive stance at the microphone. "I want everyone to watch this show without any form of violence, with a lot of peace," he said. "This band is for peace, not violence."

But from the stage, no one had any idea just how out of control the crowd had become, so the show continued on. It only came out later that over a dozen fans were severely injured and one was fatally shot.

"I'd just known about the boy's death the next day in the newspaper," Agra said. "A skinhead shot the guy. We heard the boy belonged to a gang too, but we never knew the truth. The fact is that event had a very negative impact on the band, and it took years for people to realize they never had any responsibility for that."

"The band, of course, never wanted to promote a concert to hurt anyone," Toninho added. "But the press at the time wanted to see rock n' roll involved in all crap possible. The audience was not welcome by the authorities and media. Anything that happened in an event of this size, obviously [the media] would take maximum advantage of the bad side. The death at the concert was everything they wanted."

"The media was not wrong," Agra recounted, "when saying the audience was violent, because part of the audience really was."

Toninho agreed. "All specialized media took advantage both to help [and] to damage the band's image," he said.

The media found their scapegoat. While Sepultura had always insisted their music was a reflection of society, the press vehemently opposed the idea. They claimed that the loud, hyperspeed music and antagonistic lyrics incited violence in the people. In later interviews, Max would go toe to toe with these journalists, pointing out that the band and the fans were unified in frustration. Sepultura fans, he said, went to concerts *already pissed off* that they were criticized for having long hair and tattoos, and didn't fit the mold society had reserved for them. They were *already pissed off* that the government was more interested in feeding their own bottom line than in feeding their poor. They were *already pissed off* about the injustice, the corruption, the crime, the poverty. Like the artists during the military dictatorship who voiced their discontent through protest music, Sepultura were a megaphone blasting the anger of the people.

But the band didn't get a chance to retaliate against the media accusations then. Less than a week after the incident at Praça Charles Miller, they'd be in the Netherlands to begin the *Arise* tour cycle, which would see them on the road for almost two years.

Following a couple of warm-up shows and a festival slot in Germany, the European tour officially kicked off with Sacred Reich as special guests, and short-lived Bay Area thrashers Heathen opening. The metal press—those who supported heavy music, not those who condemned it—was abuzz with stories of Sepultura's already renowned concerts. At the end of May, to show everyone else exactly what they were about, the band recorded two shows in Catalonia to later be released as their first home video, titled *Under Siege: Live in Barcelona*. For the uninitiated who hadn't yet seen Sepultura in concert, it became clear that this band was hungry, firing on all cylinders. The incendiary live performance made up the meat of the video, interspersed with revealing interview segments.

Gloria and Sepultura (and Sacred Reich) dove right from Europe into the aptly named *New Titans On The Bloc* tour crisscrossing the US, adding Napalm Death and Sick Of It All onto the bill. Despite a threat of lawsuit by the managers of teen pop sensations New Kids On The Block, the trek was an achievement of impressive proportions. Bands, crews, and fans got on famously during the two-month tour. In nothing but good nature, Sepultura drank all of Napalm Death's Heineken beer. A pair of

Japanese girls followed the band religiously up the west coast, never missing a single show. At a date in New York, where Sick Of It All was unable to play, up-and-comers White Zombie filled the slot.

Across America's bible belt and the Midwest, where nothing much of consequence ever happened, Sepultura were—for many—a strange breath of exotic air. As their notoriety increased, so did the number of interview requests. Media and press were drawn to them and their accents, asking about the social injustice, the drug problems, the favela gangs in Brazil. The guys were well spoken, now with polished English. They explained that their lyrics weren't always meant to target Brazil specifically, but to raise awareness about similar problems all over the world.

With Roadrunner Records crew (notice Andreas' broken arm).

Paulo, who detested interviews, pretended that he didn't understand English so he wouldn't have to do them.

A three-month break was in order during the final quarter of the year. In December, just days after the band's first concerts in Mexico (bootleg videos of which show a highly out-of-control audience welcoming their Latin American brothers with furious passion), Andreas broke his right arm in a Jet Ski accident. The timing was unfortunate; Sepultura had been booked for the Christmas Metal Meetings European tour with Motorhead, Morbid Angel, and Kreator, to begin on the eighteenth of the month. Rather than cancel their participation in those six dates, Igor, Paulo, and Max went on with Korzus guitarist Silvio Golfetti filling in. Kisser was disappointed that he couldn't contribute, but he commended Golfetti for doing a fantastic job on such short notice.

The band took another short sabbatical, this time for the holidays, returning to the road in March of 1992 with Andreas' arm

From Brazil to the world.

Tourism in Moscow.

A kilted photo session.

caged up in a metal brace and UK noise metallers Fudge Tunnel as support. The tour nurtured a friendship between Max Cavalera and Fudge Tunnel's Alex Newport that would later culminate in a half-industrial, half-metal, all noise collaboration dubbed Nailbomb.

Indonesia, of all places, took to *Arise* in a way few other countries had. Fans there felt an affinity with the Brazilians, as the struggles they faced daily in their own land weren't so different. Since earning its independence from Dutch colonialists in 1945, Indonesia had dealt with poverty and rapid economic change, political corruption and violence. The lyrics on *Arise* that pertained to Brazil, as the guys had explained earlier, could just as easily apply to any developing Third World nation. Including Indonesia.

And just like Brazil, Indonesia suffered from a massive gap between the rich and the poor. Millions of citizens lived in destitution and poverty even as the rich grew richer. One of these influential businessmen invited Sepultura to his palace for a private performance, showering the band with gifts, food, drink, and culture. This was a stark contrast to the concert in Jakarta, where 40,000 of the not-so-wealthy fans were descended upon by the police, struck with bamboo rods, and forced to sit in silence after the authorities deemed the crowd wild and disorderly.

Indonesian photo shoot.

It was such a shock that Max stopped the show to say he was sorry for all the problems, and wished they could do more than just apologize. In the States, Cavalera would start fights with security for beating up fans. In Indonesia, he was at a loss.

The gargantuan partnership of that summer belonged to Metallica and Guns n' Roses, who teamed up for a co-headlining North American stadium tour with Faith No More as special guests. On August 8, during Metallica's set in Montreal, James Hetfield missed a stage cue in "Fade to Black." He stepped into hell as a volcano of flame blasted up from beneath his feet. Through the PA system, as the song petered out, the audience could hear the strings of Hetfield's guitar melting and snapping in the heat.

Luckily, James had been playing a new double-neck guitar that night, and the sheer size of the instrument—while not protecting him completely—may have saved his life.

Always the trooper, Hetfield returned to the stage less than three weeks later, albeit with a severely burned arm and unable to play guitar. Metal Church's John Marshall filled in, just as he had on the *Master of Puppets* tour when James broke his arm skateboarding.

But Marshall almost didn't get the job that second time.

Shortly before resuming the tour, Metallica bassist Jason Newsted had been speaking to Phil Rind of Sacred Reich, an old friend from the Phoenix, Arizona club days when Newsted kicked around town with Flotsam and Jetsam. Jason told Rind that Metallica was seeking a guitarist to fill in for James after the accident. Phil told Jason that Andreas Kisser was free.

Sepultura had recently wrapped up five shows in Brazil and found themselves with a short break before their next North American leg, which would start in October, opening for Ozzy Osbourne and Alice In Chains. So, in the middle of August,

With Black Sabbath's Tony Iommi.

Metallica flew Andreas into Denver, Colorado to audition for the temporary gig.

Newsted and Kisser had met briefly a couple of months before, at the MTV Video Music Awards in Los Angeles, California. Metallica had performed that night, and Sepultura's "Orgasmatron" clip was nominated for—and won—the International Viewer's Choice Award for Best Brazilian Video.

In Colorado, Kisser stepped off the plane to an awaiting limousine. This was much more intense that chatting up his childhood heroes backstage at an award show. Now he was about to jam with them.

He stayed in Denver for a couple of days, rehearsing twice with Metallica, the first day without James, the second with the vocalist present and singing. Andreas knew the older material—everything up to and including ...*And Justice for All*—like the back of his hand. They ripped through "The Shortest Straw" and "One," even newer songs "Enter Sandman" and "Sad But True," with Kisser's spirit soaring. Unfortunately for Andreas, Metallica was touring on the so-called "Black Album." When it came time to play tracks like "Nothing Else Matters" and "The Unforgiven," two of the album's biggest hits, the guitarist struggled. He didn't know the songs very well, and there wasn't enough time to learn them.

With Sabbath's Geezer Butler and Tony Iommi.

Even though he didn't get the gig, Kisser could not possibly be disappointed with the silver medal. As a consolation prize, the audition sparked a lifelong friendship with Jason Newsted.

The rest of 1992 played out like a highlight reel. The Brazilians got on famously with everyone on Ozzy's crew, partying every night with Layne Staley and the guys from Alice In Chains, whose recently released *Dirt* was screaming up the charts. On the final night of the tour, November 15, they witnessed history as Ozzy reunited on stage with Bill Ward, Tony Iommi, and Geezer Butler, to perform with Black Sabbath for the first time since 1979.

Even sickness couldn't derail Sepultura. When an illness forced Max to miss a show, the others plowed onward, playing as a three-piece out of respect for the fans. This had happened once before, during a tour in 1989, so it wasn't the first time they'd performed without the vocalist.

Of course, it wouldn't be the last time, either.

An opening stint on an unlikely arena tour (many of the venues holding 10,000 or more people) closed out the year in explosive fashion. Ministry was the headliner, riding high on the popularity of *Psalm 69*, with Helmet feeling the weight of their hit song "Unsung." To many, the inclusion of Sepultura seemed odd, though in truth, Helmet was the most dissimilar of the three.

The Brazilians adored both bands. And the influence of Ministry, especially, would be felt on the following record.

Still, many wondered how the tour would play out. Industrial, alternative hardcore, and thrash metal all on the same bill?

It turned out to be one of the most consistently violent tours, as far as crowd interaction went, of Sepultura's career.

In venues that were general admission on the floor, with no seats, the ground level became one giant mosh pit for the entire evening, from the back to the front and side-to-side. Night after night, fans were knocked unconscious or carried out on stretchers, many claiming they actually feared for their lives in those pits. At the show in San Francisco, a (presumably intoxicated) fan fell from one of the balconies, slamming into the concrete below with his pants around his ankles.

The concert in Atlanta, Georgia, however, may have taken the award for most brutal. When Helmet was forced to cancel, Ministry's infamous leader Al Jourgensen called up his friend Ice-T. The rapper was in town with his extreme metal project Body Count, and they did not hesitate to replace Helmet that evening.

Body Count's name could not have been more fitting for such an occasion.

And the tour with Ministry and Helmet could not have been a more appropriate ending to the *Arise* cycle. Paulo, Igor, Andreas, and Max closed the year feeling electric, high on music and experience, ready to turn their collective gaze on the next album.

FIVE

CHAOS IN ALL FORMS

At the beginning of 1993, heavy music was changing. As far as rock music went, the likes of Nirvana and Pearl Jam had taken over the airwaves, and metal bands were gradually being pushed back into the underground. Metallica's infamous Black Album, which was both loved and hated in equal measures, was nearly two years old at that point, and Pantera wouldn't release their chart-topping *Far Beyond Driven* until the following year. Two hugely successful British heavy metal bands—Iron Maiden and Judas Priest—lost their iconic singers when Bruce Dickinson and Rob Halford almost simultaneously announced departures from their respective groups.

Still, 1993 had its moments of metal in the spotlight, just not many of them. Anthrax released the well-received *Sound of White Noise*, their first album with Armored Saint vocalist John Bush replacing Joey Belladonna. Sweden's Entombed made a small splash when their disc *Wolverine Blues*, a shift from their death metal roots to what they termed death n' roll, was packaged (allegedly without the band's knowledge) with a "lost" comic featuring the popular Marvel character Wolverine. And Rob Halford came out swinging after his exit from Priest, unleashing *War of Words* with his new band Fight.

Having wrapped up the *Arise* touring cycle at the end of 1992, Sepultura returned to Brazil for the holidays, in dire need of a recharge after two years on the road. But almost immediately, back in Santo André, Max and Andreas began writing. The first song they completed, "Propaganda," came quickly and easily, before either of them had a solid concept in mind for the next album. Musically, the song sounded as if it belonged somewhere close to the *Arise* era while reaching out to new and unexplored territory.

In January of 1993, the four traveled back to Phoenix, where Gloria lived, to settle in and finish the writing (though Igor, who loved to surf and missed the ocean, would eventually move to San Diego, California, with Monika). A permanent move to the US had actually been in the works since the release of *Arise*. Logistically, it made sense, because the corporate structure of the band – label, the lawyers, the agents–was at that time based out of the United States. Gloria ran the management offices out of her house, and while half of Sepultura's road crew was Brazilian, the other half called Phoenix home.

The legion of homeland fans had mixed feelings about the relocation, understanding that it was a necessary decision for the band to continue on their upward trajectory, but also disappointed that there would be far fewer opportunities to see their heroes in Brazil.

For Max, there was another reason for the move. He and Gloria had developed a relationship that was kept fairly quiet until then, and the couple were about to have their first child together.

All this time spent away from native soil would greatly impact the sound of the next album. They had established a reputation as more than just *a heavy metal band from Brazil*. They were uniquely a *Brazilian heavy metal band* now, and the subtle change in wording made a world of difference. For fans all over the globe, Sepultura had altered the image people had of the South American country. For many fans, in fact, Sepultura represented the *only* image they had of Brazil.

As a result, Max, Paulo, Andreas, and Igor felt a sense of responsibility in the way they represented their nation. The more

Roadrunner Records press kit photo.

cultures and countries they experienced, the more pride they took in being Brazilian, for all the positive and negative connotations that entailed.

And even though they were expatriates, they felt a need, Andreas later explained, to remind the world that they were still a Brazilian band.

Igor, already considered by many of his peers as one of the best of all metal drummers, wanted to distance himself even further by focusing more on his individual strengths, allowing those natural Brazilian rhythmic tendencies to shine through. Bringing in the tribal rhythms felt exceedingly natural to him, since he'd grown up hearing and playing them. They were under his skin.

More than anything else, with this new album, Cavalera's drumming would set Sepultura apart from the other metal acts of the day.

But the influences behind *Chaos A.D.* were many and varied, precisely because they had spent so much time outside of Brazil.

For starters, they sought a thicker, refined sound that favored groove over speed. Some of the thrash purists vocally disapproved of this, crying "sellout," worried that Sepultura were going the way of the Seattle-based bands that were popular at the time. Though Max insisted grunge was never an influence, there would've been no shame in admitting such growth. After all, the heavier bands of the grunge era, Alice In Chains and Soundgarden among them, evoked Black Sabbath in the their music just as much as Sepultura did, and no one argued against Sabbath as a patriarch of the metal pantheon.

But such harsh criticism, even from their own fan base, was nothing new for this band. They had been criticized for selling out since they shifted their sound from black metal to the visceral mix of death metal and thrash, some "true" fans refusing to listen to anything post-*Morbid Visions*. Even more absurdly, some would say the band sold out after they learned how to tune their guitars, or even further back, after the split with Wagner.

Having perfected their own unique brand of Third World thrash, but refusing to be confined by it, Sepultura dialed back the pace and brought the low end closer to the forefront in these new songs. As musicians, they not only studied their craft, but also how audiences reacted to the music they played. They cross-referenced new ideas with their experiences watching the crowd go nuts during the breakdowns of songs like "Dead Embryonic Cells" and "Desperate Cry," and focused on the maxim that one note played *just right* could be the heaviest sound in the world.

"The songs won't be as fast," Max explained to a local newspaper, "but they'll be more pissed off [and] aggressive."

After spending a weekend with their wives in Sedona, a northern town in Arizona where native American Indian tribes still live and the sun colors sandstone structures a brilliant crimson, Andreas (who never left home without an acoustic guitar) and Max began working on an idea for the band's most dramatic experimentation yet. It wasn't pissed off and it wasn't aggressive. At all. It even incorporated some of the caipira melodies, the countryside music Kisser's father used to play around the house when Andreas was a kid.

The quartet set up shop in an Argo warehouse in south Phoenix, the same facility where Sacred Reich rehearsed, and got straight to work completing the writing of *Chaos A.D.* Each member's confidence was at an all-time high, and collectively as well, their musicianship finely honed after such extensive touring. The rehearsal space was electric with excitement and creativity, and the cautious belief that Sepultura were about to break even more barriers; Roadrunner had recently partnered with Epic/Sony to provide major label distribution for the album in the United States.

Once the musical direction was resolved, the first three tracks—"Refuse/Resist," "Territory," and "Slave New World" (all of which were filmed as music videos and released as singles)— were written in no time, almost as if some otherworldly force were streaming the songs through the band's instruments. The lyrics were as volatile as the music, Max livid as he shouted about violent, global uprisings against despotic leaderships, territory wars, and censorship.

The band knew already they had something special on their hands, and the overall theme of the album soon became evident: chaos, in all forms.

When it came time to record, a couple of changes were in order. Scott Burns had become a highly sought after producer in death metal circles, a scene that Sepultura were intentionally steering away from. They chose Andy Wallace instead, since he had done such a masterful job mixing *Arise*, but they decided not to return to Morrisound because there had always been too many people around, too many distractions. In search for a quieter, out-of-the-way place where they could focus, they settled on Rockfield Studios in Wales. If it was good enough for Black Sabbath and Motorhead, who had both tracked seminal albums there, it was good enough for Sepultura. In fact, their childhood heroes Queen had even recorded most of their classic "Bohemian Rhapsody" at Rockfield.

And for the first time, Paulo would not only have the luxury of time, but also the poise and self-assurance to lay down his own bass tracks in the studio.

Opening with the ultrasonic rhythm of a fetal heartbeat—that of Max and Gloria's first child together, a son named Zyon—*Chaos A.D.* explodes into life with an abrasive tribal drum intro. Igor's snare cracks are reminiscent of machine gun fire, paving the way for a simple—yet crushing—two-note riff over which Kisser's creative chording wails like a siren. Max's war cry in the chorus of "Refuse/Resist" is a virulent call of defiance, a chant just begging to be shouted by thousands of fans in concerts to come.

Those not familiar with Brazilian music—and even those who are—likely dropped their jaws upon first listen to Igor's samba-on-steroids at the beginning of "Territory." This was altogether new terrain for most metal fans. It was fairly new territory for Sepultura, too; despite the introduction, it was the slowest song they'd written up until that point in their career. However, it sacrifices none of the heaviness of previous material. The slow burning groove, in fact, may be the very reason "Territory" is as

Silvio "BBK" Gomes and Paulo during a Chaos A.D. recording break.

heavy as it is. Kisser's lyrics, bursts of four and five syllable lines, only enhance the track's simple intensity.

The short, staccato verses continue in "Slave New World," emphasizing this change from the *Schizophrenia* days when Max used to stuff as many words as possible into one line. The effects of such brevity increase the clarity of the message, here co-written by Evan Seinfeld when the Biohazard bassist brought a book of lyrics to Cavalera's house. The vocals, when not spit out at a thousand miles an hour, also sit more comfortably within the structure of the song, becoming a sort of percussion of their own.

"Amen," with its lingering guitar chords and bass lines locked firmly in with Igor's groove, shines a light on the low-end Sepultura wanted to exploit on this record. Close listeners can hear the influence of Metallica's eponymously titled album. A couple years earlier, the aforementioned worked with esteemed producer Bob Rock to bring Jason Newsted's bass tone closer to the forefront in their music. Rock's technique revolved around having Jason concentrate more on playing to Lars Ulrich's bass drums, rather than the standard heavy metal approach of simply playing the rhythm guitar riff an octave lower. Paulo does something similar here, creating a new layer of sound for Sepultura to experiment with.

While on location at Chepstow Castle for a photo shoot, a tour guide led the band to a small room with no ceiling and walls that reached over two stories high. The acoustics, as a result, were sonically breathtaking, and arrangements were made to record "Kaiowas" there at the castle. Listeners can ever hear birds chirping overhead, in the beginning, as the band tunes up and warms into the tune. Chepstow provided the perfect atmosphere for a song of this type; a stripped-down, bare bones track born in Sedona, with Igor and Paulo later developing its rhythms on plastic buckets. It is, in a sense, a Brazilian version of Led Zeppelin's darker, more acoustic moments, inspired as much by the Celtic location as the sounds of their homeland. For the recording, Max was forced to use one of Andreas' guitars, as Cavalera didn't even own an acoustic at the time.

Chaos A.D.'s liner notes explain that "Kaiowas" pays tribute to the Brazilian Indian tribe of the same name, many of whom committed suicide after the white man appropriated their land.

"Propaganda" not only musically stretches backward a bit, but vocally as well. Max returns to utilizing long sentences in the lyrics to lash out at lies and rumormongering in the press, but his words are spaced out more evenly now, accenting the single-note riff that chugs in unison with Igor's double bass drums.

The pace of "Biotech Is Godzilla" revisits Sepultura's pure thrash days, though the riffs themselves are less complex and more reliant upon groove and interaction with drum accents. The song had no lyrics when offered up to old friend Jello Biafra as a guest track.

As the infamous lead singer of seminal punk band Dead Kennedys, and the brains behind the band's oftentimes political and absurdist lyrics, Jello was a longtime hero of Sepultura's. He was also an obsessive music collector, trading tapes with people from all over the world, when he came upon a copy of *Schizophrenia* in the late 80s. He was stunned, blown away, enough to invite them to contribute to the Dead Kennedy's *Virus 100* tribute album in 1992 (they covered "Drug Me"), which also featured Faith No More and Napalm Death.

For the as-yet-unnamed "Biotech Is Godzilla," Max suggested the lyrics revisit a classic Dead Kennedys track, a sort of "Nazi Punks Fuck Off! Part Two," but Jello had a better idea. Inspired by his recent protests at the Rio Earth Summit, and the various conspiracy theories he'd developed in response to the more clandestine motives of the United Nations, Biafra's lyrics issued a controversial warning against political intervention in biotechnology.

Taking cues from Black Sabbath, "Nomad" is a slow, doomy dirge (at least until its end) with vaguely Middle Eastern lead sections that conjure up images of desert tribes moving from place to place, rarely stopping for long. It is symbolic of Sepultura's existence, living as they do on the road. The following track more explicitly describes the band with its title and only lyric, "We Who Are Not As Others." But the "we" in this track refers also to Sepultura's fans. Those six short words are a rallying cry, a celebration of individuality and community at the same time, embodied in the call and response between Max and his gang in the second half of the song. Those six words explain Max's feelings about the repression he'd felt as a kid, the repression others had felt at the hands of the military dictatorship. Those six words justify Sepultura's tattoos as freedom *from* repression, and freedom *of* expression. Those six words expose the ignorance of those with power, of those in control, such as when the military attempted to draft Igor a few years before; they'd turned the drummer away, in disgust, because of his tattoos. "We Who Are Not As Others" speaks of the society's lack of belief in, and respect for, its youth.

If, with *Arise* and *Beneath the Remains*, the band wanted to expose Brazil's darker side, they took this to the extreme on *Chaos A.D.* In "Manifest," Max plays the part of journalist, reporting on a massacre that had taken place at Carandiru Penitentiary in São Paulo only some months earlier. Designed to hold 3,000 inmates, Carandiru was far over occupied with nearly 8,000 prisoners when an uprising began in Pavilhão Nove, the ninth cellblock. The police response of "shoot first, ask questions later" resulted in the deaths of over 100 inmates. No officers were charged until early 2013, more than ten years after the penitentiary had been demolished and over twenty since the massacre had occurred.

The heavily industrialized nature of "Manifest" may well have been due to Kisser's recently discovered affinity for Ministry, whose circular, repetitive riffs and bras metallic noises could create an almost hypnotic atmosphere.

Perhaps inspired by the location where they recorded, and entranced with Celtic symbolism and mysticism, Sepultura chose to cover New Model Army's "The Hunt" on the album. It was a long overdue nod to their love of Discharge, The Exploited, and hardcore English punk rock in general. They also put down a version of Black Sabbath's "Symptom of the Universe," which they'd be including in live sets as far back as 1988, and would later be included on the *Nativity in Black* tribute album.

An appropriate ending to such a livid album, "Clenched Fist" combines the sounds of grinding machinery and grinding guitars with some of Max's most personal lyrics yet. *Chaos A.D.* closes as it opened—with a fist. However, where in "Refuse/Resist" the fist was raised in defiance, here it is clenched for attack.

Two Portuguese-language cover songs—"Crucificados pelo Sistema" by Ratos de Porão and "Polícia" by Titãs—were also recorded during these sessions. Like "Symptom of the Universe," both had been live staples for years. The American hardcore punk of Final Conflict's "Inhuman Nature" matched *Chaos A.D.*'s theme well enough to be recorded, though it was not added to the album's tracklist.

With its industrial influences and chaotic nature, the album required a cover that would represent the music *and* the concept well. Michael Whelan was given a few songs to listen to for inspiration, and set to work after brainstorming over the telephone with Max. Cavalera also had some very specific ideas in mind. The resulting artwork shows a disturbing image of a figure suspended upside down, bound and tied in bloodied cloth, his (or her) soul being sucked out and assimilated into machinery.

Andreas during filming of "Territory" video in Israel.

It fit perfectly.

In June, a few months before the release of the album, Max and Gloria were married at their home in Phoenix. Members of Sacred Reich and Roadrunner Records label representatives made appearances, as did a number of other friends and family, including Max's mother and sister. A good time was had by all at the wedding party, but beneath the joy and the celebration, on a professional level,

Paulo, the tourist, in Israel.

the union of vocalist and manager represented a rather major conflict of interest. Though it hadn't become a problem yet—and Max insisted it would not—it was possible that the seeds for future drama had been planted.

Chaos A.D. debuted to widespread acclaim in September of 1993. In celebration of the album and its worldly overtones, the band threw a massive, expensive release party at a castle in England. Organized with both medieval and Brazilian themes, there were capoeiristas dressed in jesters' garb, attendees feasting on giant turkey legs and drinking whiskey from chalices emblazoned with Sepultura's logo. The band performed "Kaiowas" and screened the video for "Territory," which they had filmed in Israel during a period of relative peace. Though Andreas hadn't written the lyrics specifically about the Arab-Israeli Conflict, the theme of the video worked for the song nonetheless. Images of war, destruction, and religious tension were interspersed with shots of Sepultura's members in the Dead Sea, and the visually striking clip won praise and awards all over the world for its socially and politically conscious messages.

Meanwhile, in Brazil, the Souza Cruz tobacco company was preparing for the next edition of their annual Hollywood Rock festival. They had announced the line-up months before, scheduling three days during January of 1994 split between stadiums in Rio de Janeiro and São Paulo. The festival would be a celebration of popular music from around the globe, including acts like Aerosmith and Whitney Houston. It would also showcase a number of Brazilian bands, such as Titãs, Jorge Ben, and Skank.

But Brazil's most popular international act was suspiciously absent from the roster.

In short, the promoters of Hollywood Rock were reluctant to book Sepultura, wary of a repeat of the tragic events that occurred at Praça Charles Miller in 1991.

Outraged, the Brazilian Fan Club took matters into their own hands.

"Our most remarkable act," said Djalma Agra, "was to bring Sepultura to Hollywood Rock."

After the announcement that Sepultura would not be invited to play, Toninho and his gang hit the streets to petition, spending several months recruiting fans to join their cause.

Kaiowas.

"Remember," Agra explained, "we had no access to the internet at that time, so we used to go to all the metal concerts to collect the signatures. I remember passing the whole queue at concerts like Pantera, Ramones, Motorhead, Manowar, and incredibly, most of the people signed to see Sepultura."

The club collected over 8,000 signatures, which even today with the viral ease of social media would be no small feat. Toninho, Agra, and Sergio Caffé compiled the petition and brought it to the Souza Cruz office, located in a large building complex in the heart of São Paulo's financial district. The trio met with Hollywood Rock's promoters, who were touched by the dedication of the club and the band's fans. Souza Cruz reviewed their decision, and then overturned it, officially inviting Sepultura to play on both January 15 in São Paulo, and a week later in Rio de Janeiro.

"I must admit we were lucky bastards," Agra said, "who had the chance to live the history very close to the band *and* be part of it!"

In recognition of their victory, a few days before the festival, Toninho manufactured a Brazilian flag that prominently displayed Sepultura's tribal "S" logo that Bozo had designed back in 1991. Toninho, Agra, and some others brought the flag to Guarulhous airport to greet the band and welcome them home, but were promptly arrested when federal police caught a glimpse of the banner.

The infamous Hollywood Rock.

"They claimed it was a crime to modify the Brazilian flag," Agra said, "so we convinced them we understood and that no one would see it."

Toninho later gave the flag to Max, who proudly displayed it to the audience following Sepultura's triumphant performance in São Paulo.

The police were waiting for Max backstage.

"After the show," Max told an interviewer, "there were 20 cops in our dressing room looking for the flag. They said I spit and stepped on the flag and that I was anti-Brazilian and a communist. It was a lie... they invented that stuff."

Video footage for the "Refuse/Resist" promotional clip had been filmed during the Hollywood Rock homecoming in São Paulo, and indeed, shows no wrongdoing. The final image of the video, in fact, is one of Max and Igor holding Toninho's flag up, proudly, for all to see.

The band—and Max especially, since he was the only one arrested—felt targeted by the police. He felt victimized because of his long hair, tattoos, and critical lyrics.

The arrest was highly publicized in Brazil, polarizing the opinions of both Sepultura's fans and critics even further. Never ones to back down from controversy, the band would strike back in a rather creative way by joining Titãs on stage in Rio to perform a raucous version of "Polícia." Barking out its highly critical lyrics, Max left no one wondering about his feelings.

Again though, the band had no time to dwell on further negative publicity due to their whirlwind schedule. A headlining tour of the US with Fear Factory, Clutch, and Fudge Tunnel supporting was scheduled to kick off only two weeks after the Hollywood Rock concerts.

Early in 1993, before recording sessions for *Chaos A.D.* had begun, Max and Alex Newport, Fudge Tunnel's founder and brain stem, created the aforementioned Nailbomb as a two-man side project, a way to kill some of the downtime. In a matter of weeks, they birthed an industrial metal Molotov cocktail titled *Point Blank*. The album was equal parts noise and naked anger, driven as much by the techno genius of Newport as Cavalera's raw fury. It boasted guest appearances by Igor, Andreas, and Fear Factory's Dino Cazares. Neither Max nor Newport considered Nailbomb a "real"—or traditional—band, so even though *Point Blank* was completed before *Chaos A.D.*, Roadrunner decided to shelve the album until March of 1994 so as not to conflict with Sepultura's release. They wanted to ride the partnership with Epic/Sony as long as they could, letting nothing divert attention from *Chaos A.D.*

But there were concerns. Though *Chaos A.D.* was selling well, it wasn't selling as well as everyone had expected. Epic had dumped a million dollars into promotion, helping the album to peak at spot thirty-two on the US Billboard chart and eleven in the UK, and earning it gold and silver certifications in Europe, Brazil, and Indonesia.

Those numbers were nothing to balk at, and were actually quite impressive for a band of their status. Still, something was not quite right. After all Epic had promised, *Chaos A.D.* should have far outperformed what it actually did in the United States especially, which was the most coveted market at the time. But in the US, radio airplay was scarce, and outside of *Headbanger's Ball*, the standard collection of publications like *Metal Edge*, and occasional pieces in guitar magazines, promotion was practically non-existent. Where were the cover stories? Where was all that "major label" support?

Andreas paying respect in Japan.

During an interview with MTV Brazil, Igor revealed that the American hip-hop artists Sepultura befriended had warned them of racism. While the rappers were victims of prejudice for being black in a prevailingly white music industry, they believed Sepultura would fall victim to a similar prejudice because they were Brazilian.

Igor and the boys didn't want to believe it, but as time went on, the signs were too strong to ignore. During magazine interviews, the band would regularly be promised the cover story, but over and over again, they'd later find another band—an American band—on the cover instead.

As if this neglect weren't enough to incense the band, they began to notice that Prong and Fight—the two other metal bands who had been signed to a similar distribution deal by Epic/Sony—were everywhere. The percussive swing of Prong's "Snap Your Fingers, Snap Your Neck," and Fight's catchy "Little Crazy" blew up rock radio in 1994. Both songs spent months in heavy rotation. It soon became obvious that the label was pouring all their money into the two American bands, and largely leaving the Brazilians to fend for themselves.

Sepultura's reputation as a live act preceded them. Igor further suspected many other bands were afraid of touring with Sepultura as openers or special guests because they were worried about being blown off the stage every night.

But there was at least one that wasn't afraid.

SIX

ROOTS...

Pantera's *Far Beyond Driven* tour, with Sepultura as special guests and Biohazard opening, kicked off in June of 1994.

Anyone lucky enough to tour with Pantera during that band's heyday reflects on those times as career highpoints, the most fun they'd ever had on the road. Sepultura were no exception. Pantera shredder Darrell "Dimebag" Abbott was the typical instigator of any number of drunken hijinx, usually armed with a video camera in one hand and a "Black Tooth Grin" (a potent mix of whiskey and Coke) in the other, insisting that everyone within his line of sight be just as inebriated as he was at any given moment.

Among the highlight of these concerts was a raucous, electrified version of "Kaiowas" that saw Max, Andreas, and Paulo trade their guitars for drumsticks after Kisser's solo. Members of Pantera and Biohazard, as well as any other musicians in earshot, would occasionally join in to slam away on a collection of drums scattered across the stage. It brought a little bit of Brazil to wherever they played.

Initially, they thought the song would never work live. They couldn't even consider going acoustic in the middle of a set. But

Celebrating Brazil's World Cup victory with a green beard (and plenty of alcohol).

after seeing Oakland's Neurosis drop their guitars and pull off something similar, Sepultura gave it a shot.

It turned out to be one of the heaviest moments of the show.

The *Chaos* tours—first with Biohazard opening and later with Prong—were loaded with special moments, the kind that many musicians are lucky to experience once or twice over the course of a career, much less a year. On June 4, barely a week before the World Cup kicked off, Sepultura (technically billed over Pantera due to a *Kerrang!* magazine readers' poll) walked out to a sea of yellow shirts and Brazilian flags for a memorable set at England's annual Monsters of Rock festival. Back in the United States a month later, in Laguna Hills, California, a highly intoxicated and celebratory Sepultura invaded Pantera's stage when the Brazilian national soccer team defeated Italy to win the World Cup. The final match had taken place only an hour's drive away in Pasadena, and Pantera graciously allowed Sepultura to play an extra-long set that night.

Sharing the stage was a common theme on that tour. Kisser jammed with Pantera on their catchy and instantly classic "Walk," as did Paulo when the Brazilians were forced to cancel a few shows after Max injured his knee. Phil Anselmo, Pantera's volatile vocalist, often joined Sepultura for versions of Discharge's "Hear Nothing, See Nothing, Say Nothing." Caught up in the moment after one such meeting, Max unstrapped his guitar

Max and Zyon at Donington.

Setting up in the Phoenix rehearsal room.

and attempted to smash it to bits. After a couple of unsuccessful swings, Anselmo motioned for Cavalera to hand the instrument over, and with one mighty thwack, Phil split the guitar in two. With a smile, he handed the pieces to Max who tossed them to some lucky concertgoers in the front of the crowd.

But Max didn't particularly care for playing larger arenas. Oftentimes with seats on the floors and uptight security, these venues were not ideal for inspiring mosh pits, stage diving, and the exceedingly crazy crowds that they enjoyed in smaller clubs. He preferred being closer to the fans, in their faces, feeling the sweat and the heat emanating from the audience. Sepultura's music, Max believed, provided a much greater impression in this type of environment.

Short runs in Australia and Japan in September brought the *Chaos A.D.* tours to an end, with the only real low points being Max's injury and an incident in Europe where police raided Sepultura's bus in search of drugs. They'd found nothing, prompting Max to revise the lyrics of "Antichrist"—turning it into "Anticop"—and drop it into set lists to vocally express his distaste for law enforcement.

But before closing the book on the *Chaos A.D.* tours, there came an opportunity in early November that the band couldn't refuse. Billed as co-headliners on the Acid Chaos Tour, Sepultura joined NYC punk legends The Ramones on a short trek around Brazil with Raimundos, a hardcore punk rock group based out of

Phoenix rehearsal room.

Brasilia. With a tagline warning "This show will drive you nuts" (Este show irá tirar você do sério), the short run more than lived up to its hype, and would later be cited by Max as a high point in his career.

A much-needed rest was in order, an opportunity for the members to partake in a semblance of normalcy amidst the chaos of their success. In December, Andreas and his sweetheart Patricia wed, and not too long after, Igor married Monika.

1995 was fairly low-key, and with the benefit of hindsight, the number of outside activities Sepultura engaged in may have indicated a slowly widening fracture within the band. Igor dove into designing album covers and pursuing his artwork. He'd enjoyed painting as a kid and wanted to get back into it now that he had some time off.

Cooperating with Alberto Hiar, Igor indulged in another activity he considered a refreshing escape from touring and playing music: fashion design. He and Hiar created the Cavalera brand, with the launch collection—called "Vision by Igor"—the drummer's take on skate and hip hop clothing.

Max continued writing and religiously following his beloved Palmeiras. Those two things (other than his family) were really his only passions, his only constants. In early June, he and Igor took off to Holland for two special shows that put Nailbomb to rest—the first, a warm-up at a dank club in Eindhoven. The second was a massive gig at the Dynamo festival that would be documented and released by Roadrunner under the title Proud to Commit *Commercial Suicide*. The following day, to close out Biohazard's set, Max jumped on stage with Machine Head's Robb Flynn and Adam Duce to join in on "Hold My Own," returning the favor after Evan Seinfeld had taken part in Nailbomb's show.

Andreas also hooked up with Robb Flynn, as well as mutual friends Jason Newsted and Exodus drummer Tom Hunting, for a not-so-serious project called Quarteto da Pinga. The band was so named after Kisser brought a bottle of cachaça for the guys to enjoy while jamming, and the theme of those sessions was formed. Drinking, hanging out with friends, playing music. No pressure, no stress, no worries.

Quarteto da Pinga had evolved out of a group begun the year before with all the same members except for Flynn. Sexoturica, as they had been called (a combination of the names Sepultura, Exodus, and Metallica) recorded a demo at Newsted's Chophouse studio in California over the course of a weekend. Quarteto da Pinga did the same, making a three-song demo they had no intentions of ever putting out. (The Sexoturica tape *was* eventually released, in 2002, on a split CD with another project of Newsted's— the aptly named IR8, which also featured Devin Townsend). Regardless, the Quarteto demo leaked out and became legendary in the underground tape trading circuit.

While the other three members remained relatively busy in some form or another, the quiet and reclusive Xisto seemed to drop completely out of the public's sight.

But Sepultura fans were not left wanting. They could view a long-form video that was part rockumentary, part live document, part promo clip collection. Compiled in the vein of Pantera's classic

Rehearsal room decorations.

Getting down to business.

home videos, *Third World Chaos* exposed a side of Sepultura that fans only got a glimpse of during the *Under Siege* interview segments. They saw a band of brothers that took their music seriously, but also knew how to have a good time. They witnessed brutal performances with Ratos de Porão and Jello Biafra, as well as the samba drum jams from the Pantera and Biohazard tour.

For non-Brazilian fans, the video itself was a sort of culture shock, introducing them to tracks like "Crucificados pelo Sistema" and "Polícia," songs they likely hadn't heard in that pre-YouTube, pre-file sharing era.

But *Third World Chaos* didn't just pay tribute to the band's Brazilian roots. It made the world a little smaller for everyone, with segments from such culturally diverse locations as Japan and Europe. There was even footage of the Debus presentations Sepultura had witnessed in Indonesia, where the Islamic faithful pierced their own flesh with knives and spears that left no blood or scars.

But before long, Sepultura were itching to get back to work, to reconvene and start on album number six.

Chaos A.D. had indeed launched them into a sort of heavy music "mainstream," as such there was in the early nineties, even though the movement that would soon play a part in metal's demise had already taken root. Nirvana and Pearl Jam ruled the airwaves in those days with a style of retro-rock music the label-happy masses referred to as grunge. The term was a bit of a misnomer; while it attempted to describe the *sound* of the music—detuned guitars and raw, unpolished performances—it was too limiting. Instead, it came to be synonymous with Seattle, the hometown of those bands that were pushing heavy metal groups back into the underground. You would not have heard "Refuse/Resist" or "Slave New World" on many radio stations outside of metal stalwarts KNAC and Z-Rock, or seen the video clips on MTV anywhere else but the two-hour *Headbanger's Ball* block on Saturday nights, yet Sepultura had spent much of 1994 headlining arenas across Europe and tearing a swath across America, playing sold-out dates both as headliners and as support for other acts. By the time they began writing the follow-up to *Chaos A.D.*, the Brazilians were Roadrunner's hottest commodity, even though the distribution deal with Epic/Sony had collapsed.

The dissolution of major label distribution was no big deal for Sepultura by then. They understood—and accepted—that Epic had been too big for them, and that they belonged on a smaller label like Roadrunner. As the band saw it, Sepultura was just another name on the Epic roster.

As work began for the next album, they referred to the native influences they only touched upon on *Chaos A.D.* Those were their differentiators, the unique elements no other band had, so they decided to take them to the extreme. Call it the apex of nostalgia or homesickness or *saudades*, as they would say in Portuguese, but the band's relocation to Phoenix was at least partially responsible for this decision.

"When we left Brazil," Max told *Rock Brigade* magazine, "it helped us see that there are a lot of cool things that we could add to our music." The title of the album, *Roots*, was a perfect descriptor of the band's desire to reach back into their cultural heritage, but not necessarily a desire to revisit the roots of their music. In that aspect, they stretched further forward. The end result was something altogether new, original, and vital.

Originality and evolution, for Sepultura, has always been key. They never wanted to be the type of band that made the same album over and over again, and this is a sign of integrity that we see revisited throughout their course of their history. As musicians, it was—and is—crucial for them to challenge themselves. They've accepted that some fans appreciate this attitude, while others abhor it and would prefer they just keep releasing new versions of *Beneath the Remains* or *Arise*. Those who had shouted "sellout" at *Chaos A.D.* would likely do the same with the new record, but Sepultura were okay with that. First and foremost, they had to fulfill their musical aspirations. First and foremost, they had to make themselves happy.

And with this new album, the guys wished to present a more balanced image of Brazil. *Chaos A.D.* was so dark, so focused on corruption and violence and death. This time, they wanted to celebrate their homeland by introducing some of the nation's musical diversity. While the songs were still aggressive, still angry, the lyrics they were penning revolved around turning that negative energy into something positive.

At the tail end of August, they interrupted the writing sessions with a return to São Paulo for the inaugural MTV Brazilian Video Music Awards. As the nation's most popular musical export, they were invited to close the show in a manner of which only they were capable. Sepultura's inclusion in a program such as this said much about Brazil's love/hate relationship with the band during those days. Lest we forget, only a few short years earlier, they had been largely blacklisted after the Praça Charles Miller incident. Max's arrest post-Hollywood Rock was still fresh. Though a Sepultura appearance always brought its share of controversy, no one could deny their impact on the face of Brazilian music and, perhaps more importantly, their hand in the spread of Brazilian awareness worldwide.

An absolutely furious "Territory" segued into an electrified version of "Kaiowas," and when a cadre of musicians came out for the drum jam at the end, a sense of triumph and pride hung thick in the air. Despite the fact that they were more popular abroad than at home, despite the fact that they lived permanently in the United States then, Sepultura were *proud* to be a Brazilian band, and at that moment, Brazil was proud to have them.

One of the percussionists who joined them on the VMB stage was Carlinhos Brown, a Bahian artist known as the leader and creator of Timbalada. A friendship was born that night, and when Sepultura decided to heavily incorporate Brazilian rhythms into the new album, inviting Brown to contribute was a no-brainer.

Some say the demise of grunge began with the death of its key figure, Nirvana's Kurt Cobain, in 1994. In October of that same year, a band from Bakersfield, California released their eponymous debut album, and the face of rock music changed again. That band was Korn, and that album—and its production— became a key influence in the making of *Roots*.

While it's arguable whether or not *Korn* is "metal" (and the band themselves eschew the aesthetic, claiming to hate it when the term is applied to their music), it is undeniably heavy. They helped popularize the seven-string guitar, and yet tuned the instruments down further to add even more low-end. The bass guitar was prominent, something not often found in rock music then. It also locked in with the drums to create a hip-hop style groove, rather than simply following the guitar riffs note for note. Jonathon Davis' lyrics were honest. The vocals dripped with vulnerability, another taboo in the alpha world of heavy music. The songs weren't fast, and there wasn't a guitar solo in sight.

The success of *Korn*, and its follow-up *Life is Peachy*, put its producer in high demand. Ross Robinson, former thrash metal guitarist and man behind Fear Factory's pre-*Soul of a New Machine* demos, would quickly become known for his creativity in the studio, as well as his spirituality and ability to pull raw, emotional performances out of the artists he worked with. Artists as diverse as Slipknot, Machine Head, and even Vanilla Ice.

Recorded in large part at Richard Kaplan's Indigo Ranch studios in Malibu, *Roots* was not created with the intent to be a classic or a breakthrough or anything more than another step in Sepultura's progression. And it couldn't have happened anywhere else than Indigo Ranch, where Kaplan had gathered an arsenal of equipment, pedals, and effects he'd collected throughout the years. The studio was like a playground or a candy store for musicians.

Roots fades into life with the sounds of crickets and cicadas and what sounds almost like a gunshot. Before the listener can ponder the noise, "Roots Bloody Roots" explodes through the speakers like a sonic kick in the teeth. This is *heavy*, but a different type of heavy than Sepultura fans are used to.

Perhaps the first thing listeners will notice is the increased simplicity of the rhythm guitar work, and that the guitars themselves are tuned far below standard. While Korn may have served as an influence here, there are other origins, as well. While writing songs at home, Max had gotten used to throwing new strings on his guitar and not bothering to tune them up.

The low frequencies, however, made it difficult to give the sound clarity. Richard Kaplan had the solution.

When working with Korn, Kaplan had built a plywood guitar pedal based off of the famous Big Muff distortion box. His creation was a hybrid of transistors and high gain tubes that kept the crushing low-end heaviness without muddying the tone. Naturally, he called it the Bigger Muff. Max and Andreas loved the pedal so much that Kaplan built them a special model they could take on the road with them.

Perhaps the next thing listeners will notice is the groove, the Brazilian swing in Igor's drumming. Even though concerts on the *Roots* tour would naturally open with "Roots Bloody Roots," it's clear this song is an anthem that will eventually earn its place at the end of the set. The perfect show closer. The chorus, with its addictive barking of the poetic title, harkens back to Max's lyrical inspirations on *Chaos A.D.*, not only in its minimalism, but in its content. It could just as much pay tribute to U2 as Black Sabbath, "Sunday Bloody Sunday" as "Sabbath Bloody Sabbath."

One song down, and for most upon first listen, the album was already far different than expected.

The surprises only continued from there. "Attitude" introduced the sound of a completely unknown instrument for most people outside of Brazil and southern Africa. The twang of a berimbau played by Max rises into an eerie guitar preface that strikingly resembles Korn's "Shoots and Ladders." As with the previous song, "Attitude" is driven by a far-from-flashy single string riff consisting of only two notes. Lyrically, listeners are already hearing a less politically motivated, more personal side of Sepultura.

This personal connection is what made Ross Robinson an ideal choice to produce the record. Music, for him, was the sound of the soul. Though the band had, in a sense, auditioned several other producers by playing the songs live for them, only Ross made his spiritual connection with the music obvious. Only Ross showed his unbridled enthusiasm about the possibilities of what he could do with Sepultura.

Much of the next song, "Cut-Throat," isn't too far removed from *Chaos A.D.*, besides being slower and tuned down to hell. In general, Max screams out against the corporate nature of big money record labels, and more specifically, he attacks Epic in inventive fashion for the way they mishandled the co-distribution deal with Roadrunner.

"Ratamahatta," though, represents the first of a few curveballs on *Roots*. This innovative track, featuring additional percussion by Ross Robinson and Korn drummer David Silveria, revolves heavily around Carlinhos Brown's maracatu rhythms and the call-and-response Portuguese verses exchanged between Brown and Max Cavalera. This "dirty poetry" is familiar to the youth of Brazil, the abstract nature of lyrics that are often chosen less for their meaning than for their rhythmic and musical qualities. Words strung together to formulate more of a concept than a concrete idea.

The first verse appears to speak of the struggle of Brazilian youth during a time of great oppression and economic hardship. The second, with its mention of folk heroes such as Zé do Caixão, Zumbi, and Lampião seems to represent freedom, a break from the norm or the typical. The title itself acts as a percussive instrument in Brown's recitations, the made-up word drawn from an image of the many rats in Manhattan, mixing together the US and Brazil.

"Ratamahatta" as a whole is quite a break from the norm, the typical, for metal bands of that day or *any* day.

Building from Igor's samba snare accented with palm muted guitar chords, the anxious doom of "Breed Apart" breeds a dark atmosphere through its groove. Max gargles his way through vague verse lyrics that crawl over sustained chords, exploding into a motivational shout that demands we all create our own paths in life without allowing the prejudices of others to keep us down. The song is a potent cocktail of dynamics, showing how the quiet and the loud can work together to amplify the effects of each. The completely unexpected section in the middle breaks down the song, utilizing berimbaus and syncopated rhythms in an almost hypnotic way, and plays like a capoeira roda on amphetamines. This segment spotlights the innovative use of Brazilian and metal sounds to forge something massive and heavy and entirely original.

Measured bass lines fatten the tones of Igor's drums and lay the foundation in "Straighthate." Chunky guitar harmonics lead into a Sepultura meets Sabbath riff and the *wah-wah* soaked verses beyond. Andreas, making his first distinct vocal appearance on the album, belts out the pre-chorus lyrics, a raw counterpoint to Max's identifiable yell. Again they exploit the single-string guitar riff to great effect, Kaplan's Bigger Muff distortion pedal lending it a ton of extra weight.

The relatively short "Spit" careens from feedback and Paulo's vicious lead-in to a sort of detuned hardcore, a pure headbanger all the way through. The track's straightforward nature makes the successive "Lookaway"—an already odd and bewildering song—seem even more so.

Showcasing the techno scratching of House of Pain's DJ Lethal (who actually pieced the song together using computers and studio magic), the warped Gregorian-like chants of Mike Patton, and twisted lyrics courtesy of Korn's Jonathon Davis, "Lookaway" is unlike anything Sepultura has done before or since. It is an unsettling, borderline industrial track, likely inspired as much by Ministry as by Max's work in Nailbomb, though it doesn't sound remotely like either band. The subject matter, too, could not get any further afield from what Sepultura fans have heard before. Davis, in his typical approach avoiding the tropes of metal, adopts the persona of a man who is disgusted by the thought of performing oral sex.

"Lookaway" is a song that could have only happened with those specific personas involved, and completely unplanned. Working with guest musicians was never something Sepultura arranged in advance or ironed out with record labels, managers, or lawyers. It was always based on a sudden idea, on who was around at the moment, and the mutual respect they had for music and the process of creation. It was about impulse. It was about art.

The entirely Kisser-constructed "Dusted" steers the listener back to a more comfortable—as in recognizable—place, sounding like it could have fit nicely on *Chaos A.D.* It also boasts the guitarist's most experimental lead section yet, with dueling solos panned hard left and hard right in the mix, possibly in tribute to Tony Iommi, who often executed a similar technique on Black Sabbath's records.

"Born Stubborn" is another track reaching slightly to the recent past, though coming across a touch more upbeat due to the major key riff progression heard in the verses. Still, the layering of weird studio effects and noises—not to mention the inclusion of the Xavante Indian tribe chant at the end—sets it nicely into the sequencing of *Roots*.

The appearance of the Xavantes here is only a taste of what is to come.

"Jasco," a short instrumental that blends in traditional Brazilian melodies, spotlights Andreas' fondness for classical guitar, a discipline he continues to study and hone for several hours a day. Though mastered as its own track, "Jasco" serves as an introduction to what will the be the next, more extreme step up from "Kaiowas."

Meaning "roots" in the Xavante language, "Itsári" was written and recorded over the course of three days the band had spent in the tribe's village in Mato Grosso. The idea for the project had been in gestation for some time, partially inspired by Max's viewing of the film *At Play in the Fields of the Lord*. The movie, and its themes of "white man" civilization causing various harms on indigenous tribes, reignited the interest Sepultura had explored in "Kaiowas."

Connecting with the Xavantes helped to flesh out the entire concept of *Roots*, and even give the album its name.

Painted and ready for work.

The band spent the better part of a year corresponding with representatives of the tribe, filling out paperwork, discussing the logistics of bringing recording equipment into such a remote area that had no electricity, no modern amenities. But there was at least one stumbling block they didn't have to worry about. The Xavantes were independent from the government, which meant there would be no bureaucratic red tape to wade through.

Arranging the visit took long enough *without* the government's interference; one can only imagine how complicated and time-consuming the process would have been with the government involved.

The core group of visitors, including the band, Gloria and Max's family, Igor's wife Monika, photographers, record label representatives, and Ross Robinson, flew from São Paulo to Goiânia, and from there split across four small Cessna airplanes headed toward the Xavante village in the Aldeia Pimentel Barbosa. The planes were old and unkempt, susceptible to turbulence as a result of even the dullest winds.

Paulo, sitting up front near the pilot, received a tutorial on some gauges. When green, the pilot said while pointing to the radar, all was well. When yellow, everyone should be advised there might be turbulence. If red, hold on tight because turbulence will be bad. Just then, as if speaking of the devil, violent

Monika Cavalera and Ross Robinson in the Xavante village sleeping quarters.

wind crashed against the airplane, tossing it from side to side, sending the passengers reeling.

Xisto, terrified, noted to the pilot that the radar wasn't red. The pilot responded that the radar was broken.

Only three planes were able to land that day, the fourth—which contained all the recording equipment—wouldn't arrive until the following afternoon. In the meantime, the Xavantes absorbed Max, Igor, Paulo, and Andreas into their culture, decorating them with face and body paint, performing for them traditional rituals and songs, even assimilating them into their dances and music.

This union was essential not just for the band, but for the tribe as well. Their leader discussed past experiences with artists who only used them for publicity and personal gain. They hoped Sepultura would be different, remaining in touch after all was said and done, and making the world aware of the richness and diversity of their people.

Once the recording equipment had arrived, and an 8-track recorder was strung up to an automobile battery for power, they all set to work. It had been decided earlier that the Xavantes would perform for the album a healing chant—in their language, *Datar Wawere*—with Max and Andreas accompanying on acoustic guitars, Igor and Paulo percussion.

The car battery ran out of juice just as they wrapped up the sessions, and Sepultura paid their respects and gratitude to the tribe by playing "Kaiowas" for them. Twice.

Continuing with this theme of honoring the roots of Brazil, "Ambush" tells the story of Chico Mendes, as inspired by the book *Fronteiras de Sangue (Bloody Borders)*. Mendes was a freedom fighter who struggled to prevent the destruction of the rainforests. As a result of the widespread protests Mendes both led and supported, a local rancher murdered him in his home. After a sudden instrumental break in the middle of "Ambush," where Carlinhos Brown again makes himself heard, Max launches into his most vicious chorus yet, ending the song with a question: *Why? Why?*

He is silenced by the rhythmic cracks of three gunshots, symbolizing those that took Chico Mendes' life.

Revisiting the dark, doomy atmosphere of some of the earlier tracks, "Endangered Species" splits off once more with the help of Carlinhos, this time in a much creepier breakdown loaded with backward-masked screams and low chants, like something straight from a horror movie soundtrack. We also hear more incorporation of Kaplan's wide array of studio effects, and one begins to wonder how Sepultura will pull this off live.

Painted up by the Xavantes.

The effects, however, are more accoutrements than necessity. While they add color to the music's tapestry, they never overpower the basic structures of the songs. This was of the utmost importance. Sepultura were—*are*—a live band, and thus had to be able to recreate any of their songs in a live environment.

As much as they may have hoped, with *Roots*, to concentrate on the more positive aspects of Brazil, they occasionally lapse right back to targeting some of the subjects that pissed them off in the first place. One of these is "Dictatorshit," a vicious tirade against the military dictatorship. Families and friends are still impacted by the disappearances of those who spoke out against the leadership all those years ago, and the band pledges to never forget.

"Dictatorshit" ends on an explosive note, one that would have been fitting—considering how the album began—upon which to end *Roots* as a whole. But there is a note even more fitting.

The uncredited, thirteen-minute track "hidden" at the end of the disc opens with the same cracking noises heard at the beginning of "Roots Bloody Roots." It's not a gunshot after all, but one of Carlinhos Brown's percussion instruments breaking. Immediately afterward, according to legend, Brown kissed the instrument, said a silent prayer, and then hurled it into the canyon behind Indigo Ranch.

Max in slave transport catacombs during the filming of the "Roots Bloody Roots" video.

This marks the beginning of the "canyon jam," which is actually the tail end of a four-hour session they'd spent there, communing with nature, becoming one with each other through music.

Sometimes the impact of an album isn't felt until many years later, only when people are able to see the effects it had on other music, on other bands. Maybe such recordings are too "ahead of their time" to be recognized as revolutionary when they're released.

Roots is not one such album. While some fans did not take well to Sepultura's drastic change, few could deny they had broken down barriers. They had made an album no other band could make. They had taken their own personal roots—the Brazilian flavor that ran thick in their blood—and created an entirely new and original sound. Some would even say they created an entirely new subgenre of heavy music: tribal metal.

Even the cover packages the tribal aspect with a bow. Michael Whelan was again commissioned for the work, developing a framework around the indigenous child seen on the one thousand-cruzeiro bill, Brazil's former currency. To top the image off, Whelan ensured that the child sported a necklace emblazoned with the standard S logo.

A few additional tracks were recorded during the *Roots* sessions, as is usual with the band. They did, after all, nod toward their musical beginnings with a sludgy, evil interpretation of Celtic Frost's "Procreation of the Wicked." Max took on Bob Marley's "War," with its lyrics lifted directly from an Ethiopian emperor's UN discourse, transforming Marley's raggae rendition back into a virulent speech. And besides these two cover songs, Sepultura brought in Mike Patton one more time for the original, and sinister, "Mine."

Musically, the band may have been on point, unified in their vision to create something altogether different than anything they'd done before. But the studio was far from peaceful. The band was drifting apart, the tribe upset by a growing rift. Andreas, Paulo, and Igor felt that Gloria was taking too much control over the band. Showing preference to Max. And when disagreements occurred, it seemed to them, Max would take the side of his wife. "During the recording there were arguments [about] how to do our business," Andreas claimed. "It was everything done at her house, and she was totally power controlling."

Some of the fans began to compare Sepultura to The Beatles in this respect, foreseeing problems, calling Gloria the "Yoko Ono of metal." But the situation was far more complicated in Sepultura, with one obvious difference; Yoko wasn't the manager of The Beatles.

Gloria, whose job it was to manage the band as a unit was also married to its singer, the guy who was a media focal point simply because he stood in front of the microphone every night.

"From my point of view," Toninho explained, "I always thought it was not going to work. Suddenly Paulo, Igor, and Andreas were in the background, Max was the boss and Gloria his right arm for everything."

They all felt that they were seeing less and less of the vocalist and, Monika claimed, "Igor tried to talk to Max once, and Max was like, 'Oh, you're wrong, there's nothing going on here,' and Igor was being more and more upset. I think Igor was the most upset because in his mind he was losing his brother. He didn't have any contact with him anymore, pretty much."

The only US show before the release of *Roots* took place in January, at the aptly named Club Rio on the north side of Tempe, Arizona. It was a special warm-up in their relatively new hometown area, after which they flew across the pond for a brief promotional tour of Europe before returning Stateside to the hit the road with Ozzy, again, plus Brooklynites Type O Negative.

Looking back on interviews and video clips from those days, knowing what we know now, it is easy to see that something wasn't quite right. The band appeared to be distant, distracted, soft spoken. During a time when they were quite rapidly ascending a ladder of popularity, they didn't seem as excited or enthusiastic as one might expect. Igor and Paulo passed the time training jiu-jitsu. Certain tour mates noticed the band members were nice enough, but mostly kept to themselves, which was quite the change from 1994's tours with Pantera.

Some of this can be explained by the fact that Sepultura had, in a manner of speaking, grown up over the last couple of years. Max and Andreas were both married with kids, Igor was married with a child on the way. They were more responsible, not partying as much, taking their profession—especially on the road—a little bit more seriously.

But it can also be seen as evidence of tension building between different band members and the demands being made on them by outside forces.

"When I got pregnant," Monika recalled when discussing the subject, "my baby was supposed to be born in February [of 1997]. So I told Igor ... this was in July ... 'You have to tell Gloria we need February off because the baby is going to be born'."

Igor made the call, but it was impossible, explained Gloria.

Monika continued, "She said, 'I can't. I have Japan already'. And he's like, 'What? What do you mean?' and she said, 'I can't cancel the tour. We're going to get a replacement for you if you can't do the tour in Japan'. So he was like, okay, fuck off, and hung up the phone. And he said, 'I'm not doing it'."

It is human nature, though, to come together in times of calamity. In the early hours of August 16, a tragedy occurred back home in Phoenix while the band and Gloria were arriving in London to perform at Donington Park's Monsters of Rock the following day. They were billed to play on the main stage as the third-to-last band, just before Ozzy Osbourne and KISS co-headlined the event.

Shortly after they arrived at their hotel, Andreas received a call from Patricia. She was back home in Phoenix, with a friend and the nanny of Max and Gloria's children, and carried the worst news any parent could imagine. Gloria's son—Max's stepson—Dana, had died in a car crash. He was only twenty-one.

Any alleged infighting immediately ceased. Gloria and the band, each of them shocked and devastated to say the least, agreed that she and Max had to fly home as soon as possible. They were unified in one other respect, too. For the fans who'd come to Donington just to see them at least, Sepultura would go on as scheduled, though as a trio, with Kisser sharing the majority of the vocal duties with guests such as Silvio "Bibika" Gomes and Biohazard's Evan Seinfeld.

Ozzy, and Sharon, his wife and manager, allowed the Cavaleras use of their private jet so they could get home that same day.

Monika remembered, "When Gloria's son died, I was in Jamaica with my boss, and someone called me and told me he was dead. And then I flew the day after [in order to attend] his funeral."

The household was a somber place upon arrival. Family and friends were heartbroken, mourning the far-too-young and gentle soul whose passion was music. Jason Newsted and Max spent a night in tears, making a mix tape for Dana so they could bury him with his favorite music playing.

Details surrounding Dana's death remain sketchy, almost shrouded in mystery. Some people claim he was murdered, his car driven off the road by gang members who had sworn vengeance on Dana's passengers. Whether an accident or something else entirely, the event became a motivating factor in Max's future works.

Meanwhile, at Donington Park, Andreas explained the situation to the understanding audience, and asked them to join in a moment of silence before leading them into "Roots Bloody Roots." The concert as a whole may not have been their best, but it was the best they could have done under the conditions.

Rather than stay home and wallow in misery and sadness, Sepultura coped the best way they knew how. Barely a month after Dana's death, they were back on the road, this time as part of a package that included Ozzy, Danzig, and Biohazard.

But not without contention.

"When Dana died," said Monika, "they were supposed to go on tour two weeks after—because it was a break—and they had a meeting with Max. Max went inside Paulo's house and I was hiding behind the door, [listening] of course," she said with gentle laughter. "They said, 'Max, we know how hard it is for Gloria, but we need to move on. This is a great opportunity for us to tour with Ozzy, and we cannot miss this, so Gloria can stay at home and you go with us'. And Max said, 'Okay, I'll go on tour. I'll speak to her and then I'll go on tour and everything will be okay'."

Monika continued. "Our tour manager, Eddie Rocha, called Gloria and said he needed to know about the tour in two weeks because the band told him to start the advance, that Max was okay, that he would go on the tour. She said, 'Are you crazy? He'll never leave me here. He's not doing the tour'. At that time, Igor said, 'So ... her son died and she cancels the whole tour. And my baby's born, and I'm telling everyone six, seven months before, and she says she wants to replace me with a new drummer. Fuck her'."

The tour went ahead with Max.

Given the circumstances, touring may not have been the best course of action. Max and Gloria were emotional wrecks. Igor, Andreas, and Paulo were still seeing evidence of favoritism on Gloria's part, and were discussing their options. Sepultura's collective skin was covered in splinters, painful daggers both personal and professional, and going back on the road only buried them deeper into flesh.

The next four months were allegedly spent in various stages of misery, and would culminate in a nasty, drawn out split that clouded everyone's holiday season.

SEVEN

...BLOODY ROOTS

The middle of November saw the band return home to South America for a series of shows, but the homecoming atmosphere was far from ideal. In a sense, the split had already occurred, with Max and Gloria on one side, Paulo, Andreas, and Igor on the other. For most of 1996, after the release of *Roots*, the two factions saw very little of each other outside of rehearsals and performances.

The tensions that had been slowly building over the last year finally came to a head in Argentina, Andreas explained during a candid discussion. "And when we were playing in Brazil," he said. "Our house, our home, Sepultura fucking roots, the biggest thing ever. We were so happy to be in Brazil. At the same time," he said, the ripple of an almost uncomfortable laugh in his voice, "it was a disaster backstage. And Argentina was the biggest fight we ever had."

On November 14, at Estadio Obras Sanitarias in Buenos Aires, an indoor arena that holds around 5,000 bodies, no one in the audience would have guessed how strained the band's relationships had become. Sepultura played as if on fire, drawing raw energy from the crowd, even though they knew the end was probably near. And there were external tensions, as well, including Max and Gloria's lingering sadness over the unresolved death of Dana Wells, and Igor's preoccupation with his daughter Joanna, who had been born premature by almost three months, and was still in the hospital fighting illness and infection. Plans were being made to bring in ex-Machine Head drummer Chris Kontos for the upcoming Australian tour in January, so that Igor could stay home with Monika and Joanna.

Even though the band was at their absolute peak of success, in the midst of changing the face of heavy music and selling out arenas all over the world, these were not happy days for Sepultura.

Max later described the Buenos Aires aftershow events, saying he was roused from near sleep in his hotel room by Andreas on the phone, with Igor and Paulo. They needed to have a band meeting, and it couldn't wait until morning. According to Max, neither he nor Gloria had any idea what the trio wanted to talk about.

"The band really broke up in Argentina," Andreas said, "after the Buenos Aires show, in the hotel. Just the band and Gloria was almost like ..." He paused, collecting his thoughts. "You know, broken glasses, and it was very heavy, very intense, very emotional, and the band really decided to fuck off."

It was the culmination of discussions that the three had begun months earlier. Igor had been the first to suggest a change, angrily, citing a noticeable shift in the band's dynamic. Everyone understood that Max, as the front man, would naturally receive more media attention simply as a consequence of his position. But as their popularity grew, it began to appear (to them at least) as if Max *was* Sepultura, and that the other three were simply his backup band. For them although Gloria wasn't actively pushing this idea to the media, at the very least—Igor, Andreas, and Paulo believed—she was not doing enough to change this impression.

Igor suggested the–to him–most logical solution: Gloria could remain Max's manager, while the other three would seek representation from someone else. But nothing was really solved that night in Argentina. The pressures and responsibilities of being a popular touring band were too great to ignore, and of course, no one wanted to even consider splitting up Sepultura.

"In November," Monika recalled, "when they decided to tell her that she wouldn't be the [band's] manager anymore, I had an early delivery. My baby was supposed to be born in February and she was born in November. She was 30 centimeters and 600 grams, and she had to stay in the hospital for three months. How can someone think that I cared what was going to happen with the band? The only thing I told Igor was, 'You guys are going to make a decision, so you have to do this tour because we have no idea what's going to happen once you say you don't want to work with her anymore. And in case Max decides not to be with the band anymore, we would be out of money. So go do it and I'll take care of the baby at the hospital'."

"After the turmoil," Andreas explained, "on the same night, we decided to go to Europe because we had a European tour booked. We had Big Day Out in January. We had Japan, a huge tour in Japan in January and February. So we decided to go to Europe and talk about it, and resolve things. Of course that never happened. Especially on tour. *Roots* was exploding around the world, and we were in Europe playing fucking arenas for 10,000 and 15,000 people. After all that, it was just a big snowball.

Nobody could really handle it. No [record] label, no manager. Nobody."

Sepultura had become a machine, an entity, much bigger than any of its individual parts, and perhaps much more powerful than any of them—Gloria included—could control. Andreas summed it up, putting into words what everyone else trapped in that machine felt: "What's the point to play in a fucking arena and feel miserable?"

The misery affected everyone differently, as individuals, though it never seemed to affect the music.

"And the end," Andreas said, "was the last show at the Brixton Academy, December 16, '96, exactly the day that Gloria's contract was expired."

The date was not coincidence.

"During the *Roots* days, things were very difficult outside music," Andreas continued, speaking with a calmness that comes with years of retrospect. "We wanted to change that system," he said. "We wanted to be a little more professional, a little more in control of things, not too much one person taking care of everything. And that was very difficult to talk about because everything was very emotional."

Since the earliest days in Belo Horizonte and then São Paulo, Sepultura considered themselves a tribe. The tightness of their live performances came from almost ritualistic practice, day in and day out, and there was, as Andreas stated, something very sacred about that. They played every day—covers of bands they loved, bands like Slayer and Destruction and Venom—and worked constantly on their own songs. They were a family, united in music and mutual struggles both within the industry and outside of it. They had grown up in, and with, Sepultura, but at the end of 1996, they weren't kids anymore. They'd established families of their own.

"We were [no longer] four guys from Brazil who practiced every day," Andreas said. "We were not that kind of band anymore. We had families, we all lived in our houses, the band was a big success. Since the *Schizophrenia* days, things were going step by step. We didn't stop, you know? So everything was a little crazier, and this family kind of vibe was the stuff that didn't really let us go to a professional level."

The Brixton Academy concert would eventually be released by Roadrunner—against the wishes of the band, who until this day refuse to consider it an "official" Sepultura album—as a sonic document of Max's final show with Sepultura. Titled *Under a Pale Grey Sky*, the recording is untouched, free of studio dubbing, only having been mixed and mastered to ensure a balanced sound. It is violent, abrasive, and human ... and Sepultura resisted its release primarily because the recording placed a spotlight upon such an awful and emotional period of the band's history.

After Max, Andreas, Paulo, and Igor walked off that Brixton Academy stage, guitars screaming feedback, Max retired to the tour bus, while the other three met with Gloria backstage. By all accounts, the meeting itself was calm and collected when the trio gave Gloria a letter—prepared by their lawyer—that officially terminated her contract. Had they not done so on that particular day, when the original agreement expired, the contract would have automatically renewed.

"She knew her contract would expire," Andreas said, "and she knew we wanted to change the system of management in Sepultura. And of course Max and Gloria didn't agree. They had the right to do that. But Max wasn't in that meeting backstage at Brixton. It was just me, Gloria, Paulo, and Igor. Max stayed on the bus for whatever reason. He wasn't there to see his wife being fired."

Andreas quickly added, "*She* was fired, not him. Max never even showed his face in that last meeting with us, or with Gloria, even. He wasn't with anybody. She was by herself, and we were by ourselves as a band. And that gave us the power to keep going, actually, because me, Igor, and Paulo were there together to stay with Sepultura, with the good part, with the name and everything, and with the bad part as well. All the bullshit ... it took a long time to put everything together."

New Year's passed, and the first couple months of 1997 were filled with confusion and uncertainty around Sepultura. Tours in Australia and Japan scheduled for January and February were cancelled. Still no official decisions had been made about the state of the band, and there was (they alleged) no communication between Max and the other three guys. Max and Gloria had returned to Phoenix, while Igor, Paulo, and Andreas regrouped in Brazil for the holidays, convinced they could solve the issues internally, without the media or the fans or anyone else being involved or even aware of the situation. But all plans for discretion were abandoned when Max faxed an unannounced statement, an emotionally charged open letter, to media outlets across the world.

The statement read, in part:

"I want to let people know that I'm feeling not different than them hearing that all our work is being forced to end; I'm crying everyday, I'm hurt, I'm sad, I'm angry, I'm in complete shock, I'm feeling like half of me has died.

"It wasn't my decision to split the band, me and Gloria were pretty much forced out of Sepultura. I have to be honest, the feeling inside the band weren't [sic] like when we started, or the first time we ever play [sic] outside Brazil, but more like too many fucking "outsiders" telling everybody what to do, how to act and all this bullshit!!!

"I got sick of it, I don't need this shit in my life. I want to enjoy being in a band again, to create, to play, to laugh, to cry, to fight, to go after that impossible dream; and I want all of those feelings back...

Kamaitachi: the trio intact.

"One of the things that hurts me the most is the fact that we were such a united tribe at one point and sadly people started changing and acting different, with envy, greed, etc., etc...

"All I can say, and that's from the deep of my heart; we were a perfect team the four of us, Gloria, the roadies, the whole organization and like they say in Brazil, 'In a team that's winning, you don't change players,' and that's so fucking true!!!

"We could have replaced members or crew for more professional people, we stuck with each other; of course we could get a better bass player, or a superprofessional roadie, but that's not the way I believed things should be, we stay true to our tribe members, we help each other!!! And then, all of the sudden they gave Gloria a letter saying she was no longer representing Andreas, Igor or Paulo, without a fucking reason, simply fired by the other three guys. This is not the tribe I believe in anymore.

"I just want everybody to know, I never quit Sepultura, I never destroyed Sepultura, and I try [sic] all I could to fix the problem, but it was far too deep, far too late and unfortunaly [sic] people forget where they came from ..."

Hearing this news in the Brazilian press, Andreas, Igor, and Paulo were surprised by the sudden missive. In response, the three held a press conference in São Paulo to announce that, solely as a result of Max's statement, Sepultura had decided to continue without him. They even left the door open for the vocalist's return, though they were adamant that the band would not wait forever. When faced with the possibility that his brother might never come back, Igor plainly stated, "Sepultura is not dead."

During an interview with MTV Brazil, the always outspoken João Gordo admitted his lack of surprise at Max's departure. Once Gloria and Max had gotten married, he said, it was just a matter of time. And according to Gordo, everyone knew it.

Shortly after their own press conference, the band heard—again through the news, never directly from Max himself, nor anyone in his camp, they say—that Cavalera had formed a new group called Soulfly, and was already working on a new album with other musicians.

Igor, though, heard from Max.

Monika said, "I remember when I had the baby back from the hospital, he called Igor, and I remember exactly where Igor was sitting because this is something that ..." She trailed off, shaking her head. "He called and said, 'Hey Igor, let's dump all of the guys and let's make our own thing, and me and you, we can have another band', and Igor was like, 'Max, you don't get it. *I don't wanna work with your wife*. It's not about the guys or anything like that. I don't want your wife'."

Monika was beside him and suggested another solution. "I said, 'Why don't you tell him he could have Gloria as a manager and you guys get another manager, and then you guys can work together like that'."

But Igor was done. Fed up.

That was it, then.

In April, the now-trio convened in San Diego, California, to begin writing the songs that would become *Against*. They had a renewed purpose. All thoughts of possibly starting over with a new band name, or maybe even retiring from the music business altogether, disappeared once they got back into the groove. Playing music together was fun. They decided to take advantage of the moment. They would channel the emotions of the previous year—all the frustration, the anger, the bitterness—into a new album. Like the phoenix, they would arise, reborn.

It was the beginning of a new era for Sepultura.

"There have been moments when we felt like giving up," Andreas revealed in an interview with *Metal Hammer* magazine. "Fortunately our music is above that, and that is the reason why we survived." But there was more to it than just the music, as Igor explained. There was also family to consider. They had their own wives, their own children. "Those kinds of things really tend to weight any decision that I make. Sepultura is something that I love and at the same time I have a chance to support my family so, I take that very seriously."

The new songs raged ferociously. Everything the band had experienced in the past year, and the difficulties they continued to experience, became inspiration. While Max remained exceedingly vocal about the split—sometimes saying he quit in support of his wife, other times that he was fired out of jealousy—Sepultura remained relatively quiet, concentrating instead on working on a new album. They felt no need to justify or defend their actions, even while the media latched on to Max as the victim, and crucified Igor, Andreas, and Paulo in the press.

"The press always need this kind of gossip to attract readers," Paulo said later, waving it off in his usual unaffected manner. "So sometimes things become like a soap opera." Unfortunately, the soap opera manipulated many fans into choosing a side, as if Soulfly versus Sepultura was some sort of prizefight, and to support one necessitated hatred for the other.

Sepultura spent most of 1997 writing, maturing both as people and musicians, and perhaps most importantly, deepening their bond as friends. Andreas decided to handle the vocal duties early on, telling *Kerrang!* magazine, "So far, we want to keep it to just us three. I'll develop my singing, and maybe later on, we'll find it necessary to bring in another musician or singer."

Performing as a trio, musically anyway, was not necessarily a new experience. Over the last couple of years, Max had been increasingly interacting with the crowd, striving to build the

The trio recording with Carlo Bartolini.

crucial rapport between band and audience that can turn a concert from a mere show into a spectacle. As a result, his attention to the rhythm guitar parts declined. On the *Roots* tour, he would even unstrap the instrument completely, instead dancing about like a man living up to his old nickname, *possessed*.

And, Andreas reflected, "When Max wasn't able to play some shows, we played as a trio." But to condition his voice in a way that would perfectly complement Sepultura's music, as well as develop his own presence as a front man, Andreas knew he'd have to divide his focus between singing and playing guitar. "That's something totally different," he said, "to try to make your own style and create your own characteristic way."

Lessening his focus on the guitar just wasn't an option.

Armed with twelve songs, the three-piece version of Sepultura returned to Brazil later that year to continue writing and to begin auditioning singers. They knew what they wanted out of a vocalist, and what they didn't want. They wanted someone aggressive, who could do justice to the anger-laden new songs, with his own personality. They didn't want a Max Cavalera clone.

In *Toda a Historia*, Igor reflected on the situation. "We could have easily called some famous singer, but we thought it would be better to look for somebody new, unknown, that brought new energy into the band." On October 24, a press release officially announced their search for Max's replacement, and the demo tapes began to flood in.

The band listened to hundreds of recordings, but only a few voices piqued their collective interest. A select number of candidates were given a rough, instrumental demo of the new song "Choke." The prospective singers were told to come up with their own lyrics and their own melodies, since the band wasn't simply looking for a hired gun. They needed someone with whom they could write. It had to be like it always was: four guys, together in a room, jamming on ideas and coming up with the material together.

For Derrick Green, the timing of his audition for Sepultura could not have been better. His band, Alpha Jerk, was in the process of unraveling. As if through divine intervention, Mike Gitter—a friend and Roadrunner Records A&R representative—informed Derrick that Sepultura were looking for a singer. This came as a surprise to the American, who until that point hadn't even known that Max had left the band.

Derrick was initially hesitant, unsure what type of vocalist they had in mind. Auditioning, he knew, would be a pointless gesture if they wanted someone who sounded like Max, because he was only interested in being himself.

Green had experienced a relative amount of success as a member of Cleveland-based Outface. Outface released their only album, Friendly Green (named in tribute to Derrick's father), in 1992, to decent reviews. Though signed to a relatively punk label, Crisis Records, and promoted as a hardcore band, those tags are far too constrictive to describe Outface's sound. They owed much more to Bad Brains than Sex Pistols or Sick Of It All. But after a short U.S. tour and a trek around Europe in support of Friendly Green, the band fell apart. While Derrick and guitarist Charlie Garriga headed east in an attempt to resurrect Outface as part of the infamous New York Hardcore scene, bassist Frank Cavanagh remained in Cleveland and would eventually join Filter (but not before, coincidentally, Sepultura and Filter both appeared on the soundtrack for the horror film Tales from the Crypt: Demon Knight).

While working security at New York City clubs, Green started a new band called Overfiend, which eventually transformed into Alpha Jerk, the mainstays of the two groups being Derrick and vocalist Sarah Cox.

Alpha Jerk released its only album, self-titled, in 1996, and played shows sporadically in the New York area. But the band was going nowhere, so with Alpha Jerk more or less on ice, Derrick relented and gave Mike Gitter his tape to forward to the boys in Brazil. Immediately hooked on the singer's raw power and range, they sent back the instrumental demo of "Choke," and Derrick got to work in the recording studio of a friend, Davide Gentile, who played bass in post-hardcore band Orange 9mm. Coincidentally, Davide had been invited to audition with Sepultura some weeks before.

"They really liked Davide," Derrick said, speaking to the Cleveland Examiner, "but he wanted to pursue audio engineering. He really helped me with my audition tape of the song..."

Derrick didn't have to wait long before receiving a call from Igor, on behalf of the band, inviting him to spend a couple of weeks in Brazil.

In October's press release, the drummer had stated that their ideal singer would be "someone who will fit with us... a person who somehow has the same ideas about life and sees things the way we see things. In other words, not the typical metal guy who just thinks about beer. We want a guy who can talk about beer and soccer!" Naturally, holding auditions in Brazil served a greater purpose.

Sepultura's homeland roots had become a vital part of their sound. And individually, growing up there had helped to define their personalities. We are shaped by our cultures, by our language, by the beliefs and the traditions of our countries, even our music. They all melt together into the puzzle of our often unconscious sense of identity. The band understood this, but they never considered limiting their pool of candidates to only Brazilian singers (though, in a humorous aside, Paulo once commented on a tape sent to them by a cowboy from the western state of Mato Grosso—the gaucho's voice was nice, but his image didn't fit).

More than just a live audition, spending two weeks with the band in São Paulo was also a test of cultural significance. Could the singer absorb and adapt to Brazil as well as absorbing and adapting to the music?

When the call came to try out with the band on their home turf, Derrick Green didn't hesitate. He nervously boarded a plane to South America.

From their first session playing together, everyone felt the chemistry. Sepultura knew right away they had found their guy, but they didn't tell Derrick that.

At least, not right away.

"His voice was of course the most important, but the arrangements he did for 'Choke' really tipped the scale to his favor," Andreas told *Spin City*.

In the meantime, Eric Guadagnoli from Italian death metallers Electrocution recorded a demo that intrigued the band, and among others, three well-known San Francisco Bay Area names also tried their hand: Phil Demmel, (guitarist of Vio-lence and Machine Head, most notably), Testament vocalist Chuck Billy, and Skinlab bellower Steev Esquival.

"I had spoken with Borivoj Krgin at the time when it happened," Demmel explained. "He was familiar with the Torque stuff I was doing and although he knew they had Derrick pretty much in the band, he talked me into writing some lyrics and recording an audition tape to send out to the dudes. He had the DATs sent out to me and I recorded with James Murphy (who had recorded Torque months previous) the song 'Choke.' After I was done he played me Chuck and Steev's versions while he mixed."

The competition was amiable between the three long-time friends.

"It wasn't awkward because it seemed like [Sepultura] already had their guy," Phil continued. "I was entrenched in my home life at the time and was pretty much done with music. Borivoj said they had deemed me 'Good, but too old school for what they were looking for.'"

A month after his live audition with the band, back home in New York City, Derrick Green was still buzzing. He knew he wanted the job more than anything, but was afraid to get his hopes up. On an otherwise insignificant day, he received another fateful call just before heading out to bounce at Lakeside Lounge in the east village. Todd Singerman, the band's manager at the time, was on the line, asking if Derrick would like to go back to Brazil, this time as the vocalist for Sepultura.

"I think my heart stopped," Derrick later said.

EIGHT

AGAINST EVERYTHING

Derrick Leon Green, born in Cleveland, Ohio on January 20, 1971, lived in the city with his parents, a brother, and a sister until the age of seven, when the family moved to a small suburb a few miles to the east. It was quite the change for young Derrick, leaving the inner city of Cleveland for Shaker Heights, a picturesque community with a population of barely 30,000 people. Established in 1912 by Shakers—a highly religious group of worshipers who promoted celibacy, the work ethic and love of God above all things— Shaker Heights was one of the first American suburbs to begin practicing aggressive racial integration in the 1950s. By the time the Green family moved there in the late 70s, African-Americans made up approximately one-third of the population, and the city already had a reputation as being one of the most racially tolerant communities in the nation.

By 14-years-old, Derrick was already attending hardcore and punk rock shows in Cleveland whenever he could, and one of the most attractive aspects of the scene for him, besides the music, was that it didn't matter who he was or where he came from. The color of his skin didn't matter, nor did his age, background or

Interviews and promotion: the work behind the work.

beliefs. Two years later, in 1986, he joined his first band, Outface, who had already gone through two singers by then.

And after just over a decade in the music scene, Derrick found himself in an enviable position. He was returning to São Paulo as the new vocalist of Sepultura, to help wrap up the writing—and begin recording—*Against*.

He had big shoes to fill, of course.

In rehearsals, Derrick fit in like a missing puzzle piece. This may be, at least in part, due to the fact that Andreas, Paulo, and Igor had spent those nine months working to rebuild Sepultura from the inside. Had they rushed into finding a new singer, writing a new album, and jumping right back onto the road, they may have buried their issues instead of dealing with them. And buried issues always eventually find their way to the surface.

As Andreas likes to say, the future is just a consequence of the present.

Still, even with a full time vocalist now in the ranks, many of the new tracks featured both Derrick and Andreas singing, trading lines and passages. It was a natural result of spending so much time as a trio, Andreas explained. "I tried my voice in many songs, in many bits, full songs and stuff like that, just for the hell of it," he said. "It was a cool experience, and then Derrick took over more because he's much better, you know. He's very focused on the stuff."

Integrating Green as much—and as early—as possible was essential for them to move forward. Sepultura felt they needed to retain that "band" spirit they'd always had, even with Max, as much as some critics wanted to believe that Cavalera had been the sole driving force. The tribe mentality was still there, even though members of the tribe had changed.

But Green didn't get a chance to really settle into Brazil yet, as most of the writing was already complete, and recordings would take place across a number of different studios—the majority of which were located in the United States. Meanwhile, on June 3, Roadrunner released *Blood Rooted*, a collection of rare Sepultura B-sides, remixes, and live performances.

While the band mulled over possible producers, Howard Benson approached them about the job. With a varied résumé that crossed genre boundaries from T.S.O.L. to Tuff, Bang Tango to Body Count, Benson worked up a pre-production tape for Sepultura that the band loved. They'd found their man.

The recording process this time around was unlike anything they'd experienced so far, and the sound of the album was a testament to that. Suddenly there was much more room in the mix for Paulo's bass, and for Andreas to stretch out. Igor laid down drum tracks in front of a piano with a microphone mounted inside, lending a taut, melodic quality to the percussion. Derrick could not only scream and growl with the best of them, but he could—and did—actually *sing*, introducing greater dynamic layers to the songs. And Benson discovered new computer technology far removed from the days of cutting reel-to-reel tape: Pro Tools. The software allowed for increased flexibility—and creativity—when editing and piecing tracks together.

Everyone knew the album would be judged first on its title alone, so they needed something powerful, one word that would sum up their entire existence at that time.

And that one word—*Against*—said it all.

Inspired by a song Andreas had written called "Against the Tide," the title described succinctly the last two years. While Max voiced his frustrations through the press, Sepultura spewed theirs out through the music. Still, some took it the wrong way. They were not "against" Max specifically, or even Gloria, for that matter. They were against everything that had occurred as a result of the split. The media mudslinging. The rumors. The lies. The pressure certain people put upon the fans to "choose a side." It was a private matter, they believed, that should not have involved anyone but those directly affected by the situation.

But the media loves drama, and critics had a field day dissecting the lyrics on *Against*, trying to translate every word into an anti-Max, anti-Gloria sentiment.

The hardcore influences are obvious in the title track and album opener, rolling into life with the speed of Igor's double bass drums. For those who expected Sepultura to continue down a sonic path they walked on *Roots*, sludgy and distinctly Brazilian, a rude awakening is in effect. The speed and ferocity, even before the vocals drop in, shows that the band again has no desire to repeat themselves. In less than one minute Derrick makes his first appearance, spitting absolutely furious words.

Of course the band sounds different, but that's precisely the point. Max was unique. One of a kind. Something indefinable, though, something very *Sepultura*, is still there on *Against*. Maybe some listeners refuse to accept it. Maybe the change is too

Igor at SOBFC Headquarters, Galeria do Rock.

much for them, the same way certain Black Sabbath fans railed against *Heaven and Hell* after Ronnie James Dio replaced Ozzy Osbourne. Regardless of opinion, the first song from a new era makes it clear that Sepultura is taking a courageous step away from its past.

"Choke," however, and the vocal arrangement that scored Derrick Green a job, respectfully nods in the direction of *Roots*. Green's voice is rough around the edges in all the right spots, slightly higher in pitch than Cavalera's guttural bark, and the song grooves with a verse riff that uses only single notes—no chords—emphasizing the low end marriage between bass and drums. It is a mixture of old and new. A tribal interlude similar to the drum jams in live versions of "Kaiowas" and "Ratamahatta" brings back memories, but then the lead break comes and the rhythm guitar drops out. This is something new for fans used to hearing Max chugging along on his four strings behind the guitar solos.

In the lyrics of "Rumors," the sensationalist media finds those scathing attacks they were seeking. Unfortunately for them, they are one of the targets. Kisser makes his most transparent statement yet, calling out those who spread misinformation and lies based on the testimonials of one person. The critics miss the point, proving the lyrics right, as they cite the song as a verbal attack against Max.

The album's first true standout track comes next, the dark and atmospheric "Old Earth." Derrick's voice, beyond the surface of just sounding different that Max's, gives the band an opportunity to explore the dynamics of a quiet, eerie verse exploding into a suddenly violent chorus, then creeping back into unsettling calm. A song of this nature would not have been possible with Max, who'd created an identifiable style based—admittedly—on his resistance to singing. Lyrically, with Green's input, "Old Earth" veers away from the topics of the first few tracks and places its rage firmly on the environmental and personal damage we, as humans, can cause. Deforestation. Pollution. Racism. Greed. These are the ways in which we kill our planet and ourselves.

Against has hit its stride, falling into a comfortable rhythm as "Floaters In Mud" again straddles the line between old and new. Igor's tribal prelude here is modified, not quite so Brazilian as Japanese now, utilizing bells and obscure percussive instruments he'd collected over the years. The standard structure of verse-chorus-verse-chorus is interrupted with a sudden, *Chaos A.D.*-style riff, but the song twists and turns into breakdowns and circular lead guitar patterns that advise listeners to expect the unexpected. The title itself describes a strange feeling that Andreas experienced when he and Max recently turned up at the same concert. They did not speak to—or even engage—each other. Once like brothers, they were now divided, separated, a surreal sensation Kisser likened to floating in mud.

Derrick and Andreas once more trade vocals on "Boycott," a pissed off tirade that utilizes the same simple, two-note riff for the verse as for the chorus. This song, in particular, illustrates the ambiguous nature of Kisser's lyrics, and how open they are to interpretation. Is he speaking of the police? The armies of the world? Regardless, the message remains the same. Those who are appointed to protect and serve, who live by the gun, suffer debilitating stress because they serve two masters who rarely have mutual motivations: the government and the people.

"Tribus," a short instrumental track, is interesting in that it can also have a number of meanings. The word itself comes from the Latin *tres* meaning "three," a number we see repeated throughout *Against*, and may represent the trio of Igor, Paulo, and Andreas as they struggled to keep Sepultura alive before adopting Derrick into the gang. But it also refers to Roman history, as meaning any one of the three original tribes. It is a powerful word, reiterating the assertion that they are still a tribe, and will continue on as a tribe now with a new fourth member.

"Tribus" segues into "Common Bonds" with the smooth perfection of a movie soundtrack. The rest of the album, in fact, with its usage of instrumental intervals and outros, plays almost like the soundtrack to a film that does not exist. In another first for the band, the fast, forceful "Common Bonds" is split in the middle by the harmonized voices of Derrick and Andreas as the two recite—nearly chanting—a quatrain of inspiration and strength.

The film connection continues with "F.O.E.," one more instrumental interlude, this time an amended version of The J.B. Pickers' track "Freedom of Expression." The Brazilians had been hearing an excerpted version of this song for years as lead-in music of the television program *Globo Reporter*. When Igor discovered the original on a vinyl soundtrack for the 70s movie *Vanishing Point*, he knew they had to cover it. Sepultura's adaptation ties "Common Bonds" nicely to the hardcore punk of "Reza," with its lyrics and vocals by Ratos de Porão partner in crime, João Gordo.

Excepting "Ratamahatta" with its few lines of English lyrics, "Reza" has the honor of being the first Sepultura song sung completely in Portuguese. After the years of friendship, concerts together, and tributes, a collaboration with Gordo was long overdue. "Reza" delivers on all fronts, a throwback to a bygone era that would not have sounded out of place had it been written for *Chaos A.D.*

Even "Unconscious" musically harkens back to the mid-nineties. If there had been an album between *Chaos A.D.* and *Roots*, this song could have been on it. For those listeners not swayed by prejudice, it should by now be clear that Andreas, Paulo, and Igor were just as responsible for helping define that "classic" Sepultura sound as was Max.

While on tour in 1991, Igor had stumbled onto a recording by a Japanese group called Kodo. The group's name carries a couple of meanings that define their purpose; the word *kodo* literally translates to "heartbeat," but can also mean "children of the drum." Exploring the limitless possibilities of sound with the traditional Japanese taiko drum, Kodo entranced Igor right away. Years later, they met in Belgium, and Sepultura were pleasantly surprised to learn that the Japanese percussionists not only knew their music, but were fans, as well. The two groups made loose plans to one day work together.

That one day became four during the recording of *Against*, when Andreas, Paulo, and Igor traveled to the island of Sado to visit the Kodo village. (Derrick stayed in L.A. with Benson, recording vocal tracks.) As they had done with the Xavante tribe, the band members immersed themselves in the culture, becoming a part of this community for a short time. Together they wrote and recorded "Kamaitachi," a song born out of legend.

The origin of this myth came from mountain dwellers who, while out walking, were sometimes overtaken by sudden gusts of whirlwinds that struck brutally fast, and disappeared just as quickly.

The monsters within these winds were most commonly imagined as a trio of violent weasels, and were thusly dubbed kamaitachi, from *kama* (meaning "sickle") and *itachi* (meaning "weasel"). They attacked in teams: the first knocked down the victim, the second sliced through flesh with razor-sharp claws, and the third weasel healed so the victim was left with no blood on them, and no wounds showing.

Metaphorically, the song "Kamaitachi" commemorates the time Sepultura spent as a trio, struggling against the critics, the naysayers. The members of Sepultura, in that limbo between Max and Derrick, *were* the mythical kamaitachi, striking out through their music. Extending the metaphor even further, one could suggest that Igor incapacitated their adversaries with his pummeling percussion, Andreas sliced through flesh with his jagged guitar riffs, and Paulo applied medication with the low-end salve of his bass lines.

Artistic representations of the kamaitachi, as well as the mit-sudomoe (a bladed triskelion symbol often seen on taiko drum-heads) were later used extensively in promotional artwork for *Against*.

A reworked version of "Kamaitachi" (with vocals supplied by old friend Mike Patton, and originally dubbed "Diary of a Drug Fiend" after Aleister Crowley's infamous novel) would later show up on the *Freddy vs. Jason* horror movie soundtrack under the title "The Waste."

If there's one song above any of the others that can be interpreted as a summation of Sepultura's emotional constitution at the time, "Drowned Out" is it. Even though Green penned all the lyrics, the vitriol Derrick spits could be about anyone; it could be about a selfish friend who betrayed a confidant. It could be about Max turning his back on the band. It could be about the media or the record label. It could be about all this. As with the bulk of the material, the band played "Drowned Out" only one time for Green to hear, and then told him to sing along. The vocal patterns were spontaneous and passionate, and regardless of where Derrick's rage was aimed, the unadorned viciousness of the music clearly inspired the lyrics.

The rage is cleared away with "Hatred Aside," written and recorded at Jason Newsted's Chophouse Studio in San Francisco. Featuring Newsted on baritone guitar, guest vocals, and theremin, the band pushes hatred aside and celebrates their strength, their determination, their unity.

Against as a whole, in fact, is somewhat of a cleansing. It spans the healing process, burning off its anger from the infuriated opening strains of "Against" until the tranquil "T3rcermillennium." The gentle tribal beats, acoustic guitars, and cellos in this final track symbolize rebirth as the second millennium comes to an end and the *tercer millennium*—the third millennium—begins. Sepultura is reborn. Interestingly, the first half of the song was recorded on a portable DAT machine at Igor's house in San Diego, while the guys were sitting around, thoughtlessly jamming and watching a football match. After later recognizing the beauty they'd created, they finished "T3rcermillenium" in the studio, building layers of atmosphere onto the short bit they'd recorded at Igor's.

With the album finished, Sepultura breathed a collective sigh of relief. They had made it through. They'd survived. They'd proved to themselves that there was life after Max Cavalera, but the new tribe was anxious to get on the road to see how fans would take to the new lineup.

A number of forces continued to stoke the still smoldering coals of the split—as they saw it. When Max released his first album post-Sepultura, titled *Soulfly* after the name of his new band, in

April of 1998, the media painted a picture of Max as a victim and the fact that he was overtly vocal about the situation only helped foster that image.

Even though Max's interviews often contradicted each other, the press ran with it because he was outspoken and that made great copy. Because he talked about it. Because he brought the drama. And in the eyes of the media, as well as some fans who were sucked into the debacle, the fact that Cavalera had put out an album before his former band mates was proof enough—for them—that the growler had been the leader of the pack all along. Whether intentionally or not, Max further cultivated this belief by using the same producer, the same studio, the same mixer the band had used on *Roots*. Even the song structures, sounds, and guitar tunings were the same. *Soulfly* was, to all intents and purposes, *Roots Part Two*.

Discussing his thoughts on this matter, Andreas said, "For the first Soulfly album, they just changed the guitar player, the drummer, and the bass player to do the album. He used Ross Robinson, he used Andy Wallace, he had the same management, he used the same studio. He tried to reproduce *Roots*, which of course *Soulfly* is not even close. Sepultura went to a different place, and we always went… if you put together *Arise*, *Chaos A.D.*, and *Roots*, they are totally different albums because that's our spirit. But I think he was still there in '96."

One need only read the lyric sheet of *Soulfly* to see that Max was writing from a place of pain. The songs were meant to sting, some attacking his former band (some even attacking an older former mate in Wagner Lamounier), leveling thinly veiled accusations of greed and envy.

It naturally impacted on the relationship between Roadrunner Records and Sepultura. Max was Roadrunner's priority, because he'd released his album first, and so the label provided major promotion and marketing, plus big tour opportunities to Soulfly. Even though the split was bitter and unfortunate, Andreas, Paulo, and Igor continued to insist they didn't regret anything that had happened. They only regretted *the way* it had happened, publicly, with the media playing a part. After all this, Sepultura were beyond ready to move on. They kept quiet, and kept working.

They had more pressing concerns anyway. The band was slated to introduce Derrick Green to Brazilian fans via a live television broadcast of the Brazilian MTV Music Video Awards in the middle of August, and then again a couple of days later for their first full concert in Brazil with the American.

To alleviate the pressure of starting off on such a big stage, they organized a trio of secret warm up shows in southern California under the name Troops of Doom.

"We did three shows as Troops of Doom," Andreas said. The first took place at the Brick by Brick club in San Diego. While it felt great and was a relief to play again, Kisser knew they had a lot of room to grow and improve. The second and third shows were successively better, Andreas recounting, "The last show was on the same day that Brazil lost the 1998 World Cup Final in France against the home team. It was a horrible afternoon watching Brazil lose so badly by three to zero, but at night we went on stage and destroyed. It was the best of the three and we felt great to keep moving on, to keep Sepultura alive."

They were, in the guitarist's opinion, maybe the most important shows of Sepultura's career.

As prepared as possible under the circumstances, Derrick, Andreas, Paulo, and Igor hit the vMBS on August 13, Green shouting an enthusiastic *"Brazil!"* to kick off the abbreviated set. They powered through a brutal performance of "Choke," headbanging like madmen, Green's braids whirling through the air as he proved without a doubt that he belonged on that stage with that band. As much as he tried to look angry while screaming the song's venomous poetry, one couldn't help but notice Derrick's occasional smile, from time to time lighting his face up with pure delight.

And if that alone weren't enough, the Paulistano fans were blessed with a real treat when Andreas announced a guest, Metallica's Jason Newsted, on baritone guitar and backing vocals. The band launched into "Roots Bloody Roots," and even the Caetano Veloso fans were on their feet.

On August 15 came the first real test of the new formation. The *Barulho Contra Fome* festival—Noise Against Hunger—took place in Anhembi, São Paulo, in front of 30,000 people. Organized by the Prefeitura of São Paulo and headlined by Sepultura, entry into the concert was gained with ten dollars and a can of food. In the spirit of the event, none of the bands received any sort of payment for the performances.

The show was a rousing success as the audience warmly welcomed Derrick into the tribe. It also contained its fair share of surprises, beginning with the "blessing" by way of Zé do Caixão's introduction (called "Prenúncio," and later released as a bonus track on Brailiain editions of *Against*, as well as the *Tribus* EP). After Jason Newsted's participation at the VMB's a couple of nights before, many expected to see him again this evening. They were not disappointed. Newsted provided rhythm guitar on a number of songs, and together he and Sepultura roared through Metallica's classic version of "Last Caress/Green Hell," the Misfits medley, with Jason providing lead vocals.

Among other highlights, Mike Patton joined the festivities on "Lookaway," and painted members of the Xavante tribe delighted the crowd with their live interpretation of the healing chant during "Itsári." Carlinhos Brown jumped in for "Ratamahatta," after stopping the show dead in its tracks by bringing to the stage a boy who'd threatened to commit suicide afterward.

But one guest appearance was most notable above all others, in the form of he who had handed over guitar slinging duties to Andreas more than a decade earlier. Jairo Guedz, much to the euphoric delight of the spectators, rejoined his mates for a crushing rendition of "Troops of Doom."

It was a fitting segue from one epoch of Sepultura to the next.

The rest of August and September saw the band on a promotional interview circuit of Europe before embarking on a short US

Destroying the European summer festival circuit.

club tour. While in Amsterdam, Derrick fell in love with the city, setting up residence there for a time. It worked within the framework of the band's schedule, considering how often and how much they planned to tour Europe. Unlike Brazil, for example, where concerts usually took place on the weekend, in European countries Sepultura could play any and every day of the week. Additionally, Amsterdam was centrally located and easily accessible to and from the upcoming worldwide dates.

A European trek rounded out 1998, with Sepultura as special guests for Slayer as part of the latter band's *Diabolus On Tour* package, and then-unknown System of a Down opening. The bill was a dream for Sepultura, considering the impact Slayer had had on their formative years. After the tragic death of founding guitarist Jeff Hanneman in 2013, Andreas Kisser repeatedly stated that were it not for Slayer, Sepultura would be a radically different band. Early rehearsal tapes (and concerts) even had the boys tearing through a version of Slayer's "Black Magic."

So when guitarist Kerry King joined Sepultura on stage for "Propaganda," the guys could not have felt more honored and ecstatic.

During the short holiday break at the end of 1998 and the beginning of 1999, before the more extensive North American

Slayer-tura.

leg of the *Fight Against Tour* launched, Brazilian musician André Moraes contacted Igor to see if the drummer was interested in doing some soundtrack work. Moraes had recently caught Sepultura's performance of "Kaiowas" on television, and thought the heavy percussion, acoustic guitars, and distinct Brazilian melodies would be perfect for *No Coraçao dos Deuses*, a project he was working on with his father, the film producer Geraldo Moraes.

Though André had a few ideas he wanted to incorporate, for the most part he gave Igor free reign to do whatever he felt appropriate. The drummer enlisted Andreas into the project and the two went straight to work, composing while screening rough cuts of the film, and within a few weeks had a finished product. The music even managed to hook Mike Patton, who just happened to be in town. He took a tape of "Procura o Cara" home with him to California, where he laid down the vocal tracks, and sent it back to Brazil for inclusion on the soundtrack.

Andreas worked with Moraes in a different format that year, too, as a guest musician on a song called "7" from the debut album of André's band Infierno.

Set lists for the American and Canadian concerts in early 1999 varied little, with Sepultura intent on showing fans that they were not interested in resting on the strength of their older material. They began creating medleys of songs like "Arise" and "Dead Embryonic Cells," "Inner Self" and "Beneath the Remains," to make room for newer music. Believing deeply in the album, they typically played more than half of *Against* every night.

In May of 1999, another dream came to fruition when Metallica brought their *Garage Remains the Same Tour* to Brazil, enlisting Sepultura to provide direct support. Metallica—and especially Jason Newsted—had felt it only appropriate that the Brazilians open these shows. Within a matter of months, they'd played shows with two of the Big Four bands that influenced them as youngsters, and had shared a stage with Megadeth back at Rock In Rio II. The only one left was Anthrax, but that connection would come later.

While in Brazil, they hit the television circuit, stopping by programs such as *Turma da Cultura* and *Programa H*. Though there were some fans who seemed almost offended that Max had been replaced with an American, claiming that Sepultura could no longer be "the voice of Brazil," most fans took well to Green. Sepultura continued to grow with Derrick, strengthening the band as a live unit with visits to Australia and New Zealand, Japan, and finishing out the cycle with a round of European summer festivals.

After a short vacation back home in August of 1999, the band was ready to open the book on their next chapter.

NINE

THE BIRTH OF A NEW NATION

Once beyond the emotional intensities of the moment, Sepultura could see that *Against* was a somewhat confusing record, stylistically, certainly reflecting the turmoil and confusion they'd been feeling at the time. While not a weak album by any means, *Against* was more transitional than anything, bridging the gap between two distinct eras of Sepultura.

After a solid year of touring and gelling as a unit, they were ready to begin writing an album that would more accurately represent the band they'd become in the wake of Max Cavalera's departure. To do this, they felt a return to Brazil was necessary. They wanted to take their time on the material, experiment with new thoughts and ideas, assimilate Derrick's own musical identity to forge something bigger and better—and perhaps slightly more optimistic—than *Against*. Being in Brazil also offered the opportunity to relax and not force the material due to time constraints or longing for family.

Derrick found himself making an international move for the second time in almost as many years. "I moved so we could be closer to work on the composing of *Nation*," he said. "I loved living in Amsterdam but it was better that I was in Brazil."

It wasn't easy for him in the beginning. He lived in São Paulo alone, unable to speak Portuguese very well at all. He was familiar with culture shock after having lived in the Netherlands, but the strangest aspect of it all was the instant celebrity. Everywhere he went, people knew him as the "American guy" in Sepultura. The fans, though, were always respectful, demonstrating their warm and welcoming Brazilian nature by oftentimes attempting to speak in English, just to make it easier on Derrick.

It is fair to say that Sepultura, at this point, had transcended the tag of "Brazilian band," even though they were beginning a process that would see them all move permanently back to the country. In the early 80s, as kids in Belo Horizonte and São Paulo, they'd ingested as much foreign influence as they could stand. It was only their international success and relocation to the United States that really drew out their "Brazilianness." But living abroad, and experiencing scores of new cultures through endless months on the road, changes a person. It changes a band. When Sepultura put their roots down in Brazil on the cusp of a new millennium, and with a new American singer, they were—perhaps without even realizing it—closing the circle. They'd brought Brazil to the world, and now they were bringing the world back to Brazil.

Derrick in the zone.

And really, a band like theirs could have only come from Brazil. With a musical tradition so rich, so varied, Brazil's influences ranged from locations all over the globe—Africa, Europe, even North America. The country is a true cultural melting pot. Sepultura embodied this attitude of acceptance, plucking musical inspiration from everywhere and every style. Even in the early days, when they claimed to hate samba and sertanejo and MPB, those sounds were being embedded into their collective psyche, later spilling out in tracks like "Kaiowas" and "Ratamahatta." Whether painting their faces and copying Venom's seeds of black metal, or jamming with Japanese Kodo drummers, Sepultura never set limits on where the muse could be found.

This profound global awareness would heavily shape the concept behind the forthcoming album, and in more ways than one.

Despite a summer break in 2000 to join Slipknot's *Tattoo the Earth* festival tour, also featuring the likes of Slayer, Sevendust, and Lamb of God (not to mention Metallica for one show in New Jersey), Sepultura spent most of the year hard at work in rehearsal. Roadrunner offered up a miniscule budget for the production, just as they had for *Beneath the Remains*, so when time came to record, the band decided to stay in Brazil not just out of convenience, but also financial necessity—as they had back in 1989—since it was cheaper to record there.

To be titled *Nation*, the album made a bold declaration straight out of the gate with the track "Sepulnation" and its typically Igor intro.

Judging by the main riff's unconventional, but highly catchy, chord progressions, and the title alone, it is apparent this song will be an anthem, a live staple for many years to come. It sets the tone, the theme of the album: an idealistic creation of a new, global nation, a sort of utopia with no borders, no guns, no violence, and no hate, that functions solely on respect for everyone and everything.

How can we create this?

The one-minute burst of hardcore energy, "Revolt," tells us how. This is the beginning of the rebellion, the violent war that always precedes peace.

"Border Wars" pulls back the aggression a bit, speaking of the ills of the system and how they affect the people as individuals and as an entity. Derrick's shouts of resistance—*No! No!*—in the chorus are heavily laden with echo, as if he's bellowing into a megaphone, holding court at a rally or manifestation. Igor's fascination with dancehall, a Jamaican variant of techno music with roots in raggae and dub, makes an appearance in the rhythms of the track.

Tagged at the end of "Border Wars" is the first of four spoken word interludes, famous quotations of Mother Theresa, Mahatma Gandhi, Albert Einsten, and the Dalai Lama, each recited in a different language to illustrate tolerance of all religions and beliefs, and the ultimate purveyance of peace.

"One Man Army" has Derrick addressing directly, calmly, confidently the administration with a sort of vocal manifesto, its simple chorus declaring that one man can make a change. The opening verses are presented as a first person singular narrative, utilizing the "I" of the individual, but the successive verses are first person plural, transforming the "I" into "We" as the people band together and become one. The breakdown returns a sense of tranquility, the speech of truth sounding almost like a chant, but the hostility soon circles back, perhaps signifying that change isn't just coming... change has already begun. The track ends with a gentle tribal beat and hypnotic melody as the revolutionaries rest assured of their impending victory.

"Vox Populi"—Latin, meaning "the voice of the people"—is a call to arms, a war cry, with Andreas' alarm-like riff repeating through the verses. The narrative now is almost completely first person plural, all "We" and "Our," in support of the forces that are destroying the system and building a new one upon the ashes of the old.

"The Ways of Faith," with its use of sitar and Middle Eastern melodies, is yet another song that begins and ends on a mellow note, alternating passivity with distorted aggression. It speaks of the corruption of organized religion and the wars that are fought over whose is the "real" god. It is a call for acceptance, a desperate cry if you will, for complete religious freedom, to worship and have faith—or to *not* worship, to *not* have faith, if one so chooses—without fear of persecution.

The following track takes a philosophical look at history, where it all went wrong and how easily it could have been avoided. Still, Derrick implies, it's never too late. There's always a cure for the ills of humanity. Featuring tribal rhythms and an indigenous African inspired bass line, "Uma Cura" begins by telling of how we as humanity, quite simply, fucked up. The song ends the way it began, revisiting the first verse, but this time with a slightly more upbeat outlook. Yet the listener wonders; will we make the same mistakes the next time around?

A straightforward, verbal lashing out against death penalties and the governments that employ them, "Who Must Die?" seeks to answer a question of morality. Who are we—who are *they?*—to decide who can live and who must die? Capital punishment is nothing more than approved murder, the lyrics of Kisser and Green suggest, and who pays the price in the event of a mistake or false verdict? It's a tough but compelling question, the sort a group like U2 might ask, and one can speculate if it is coincidence that Andreas utilizes heavy delay and echo reminiscent of U2's guitarist The Edge.

Though "Saga" was inspired by Kisser's actual life history, the lyrics take on a double meaning when associated with the concept of *Nation* as a whole. Opening with its drums of war and Derrick's call to battle, the track is violent and tense, yet with moments of glory. The people are done taking shit, now they're taking the place down.

A collaboration with Dr. Israel, a deeply underground artist from Brooklyn, New York, who specializes in dub and raggae and the mixing of sounds from all over the musical spectrum, follows. The first half of "Tribe to a Nation" features Israel's lyrical raggae speech as if signifying the spread of a new language, a universal language of unity. The title itself speaks to unity as the tribe rises up and becomes a nation of its own.

The frenetic pace and furious vocals in the song's second half were inspired by a dub step keyboard riff Derrick and Evetts had heard at a nightclub in São Paulo. Andreas transformed the riff into a Sepultura product, and Igor laid a techno beat over it. From beginning to end, "Tribe to a Nation" may well be the band's most radical experimentation up to that point in their career.

The tribe of *Nation* is metaphorically out for blood. Just when the rebellion seems on the verge of victory, the administration fights back through the voice of Jello Biafra.

The album needed an antagonist, someone to play the role of devil's advocate amidst all the positivity and optimism. Jello plays the role perfectly. Recording his tracks in San Francisco while Sepultura continued to record in Brazil, he speaks for the system on "Politricks," consumed with hubris and ego, insisting that the people need the government much more than the government needs the people. "Politricks" sounds like exactly what it is, a villain's theme song, not so different in atmosphere from Darth Vader's Imperial March in the *Star Wars* films. Derrick strikes back in the chorus, resisting Jello's slick speech, screaming for protest.

In another short blast of hardcore rage, Jamey Jasta joins the resistance on "Human Cause." Jasta's band, Hatebreed (who were also linked to the Brazilians via mutual producer Steve Evetts), had formed a friendship with Sepultura during their stint together on *Tattoo the Earth*, where Igor had designed Hatebreed's touring mascot; a tattooed, punkish piece of toast dubbed Hatebread.

In just under one minute, "Human Cause" reminds us all that there is always hope, even in darkness.

Resist, *Nation* urges next, the temptations of "higher" society. Reject the mad obsession with wealth and fame and the perceptions that money will not only provide for you a better life but will also make you a better person. The mass media will feed you lies, brainwash you, make you believe in *their* dream and not your own. Put on a suit and tie, get in line, keep their machine functioning, and everything will be just fine. "Reject" is about the confusion we sometimes feel when realizing the truths we've been fed are not really true at all.

"Water," like its name, flows calmly, expounding upon the premise of the previous track. Driven mostly by percussion, with bass guitars as the only stringed instruments, and the gentle, more dulcet tones of Derrick's voice, this is a song of promise, but also one of counsel. The war for a new nation is over, the battlefield a

Djalma Agra, Toninho, Andreas Kisser, Derrick Green, and the SOBFC at Teatro Municipal in São Paulo.

mess of bodies, the victorious we cannot ascertain. Whether the system has fallen or thrives as strong as ever, the track—both lyrically and musically—reminds the listener that we can either be suppliant, like water at its most tranquil, or we can be forceful, powerful, like a torrent capable of penetrating even rock.

"Water" pours into "Valtio" with the thoughtful melodies of a nylon stringed guitar. Written by Andreas on a classical acoustic, the album closer was arranged by Finnish cello group Apocalyptica, in their unique style. Literally translating to "state," the title—in the context of the record as a whole—can refer to a nation without government, a blissful utopia the band sought to create in the first place.

During the recording sessions, Sepultura threw down a few cover songs for the special edition of *Nation*. Two of them—"Annihilation" by short-lived San Franciscan hardcore punk rockers Crucifix, and "Rise Above" by the Henry Rollins-fronted Black Flag—fit the theme of the album perfectly. The addition of Bauhaus' "Bela Lugosi's Dead," a slow and doomy tribute to the actor who famously portrayed Dracula, was the only curve ball of the bunch.

Though composed and recorded entirely in Brazil, Sepultura used their homeland influences sparingly, and really only to tie the whole theme of *Nation* together. They had already explored—and exploited—that avenue with *Roots*, and it was in keeping with the spirit of evolution that they largely avoided it this time around.

Shepard Fairey, a graphic artist known for his OBEY brand, designed the artwork of *Nation* using colors and motifs, such as raised fists, typical of resistance propaganda. Incidentally, Fairey would become notorious years later for his iconic red, white, and blue campaign poster of U.S. President Barack Obama with the bolded word HOPE tagged at the bottom.

On the 19th of January, 2001, a couple of months before *Nation* was slated for release, Sepultura performed for over 150,000 people—though it could have been many more had the promoters not decided to stop selling tickets before the event sold out—at Rock In Rio 3, almost ten years to the day since their first appearance on the bill. The circumstances, though, were vastly different. In 1991, no one in Brazil—outside of their passionately dedicated fan base—took Sepultura seriously. By 2001, they were already considered hometown legends, playing in the evening instead of opening the festival under the blistering sun. They had lights and a sound system this time, and were given over an hour for their set. Rob Halford followed, then the night was headlined by Iron Maiden (who, recently reunited with vocalist Bruce Dickinson and guitarist Adrian Smith, were filming a DVD), and it was startlingly clear to all who hadn't realized it before; Sepultura had achieved the impossible. They were on equal footing with their heroes, having progressed from mere fans to peers.

During pre-release promotional tours that found Derrick in Japan and Australia, Igor doing press at home in Brazil, and Andreas and Paulo working Europe, the band received fantastic news. Still riding the high of Rock In Rio, Sepultura celebrated February 20 as a historic day when *Roots* and *Arise* simultaneously broke barriers in the UK. *Roots* was awarded a gold certification of over 100,000 copies sold, and *Arise* went silver, with 60,000.

It was a great start to a year that would hold its share of complications.

The *Sepulnation* tour kicked off on March 9 in Columbus, Ohio (at Alrosa Villa, the infamous venue where Pantera's Darrell "Dimebag" Abbott would be tragically killed, onstage, a few years later), not far at all from Derrick's hometown. Support was provided by Hatebreed, Puya, and Flybanger after Vision Of Disorder pulled out due to logistical issues. The mentality of crossing borders and playing everywhere they could had never seemed more appropriate than with the new *Nation*, and dates in Europe, again with Hatebreed, as well as South Korea, Japan's Beast Feast festival, and South America were among the first on the itineraries to be confirmed.

Nation hit the streets on March 20 worldwide, and a day earlier in the UK. It shipped gold in Brazil with 50,000 copies, cracked the Billboard Top 200 at number 134, and landed on the U.S. Independent Albums chart at number 4 despite receiving next to no promotion or advertising from Roadrunner. Still, overall sales were down. The label scrapped a planned video for "One Man Army" instead paying for an electronic press kit to be filmed while the band was in Paris. Unfortunately, the EPK would never have a chance to serve its purpose, even though critical acclaim for *Nation* was high. Those who were able to see the album objectively, judging it for what it was instead of what it wasn't, understood and accepted that the band had changed but the spirit was the same.

Sepultura's frustration with Roadrunner's perceived lack of support increased as the months went by. Each member made his distaste clear, vocally condemning the label for refusing to back the band at such an important moment. Roadrunner responded in July by issuing a press release announcing that they'd let Sepultura go.

The separation was mutual.

It was also the closing of another circle; *Beneath the Remains*, the first Sepultura album to be released by Roadrunner, was also the last to be recorded in Brazil until *Nation*, the record that ended their contract.

However, Roadrunner had an ace up its sleeve in the form of soundboard recordings from the show at London's Brixton Academy, the fateful night in 1996 that documented Max's final performance with the band.

Much of 2001 was a struggle to show the world that Derrick had really grown into his position as a frontman and an equal member of the band. He wasn't just a hired gun. That wasn't how Sepultura functioned. The adaptation phase took time, naturally, after replacing such an important figure as Max, and some fans never accepted it. But Green's confidence—and Sepultura's as a whole—was much stronger both on the new album and on stage, mainly because they'd started and ended this project *together*. The band was exceedingly proud of *Nation*, and rightfully so.

And they felt a strong sense of relief to be operating as a true band again, without all the drama they'd experienced during the mid 90s.

Tour schedules were typically relentless, often lining up five or six nights in a row with only one day off in between. Igor, Paulo, and Andreas were no strangers to such an intense workload, and Derrick slid right into the routine. A consummate professional, Green lived for the stage. He didn't smoke, he didn't drink, and he didn't partake in excessive partying, always concerned about how such activities would affect his voice and his performance.

They weren't kids anymore. This was their livelihood, and they had to protect it at all costs. But deeper than this was a profound respect and gratefulness for the fans that had stuck with them through all the changes, all the chaos. They felt obliged to always give the best show they could possibly give. For the Brazilians, this stemmed from their own childhoods, when they considered themselves lucky if they saw one international rock band a year. As matured, professional musicians—but still fans themselves—they remembered what it was like, and they refused to risk disappointing that kid who might only be able to attend one concert every couple of years.

As established as they'd become, with friends from every genre, the opportunity to stretch out musically was always available. 2001 saw everyone but Paulo contributing Biohazard's *Uncivilization*. As a group, Sepultura collaborated with O Rappa on the latter's *Instinto Coletivo* album. The track "Ninguém Regula a América," a caustic mix of metal, raggae, and hip hop, saw Derrick and O Rappa vocalist Marcelo Falcão trading barbs—in English and Portuguese, respectively—at George W. Bush, Wall Street, and U.S. foreign policies, among other targets.

But 2002 was particularly bleak for Sepultura. They didn't tour much outside of a scattering of dates across Brazil, where they played one of only a few new songs they had written: the excessively angry "Corrupted." They parted ways with yet another management company, and negotiations with Iron Maiden guru Rod Smallwood's Sanctuary Records fell through.

The guys worked on new material at a leisurely pace, concerned that they had no record label, yet relieved to be untied from Roadrunner. Igor planned a side project with Biohazard's Billy Graziadei (that never actually came to fruition), who had recently moved to Brazil. Andreas composed music for the film

Bellini e a Esfinge. Still, *Nation* continued to sell, nearly topping 100,000 copies in the United States in just over a year, during a time when media outlets across the world declared heavy music "dead." 2002, in fact, marked the demise of a number of bands populating Sepultura's back story, such as Alice In Chains (after the death of singer Layne Staley), Godflesh, and—albeit temporarily—Fear Factory and Megadeth.

It was not a good year for metal.

But Sepultura soldiered on, entering São Paulo's Trama Studios with Steve Evetts in August to record an EP of cover songs. The intention was both to keep themselves warm before starting on the next album and also to release all external influences so they could concentrate on creating something raw and straightforward, something purely Sepultura.

In October, the skies began to clear a little for them. The band signed a record contract with SPV/Steamhammer for European territories, and forged new agreements for distribution in Brazil and Japan. An elusive North American deal, however, failed to materialize.

It felt like starting over. Again.

Meanwhile, Roadrunner announced the impending release of *Under a Pale Grey Sky*, the complete, unedited musical document of that final show with Max.

Sepultura vehemently fought the release. They even tried—though they were no longer obligated—to work with the label, suggesting they pick any other show from the *Roots* tour, one that didn't shine a light on overtly negative circumstances. There were plenty of other concerts from the tour, the band said, that represented that era better. Technically, the Brixton Academy show had its flaws, Igor missing a measure at the beginning of "Troops of Doom," for example, and nearly derailing the song. But mistakes, under the circumstances, were to be expected. Everyone had been preoccupied on stage, knowing what was to come afterward.

Despite Sepultura's resistance, Roadrunner knew the album would sell based on the nostalgic, dramatic, and curiosity factors alone, and so in September, released *Under a Pale Grey Sky*. It was just another bump in the road for the band. They took it in stride, and moved on with their career.

TEN

BLACK PROPAGANDA

In EP form, *Revolusongs* saw release exclusively in Brazil and Japan in the first quarter of 2003. One could say it was Sepultura's version of Metallica's *The $5.98 EP: Garage Days Re-Revisited*, all the way down to the final couple of minutes. While Metallica's EP faded out on a sloppy, out-of-key excerpt of Iron Maiden's classic "Run to the Hills," Sepultura's did so with an equally sloppy rendition of Metallica's "Enter Sandman" (though they atoned for this with a brutal and tantalizing tease of "Fight Fire with Fire").

Of the seven covers on *Revolusongs*, only two of them are tracks a fan might actually expect the band to cover. The other five, like the Bauhaus bonus on *Nation*, took many by surprise. And that was the intention. It would have been far too easy—and obvious—to just record a bunch of thrash songs, their takes of metal stalwarts like Slayer and Vio-lence.

Revolusongs makes its introduction with "Messiah," originally by Swiss black metal progenitors Hellhammer, who were led by future Celtic Frost main man and early Sepultura hero Thomas Gabriel Fischer. It ends with "Piranha" by Exodus, closing out the circle of metal, but the middle tracks ride a rollercoaster of genres.

The almost gothic take on "Angel," by trip hop creators Massive Attack, segues nicely into "Black Steel in the Hour of Chaos." The bulk of this fairly obscure Public Enemy track is rapped in Portuguese by Maurinho "Sabotage," a hip hop artist considered by many to be a sort of Brazilian Tupac Shakur. *Turntables and scratching?* fans thought, shocked, upon the first spin. *Rap?* Lest they forget that Andreas sported Public Enemy t-shirts on stage as far back as 1989, and Igor had been a fan of hip hop beats almost as long as he'd been into metal.

Devo's "Mongoloid" comes next and the listener can hear Sepultura really enjoying this one, having fun with a track they never could've gotten away with in the context of an actual album. "Mountain Song," and its palm muted guitar riffs of Dave Navarro and Jane's Addiction, toes the line between expected and unexpected. Heavy, no-frills rock, "Mountain Song" practically sounds as if Sepultura had written it.

The standout track, however, remains their spirited version of U2's "Bullet the Blue Sky." This shouldn't be much of a shock. Astute fans will remember the Irish rock legends' influence on Sepultura as far back as *Chaos A.D.*

Both the band and SPV thought "Bullet the Blue Sky" was strong enough to demand a video clip, and in November of 2002, months before *Revolusongs* was leaked to the public, they began filming in São Paulo with Derrick playing a major role both in the production and as a character in the video itself.

"Film and photography is something I have been doing for a while now," he said later, "but I would really like to work more at filming and directing. There are a lot of clips that I would want to get involved in the process of their creation and direction, at least coming up with ideas because I can feel it—visually—from the music."

The very fact that SPV was willing to fund a video production for a song off of an EP only released in two countries, neither of which were even the band's biggest markets, said a lot about the difference between the label's belief in Sepultura. Roadrunner had financed one video across two albums and four years, and that one consisted of clips spliced together from a concert that had already been filmed.

"So," Derrick continued, "'Bullet the Blue Sky' was the first clip that we actually had a pretty good budget." The vocalist had written out the basic premise of the video: "A young boy running. There is someone chasing after him, or he is running to something, running to the city and going through this crazy stuff."

Green waded through sample reels that came in from everywhere, and eventually discovered the incredible Ricardo DellaRosa. "I do not know if he actually has even made a video, since he was a cinematographer," he said. "An actual director."

Derrick in São Paulo during filming of the "Bullet the Blue Sky" video.

Andreas and Paul Di'Anno at Mainfesto Bar.

After discussing the concept with Derrick, Ricardo suggested the vocalist play the lead role in the video.

Green explained, "He liked a lot of the ideas, little things: working out in the gym, there were TV monitors everywhere ... I could see each of us in the TV screens, in the windows, in the stores. I could see us in the white room only wearing black. But the video itself was dirty and gritty."

From those ideas, they created something "very special," Derrick added. "A really good video, I thought. And I love working in that aspect, with the director, writing ideas. So it is something I want to do more in the future, for sure."

Apparently the rest of Brazil thought it was a "really good video," too; it took a prize—best direction of photography—at 2003's prestigious Brazilian Cinematography Association Awards, as well as clinching the Best Photography category at that year's Brazilian Music Video Awards.

And with *Revolusongs*, Sepultura not only paid tribute to other bands they adored, but also the s.o.b.f.c. who had adored Sepultura for so long. They put a masked Toninho on the cover, and cast Thrashão in the clip for "Bullet the Blue Sky." He can briefly be seen running alongside Derrick about a minute-and-a-half in.

Though Sepultura may have momentarily dropped off the radar in the United States, they continued working in Brazil on various projects. One of which, the award-winning film *Lisbela e*

Paulo and Andreas, Roorback recording sessions, Rio de Janeiro.

o Prisoneiro, contained on its soundtrack collaborations with the likes of Zé Ramalho and João Falcão.

But in January of 2003, the band returned to Rio de Janeiro to begin recording in earnest their next full-length release at AR Studios, bringing Steve Evetts along with them.

A year or so earlier, during a friendly jam session at Manifesto Bar in São Paulo, Andreas and Paul Di'Anno—the original, well-loved Iron Maiden vocalist—had ripped through three Maiden classics spanning the records Di'Anno had leant his pipes to. They played "Killers," "Wrathchild," and "Phantom of the Opera," afterward making plans for Paul to return to Brazil and record a guest spot on the new album. But Di'Anno couldn't make it, which in a way worked out for the better.

This time, they decided to stray away from having too many guest musicians. With the exception of João Barone, drummer for Os Paralamas do Sucesso, adding a touch of percussion on "Urge," the album would be pure, raw Sepultura.

Rolling in with the creaking gears of war and stomping political machinations, "Come Back Alive" sends a message quite succinctly: this band is out for blood, ready to show the world that they may have lost their longtime label, but in the grand scheme of things, that didn't matter much. They still had the passion, the fire. Paulo's bass is more prominent than ever, pulsating out of the speakers like a sub-atomic bomb. Alternating pace from the heavy, mid-tempo chorus groove to thrashy verses and then back again, "Come Back Alive" also sets the lyrical tone of the record, sympathizing with the American soldiers who were thrust into a largely unpopular war after the September 11, 2001 terror attacks in New York City.

While streaming excerpts of the recording process on the internet, Sepultura's Webmaster stumbled onto a word that seemed to nicely sum up the overarching themes of the new songs. *Roorback*, also known as black propaganda or political slander, earned its origins during the 1844 United States presidential elections, when the Whig party used a fictitious character, Baron von Roorback, to accuse opposing candidate James K. Polk of being a slave owner.

Tweaking sounds, Roorback recording sessions, Rio de Janeiro.

Though not quite a concept album on the scale of *Nation*, *Roorback* is its own kind of propaganda, striking out at corrupt governments and political systems and the power hungry that manipulate people for their own gain. Even the cover, the image of a figure looming over the Earth with its fingers plunged into the soil, touched upon the theme. (Incidentally, Derek Hess's cover later created for In Flames' *Come Clarity* would bear more than a striking resemblance to his work on *Roorback*.) And the title itself could also be considered a type of wordplay; in a very real sense, the band was *roaring back* at their various targets.

Criticizing the US electoral process, presumably in reference to the 2000 election when Democrat Al Gore won the popular vote but still lost the presidency to George W. Bush, "Godless" indicts politicians for being self-consumed, answering to no one, not even the people who elect them. Utilizing long, sliding riff progressions reminiscent of tracks like "Sepulnation" and their crushing, signature single string riffery, "Godless" seethes with anger.

"Apes of God" continues the assault, a forceful number that would open shows on the upcoming *Roorback* tours with Derrick on guitar. Kisser's lead here is unconventional, soaring notes overlaid upon each other to create a majestic tapestry of sound before careening to a slow, plodding wall of noise. The song borrows its title from a novel by British writer Wyndham Lewis in which the "Apes of God" are described as mocking, spiteful characters who imitate those they—at the same time—admire and hate. Though the lyrics are vague, given the context of the novel and the album, these "Apes of God" could represent anyone who functions out of jealousy and envy.

"More of the Same" is far from more of the same for Sepultura, with its smoky, lounge music middle section. His voice soaked in reverb, Derrick flexes vocal muscles with soft, jazzy melodies as the band pulls back on the volume in a musical reflection of the song's message. It seems to be one of reluctant acceptance; the leaders, the politicians, they're all corrupt with their priorities lying everywhere except where they should be. Wars are still fought for oil, for land, for money, and—counterproductively—for peace. Nothing has changed, and in times as desperate as these, it seems as if nothing ever will.

Kisser's lyrics on "Urge" are some of the most direct he has penned so far, making obvious reference to the situation in Brazil specifically, and revealing the evolution of the guitarist's—and the band's—writing. "Originally," he said, "it was a copy and slowly, we start traveling to play—first, outside our own state, going to the north and south of Brazil, and then to Europe. So, we gradually start seeing that we can talk about our own experiences, about being from Brazil, comparing Brazil to other nations and to other ways of seeing politics and religion. It is just a more honest and interesting way to talk about the things you live by yourself, to talk over your own experience, you own point of view—not over a fantasy. In life, when we get older, we also change certain concepts, certain ideas mutate."

Writing the truths, as they see them at the time, is not only a way to reconnect with what's going on at home, but it's a way to regularly connect with the fans, as Andreas explained. "We

Igor on break, Roorback recording sessions, Rio de Janeiro.

have put everything on music. We have expressed what we feel and what we think throughout it, and we have gotten responses from people everywhere in the world saying that the music of Sepultura—the lyrics—really helped them to know what is going on in the world. We have received letters from the frontline telling 'Sepultura help us survive day by day," so, it is the way how we relate to people better."

"Corrupted," one of the tracks they'd tested out on the road before recording, grinds forward with a riff like a steam engine train. Much of the song, though, is driven by a simple percussive harmonic on Kisser's guitar, repeated over bass guitar and drum accents, allowing Derrick's pissed off vocals to take center stage.

The vocals again shine on "As It Is," a track that revisits the dynamics of a quiet verse in contradiction to a loud, screaming chorus, though in a way they've not yet done before. Derrick calls up that lounge singer vibe again, as with "More of the Same" preaching acceptance for the way things are, yet warning of the dangers of contentment. Should we accept as it is? It's an interesting question, another point of view to consider, the flipside of straight refusal and resistance presented in a sarcastic—almost ironic—manner. Despite the middle section that is signature Sepultura, "As It Is" shows the band again experimenting, playing with Indian melodies and rhythms and a reverse guitar lead that comes across like the soundtrack to a dream or a meditation.

"Mind War," on the other hand, is all Sepultura, but with a slightly polished hardcore edge. As one of the most accessible tracks on the album, it would also receive video treatment from Ricardo DellaRosa. The clip takes place in the mind of a mentally disturbed character played by Paulo, telling of the internal struggles we all face in our minds, with performance pieces being filmed in the freight elevator of a thirty story parking garage in São Paulo. Toward the end of the clip, the music suddenly ceases, as if a light in the character's mind has been extinguished. In a rather confusing interlude, the viewer is led into a store where a pair of Japanese Brazilian women argue over what happened and how to restore the light before it goes dark. In an interesting bit of trivia, the woman shopping during the argument is none other than Vânia Cavalera, mother of Max and Igor.

A two-and-a-half minute blast of rage, "Leech" recalls Sepultura's earlier English punk rock indulgences in the vein of G.B.H. and the Subhumans.
Harboring an immediate energy that just begs for the song to be performed live, Green spits venom at those who feed off of others. "The Rift" continues down this path, another number fast and short and to the point. It speaks of religious wars and death, a rift that has formed between man and his spirituality, and leaves the listener wondering where it all went wrong.

Paulo enjoying some fresh air, Roorback recording sessions, Rio de Janeiro.

"Bottomed Out" is Sepultura's most curious moment yet, as close to a "ballad" as they have ever come. Gentle verses flow like the running of musical water, and Derrick croons about his struggles—*our* struggles—with anger. We're all fed up with the system; though we don't know how exactly to change it, we know it has to change. When mellow gives way to heavy in "Bottomed Out," it is a different sort of heavy for Sepultura—slow, drenched in low end, with little distortion, and opening into a morose and melodic section that brings Jane's Addiction back to mind. This breath of relief, of relative calm, rolls to a halt with placid drums, making the strike of "Activist" that much more powerful.

A very hardcore song with a hardcore message and an atypical chorus (no guitars at all, only drums and Derrick's shouts), "Activist" is quite representative of the album as a whole. Much of *Roorback* deviates away from the use of palm-muted guitar riffs, a heavy metal staple, in favor of a more loose and open approach. The record is not so traditional, not the typical metallic, taut and highly-strung metal. Rather, it is the most potent mix of hardcore and punk rock that we've heard out of Sepultura yet. Since the early days, they—especially Max and Igor—were drawn to these influences, Kaaos and Terveet Kadet and Exploited, and with Derrick's roots in a similar scene, *Roorback* pulls it off exceptionally well.

Though the vibe in the studio was relaxed and positive (and videos of the sessions attest to this fact), Djalma "Thrashão" recalled a somber, heavy day when he was interviewing the band and taking photos for publicity. That day, they'd learned of the death of rapper Sabotage, who was gunned down in what was suspected to be a drug related incident.

In the middle of April 2003, Sepultura set out on a short US tour with Canadian legends Voivod, though *Roorback* wasn't scheduled for release until the twenty-seventh of that month. Even then, it would come out nearly everywhere *except* the United States, where negotiations with spv/Steamhammer's North American division were still underway. They teased those American audiences with only a couple of new songs, playing "Mind War" at all of the gigs and "Corrupted" at some, and threw in a few selections from *Revolusongs* for good measure. And with Jason Newsted having joined Voivod as a full-time member the year before, it was only natural that he'd occasionally accompany Sepultura on stage to play rhythm guitar on some of the classics.

The band was happy to be back in the States—after all, they'd lived there for years and still felt it a sort of "second home"—but more importantly, they were happy to see that US fans were glad to see *them*. It was always a tough market, not just for metal bands but for musical acts in general, because everything was so media driven. Trends come and go very quickly in America, and if bands stay away for too long, they risk being forgotten. And since *Nation* hadn't been promoted well at all, it seemed like Sepultura had been away for a very long time.

In the rest of the world, the surprise hit "Bullet the Blue Sky" was added to the standard issue of the *Roorback* disc, while special editions were packaged with the full *Revolusongs* EP. A month later the North American deal became official, and on August 26, Canada and the United States officially got their hands on the new material.

But the three-month gap between release dates was unfortunate. Many fans in Canada and the US had already downloaded digital versions of the foreign editions from file-sharing sites such as Napster, Kazaa, and Soulseek. The internet was only beginning to change the music industry in ways no one could have predicted.

After the US tour finished, the summer of 2003 was reserved for festival hopping: Download at Castle Donington, Sweden Rock, Wâldrock in the Netherlands. Wanted in Hungary, Belgium's Graspop Metal Meeting, With Full Force in Germany, Metalmania Festival in Spain. The list went on and on. All of June and most of July was spent in Europe, with August set aside for vacations before South America, Australia, and Costa Rica brought the year to a close.

Touring in 2004 was scant, at least by Sepultura's standards. They eased back on the gas pedal just a bit, leaving more space than usual between shows and extending breaks between legs a little longer than in the past. Again they ruled a Rock In Rio stage, on June 4, this one an international edition taking place in Lisbon, Portugal. But with Derrick living fulltime in Brazil now, it was easier for the band to mount one-off local concerts whenever they were home.

In activities outside of Sepultura, Derrick and Paulo invested in a bar in São Paulo, the Bunker Lounge Café, which was appropriately decorated like an underground military bunker and highlighted mellow, eclectic wartime music like blues and jazz. Andreas jammed with Os Paralamas do Sucesso, German thrash legends Destruction, and Brasil Rock Stars, and Igor sat in with Mexican musical terrorists Brujeria.

They deserved the reduced workload. They'd earned it. Remarkably 2004 marked the band's 20th anniversary.

To celebrate this momentous occasion, they launched their own festival—the appropriately titled Sepulfest—taking place in São Paulo, on September 25. Planned as more than just a party to commemorate their career, it served another purpose. As Paulo explained, they hoped to open the doors of exposure for other Brazilian bands they all enjoyed. A few of these bands were also represented by Monika Cavalera's newly created Base 2 Productions, from which she now officially acted as Sepultura's manager.

In a way, and unknowingly, she had been preparing for the job for years. "I've been with them since '89, taking everyone around with the gear, and on the weekends to the beach and to the country house my father has. And then when I did my travel agent course, I told Igor I wanted to work with the band because I could do good business for them in terms of flights and hotels and all that. And then they allowed me to do that. [Gloria] gave me permission to do all the jobs. Why would we stay in a five star hotel for three hours when we could stay in a hotel that costs forty dollars instead of three hundred? This is an issue that I always talked about with Igor. Why do you have to spend so much money in airline tickets or even buses? Why can't you stay in one bus instead of three buses if you have to pay all this in the end? You're not getting this for free. I wanted Igor to bring money back to the house, not spend money on tour because all this money just goes like that, and then the record label would get all this back with the sales and all that."

And after going through three managers since Gloria, Sepultura ended up with Daise Simões, the famed manager of Titãs. "But I knew what was going on with the band," Monika said. "Everything." Eventually, Daise came to Monika and suggested she take over because she knew the band better than anyone. "I started doing things for them here in Brazil, and then, when Igor and I split, I came to the band and said, 'Well, so far I did everything for free, now I need to get paid'. And that's when everything started for real."

Among the acts on the premiere Sepulfest bill were Ratos de Porão, Claustrophobia, Naçao Zumbi, and Massacration. Massacration, which was the brainchild of Bruno Sutter (aka "Detonator") and a piss-take of the heavy metal stereotype, was an important inclusion, Derrick pointed out. Born out of the comedy program *Hermes e Renato*, Massacration introduced some fun, some humor, and a whole lot of laughs into a genre that was defined by aggression, scowls, and anger. Even head-bangers needed to smile sometimes.

But Igor wasn't smiling much then, his personal life in a period of transition. His hopes to reunite with his brother—a desire he'd never made secret—grew stronger as his marriage to Monika fizzled out. At several points after Max had left, in fact, she'd been the only person able to keep Igor from leaving too. Few people knew just how close Igor had come to quitting Sepultura on a number of occasions. Monika had convinced him otherwise, that he shouldn't live in the past, that he had to move forward. Now, without her intimate influence, without *either* relationship—and perhaps feeling a bit uncomfortable as Monika continued to work with the band in a professional capacity—it was only a matter of time before Igor drifted fully away.

After six years and three strong (and getting stronger) albums, Sepulfest also honored the fact that Green had unquestionably earned his place in the band. Still, from time to time, interviewers treated him as "the new guy," asking about the integration process, how it felt, if he was ever intimidated by stepping into Max's shoes.

The answer, of course, was no, since he wasn't stepping into Max's shoes at all. He and the other three had spent those six years developing something new, something different, while fighting to keep the soul of Sepultura alive. Green was aware of the magnitude of the position, and very much respected Cavalera and his place in the history, but those days were over. Sepultura had moved on, even if a portion of their fan base hadn't. Derrick understood that some people wouldn't like him simply because *he wasn't Max*, but he was okay with that. The negativity never bothered him.

It was an attitude born in his early Cleveland club days. If people liked him, great. If not, he didn't care. It's an attitude that all artists would be wise to adopt if they wish to survive in this business, since there will always be critics. There will always be people trying to cut you down.

A European run with Motorhead filled November's schedule, and the beginning of 2005 marked another anniversary, this one a 25th for Roadrunner Records. The label's tribute to their place in heavy metal's legacy came in the form of an all-star album called *Roadrunner United*. The record brought together as many disparate names as possible, all of whom had been signed by the label at one point or another. Four "team captains" were picked to write and assemble songs with their chosen collaborators. One of the captains was Dino Cazares, who recruited Andreas Kisser as his lead guitarist. Another captain was Robb Flynn, who wrote a song for Max Cavalera to sing. It would be the first time Kisser and Cavalera appeared on the same album—though on different tracks—in a decade.

An "in concert" version of the tribute took place later that year, with Andreas as the house band's guitar player. Max was rumored to attend the event as well, causing many eyebrows to rise at the unspoken possibilities.

Perhaps unsurprisingly, Cavalera didn't show up.

ELEVEN

THROUGH HELL AND BACK

At the end of 2004, tentative planning had already begun for the next album. This was a landmark achievement regardless of any other factor. Some bands don't survive long enough to make a second album, never mind a tenth. And considering the difficulties they had slogged through since 1996, their determination to continue on in the face of adversity was nothing short of inspirational. A less passionate, less focused, less motivated band would have collapsed years before.

This time, Paulo suggested they work around a theme, an overarching construct to give direction to the writing sessions. Andreas and Igor mulled over an idea to write the soundtrack to a book, inspired by their work for *No Coraçao dos Deuses* and *Lisbela e o Prisoneiro*, and Derrick had the ideal subject. It was a story he'd read in school years ago: *The Divine Comedy*, an epic Italian poem by Florentine Dante Alighieri. With its detailed, explicit descriptions of Hell and suffering, and underlining themes that could easily be drawn parallel to modern day events, everyone agreed that this was an idea worth exploring.

Band and crew preparing for a match.

Though they were all relatively familiar with the book's concept—poet Virgil shows Dante the path to salvation by leading him through Hell, Purgatory, and finally Paradise—each member picked up a copy and read it through, making notes and bringing their own ideas to the creation of what they would be their most ambitious undertaking yet.

Discussing the routine they'd spent years establishing, how it made the process of creation as easy and smooth as possible, Andreas explained, "I just express the ideas I would like to develop, and I try to keep it interesting. Since everybody has his own voice, we debate a lot, we talk a lot. And as soon as there is a direction, we follow it."

Sepultura has never worked according to the principles of democracy. It's all or nothing with them, everyone or no one. Even though all four write and practice at home, compiling melodies and riffs and lyrics, the final decisions on what gets used and what doesn't must be unanimous.

"We discuss up to the point when we all agree," Andreas said, "then we go. I could come up with great ideas but I cannot force anybody to do something, especially Derrick, you know. I could not write lyrics for Derrick about eating meat—" (as Green has been vegetarian since he was fifteen) "—or killing animals, or something like that. He really has to believe in that, to portray it, to represent it."

This may sound like a rigid, constrictive way to create music, but in reality, band democracies usually lead to infighting and grudge holding. Sepultura has always understood the importance of ensuring each member's approval. Since Max's departure, the concept had really been driven home; the whole is always greater than its individual parts.

"We make the songs for ourselves," Paulo said, "in first place. We need to be happy with what we are doing. Everything starts for me and for the band. We don't make music for a record label or anybody else; we make it for us and then the rest is consequence."

Andreas concurred. "It is a very free and open process which we have to enjoy. Although it is a job, it is not like a firm one—we are dealing with music. It can be a good mood day or a bad mood day, but everything helps to express what we feel in music."

To co-produce, Sepultura chose André Moraes for his extensive experience in film scoring, and Stanley Soares, their front of house live sound engineer. About Soares, Andreas said, "He's been with us for many years and he knows the music. He's a great guitar player as well. He has that musician's sensibility. He knows how we should sound."

The album, like the book, is split into three parts—Hell, Purgatory, and Paradise—with each section musically reflecting the atmosphere of each. In Hell, for example, the musical structure is simple and straightforward. Just four guys playing loud, heavy music. Sepultura doing what they do best. In Purgatory, the songs become more complex, with the addition of horns and string sections, and in Paradise, which is only represented by one song, a greater arsenal of instruments paints an aural picture of unity and hesitant peacefulness.

The album fades in with the particular sinister vibe of "Lost (Intro)," setting the proper atmosphere for this first canticle. Dante, in both the book and the song, is lost in the woods, overwhelmed by a deep sense of fear. He has essentially lost his way in life. Phantom voices call to him from the darkness, and he feels woozy, as though he's asleep and dreaming. On the track, Derrick Green's reversed chant is underlaid with a poetic verse that will be repeated throughout the album. The voices grow louder, more intense, more threatening, and Dante begins to run.

The first real song of *Dante xxi*—"Dark Wood of Error"— opens with a rhythmic, galloping palm-muted riff and matching drum pattern as Dante flees further into the forest. The guitars, bass, and drums pound in unison, building in intensity, punctuated by full chord accents as Dante breaks through the trees into relatively open areas. The forest swallows him again and his breath grows heavy. Dante senses the beasts all around, lurking in the darkness, and the song finally explodes into violence with Derrick's voice as Dante is overcome by terror.

Dante, the writer, utilized metaphor and imagery in his poem to reveal sometimes hidden truths about politics and society in the Florence of his day. Rather than relate those tales specifically, Sepultura approached *The Divine Comedy* in the same way as Dante; they used it as a guide to provide commentary on the world as they see it today. In "Dark Wood of Error," Derrick plays the role of Dante, but *we are all Dante*, in this age of war, hate, and chaos. Dante tells of the light beyond the forest edge, a light he is unable to reach for it is blocked by three beasts, each representing a type of sin. Via Kisser's lyrics, Derrick thrusts the listener into a similar predicament, warning of *our* three beasts—the United

Kingdom, the United States, and the United Nations—who hold the ultimate power and thus are susceptible to the ultimate corruption.

At this point in the story, Dante meets Virgil, the Roman poet, who tells him there is only one way out of this dark wood. Derrick, then, leads us on a detour to Hell.

The fast, double-bass drum intro of "Convicted in Life" is signature Igor Cavalera, perhaps signifying the rattling of Hell's gates as Dante passes through, his senses awash with the howling, tortured spirits that have been removed from God's light. Their choices in life convicted them in death.

Inspired in part by the stories of Brazilian favela dwellers, many of whom are born into a tragic life they'll never have the opportunity to escape, the lyrics of Kisser and Green are practically a lament, and Andreas' lead guitar solo wails like a thousand voices, the moans and screams of those lost souls.

After crossing the river of Acheron, Dante is led down through the first five circles of Hell, bearing witness to the most awful and graphic punishments. After the first, Limbo, each successive circle is reserved for a particular type of sinner, from the lustful and gluttonous to the greedy and wrathful. Dante then enters the city of Dis, encompassing the sixth through ninth circles, where the most offensive of all sinners suffer: the murderers, the suicide victims, the torturers.

Sepultura marks this passage with sitar melodies and pounding drums that conjure up images of a massive, walled city engulfed in flame, demons and devils perched upon the parapets, just as Dante describes. In the first track with lyrics written entirely by Derrick Green, "City of Dis" lashes out at those who suppress individual belief and opinion with threats of damnation. If we have faith in ourselves, Derrick claims, we can do no wrong.

Having survived the lowest circles, Dante at last encounters Lucifer, the towering beast with faces in triplicate, buried up to the waist in ice. With "False," Sepultura has also reached the bottom end of Hell. They arrive with furious pace, calling out those who abuse power and use status to influence the weak. The track slows halfway through, horns and trumpets announcing the appearance of Lucifer. Kisser's lead is frenetic, almost unmelodic and intentionally so, perhaps mirroring Dante's perceived *unreality*, his awe at the sheer impossibility of it all. In *The Divine Comedy*, the reader sees each face of the beast chewing on a different historical figure. Brutus. Judas. Cassius. In Kisser's lyrics, it is those false leaders who are paying the eternal price.

After facing Lucifer, Dane climbs the beast's fur and falls upward in a swoon, thus ending his journey through Hell. The Sepultura song "Fighting On" closes out the Inferno canticle with a slightly distorted guitar introduction and a circular repetition of the mantra Derrick spoke at the beginning of the record. It is a mid-paced track, confident in its stride, a testament to the strength we all carry inside. The final guitar chord fades out, heavily distorted, sounding something like a fire that is dying as Dante escapes the Inferno.

Sepultura's "Limbo (Intro)" interlude marks the transgression from Hell into Purgatory, a taut symphony of strings mimicking the guitar riff that will drive the next track, "Ostia." But the overlaying of harmonics and usage of the "devil's tritone," a musical interval historically utilized in classical music to create a dark or evil atmosphere, warns the listener that Dante is not safe. We are not quite safe, yet.

The word "Ostia" can be defined as a small opening that leads from a dark, confining space into a wide-open expanse. Musically, the song sounds like the skies are opening up over Dante as he ascends the Mountain of Purgatory. The extensive use of horns signals the poet's rise out of the underworld and into the light. Kisser's lyrics show Sepultura's Dante watching the souls of the Late Repentants—those who died before receiving last rites—flying about, begging for prayers from the living to assist them in moving on.

A morose, depressing violin solo interrupts the crushing heaviness, perhaps as an expression of regret for those that will remain trapped in Purgatory. But Sepultura's Dante soon realizes these specific souls are not to be mourned; they are the spirits of those who used love as a gateway to sin, and the music responds in kind, circling back around to its original heaviness.

Further exploring the concept of psychological sin, the band launches into "Buried Words." This furious track opens with Andreas again using the tremolo and heavy distortion of his guitar to imitate the sound of fire. Derrick's vocals are raw, angry, his words vicious as he adopts the role of victim in a play about abuse. This character tries to bury the words, bury the trauma dealt by the hands of a priest who uses love as an excuse to do harm.

"Nuclear Seven" deviates a bit from the story of Dante specifically. The song stomps along, building dynamically as Kisser thematically ties the seven cliffs of Purgatory, each representing one of the seven deadly sins, to the seven nations that (at the time of the song's creation) had developed nuclear weaponry. With its message of warning is one of hope, a plea for change, as Dante returns and steps into the last track in Purgatory.

"Repeating the Horror," with its vaguely techno rhythm and medieval phrasings, sounds quite different from the rest of the album, marking not only physical movement in the story, but also a progression in Dante's character. Dante wants redemption, and Derrick shouts for it, too. We always have the ability to change, he seems to say, but first we have to take a close look at the horrors we'd otherwise wish to avoid. We must first stare the truth in its face before we can hope to change it. We must first be honest about our faults, our frailties, our failures, before we can hope to change ourselves.

The instrumental "Eunoé (Intro)" designates Dante's passage from Purgatory into Paradise. After washing away the memories of sin in the river Lethe, penitents bathe in the waters of Eunoé to strengthen memories of all the good they had done in life. Sepultura blasts from this frantic interlude, this desperate cleansing, into the Earthly Paradise of "Crown and Miter." In a symbolic gesture, Virgil crowns Dante, declaring him lord over himself and his own actions. Sepultura's message is the same: the journey to salvation is long and painful, but with compassion, individuality, and belief in ourselves, we can all achieve the impossible.

A final brief interlude, the majestic yet still tense ninth circle of Heaven, "Primium Mobile (Intro)," gives way to the André Moraes co-written "Still Flame" that closes the album. Featuring almost Gregorian chant, repetitive triplets, sitars, strings, and keyboards, the track alternates between moments of pure tranquility and progressions of intense, anxious notes, culminating with Derrick's final deliverance as Dante is united with God.

The band commissioned Brazilian artist Stephen "Calma" Doitschinoff to paint the album's cover and interior artwork, a series of ten images based on *The Divine Comedy*, in his unique, blocky style. Calma's work, known for its colorfully eye-catching illustrations and religious connotations, lent the perfect imagery—at the same time modern and traditional—to Dante's soundtrack.

March and April brought two special events. In March, the band traveled to Dubai, a wealthy and heavily westernized city in the United Arab Emirates. Among others, Sepultura, Machine Head, and British rockers The Darkness were on the bill for this first ever Desert Rock Festival. As a treat for the crowd, some of which had traveled from all over the Middle East to attend, Robb Flynn (vocalist and guitarist of Machine Head) invited Andreas Kisser on stage with his band to rip through Metallica's "Creeping Death."

Sepultura returned home and, the following month, put on a show in São Paulo to be recorded for a CD and DVD release. "Live in São Paulo," the first live album to be officially sanctioned by the band, celebrated their history from the earliest days until the present. Guests included João Gordo, Krisiun's Alex Camargo Kolesne, DJ Zé Gonzáles and rapper B-Negão, and once again, Jairo jumped in for "Troops of Doom," and this time "Necromancer," as well.

Guedz's recurring presence on Sepultura's stage got many fans to wondering whether the band might re-induct him as a full-time member. Though Derrick played guitar live on a few songs here and there, he was a vocalist who needed the freedom to roam around without being confined to a microphone stand.

"There was a time that we even thought about it," Andreas explained some years later, "to talk to Jairo about doing something together. He wasn't ready. He said, 'Oh, I don't know ... I have this and that going on,' and then it didn't happen. Years later he came back, 'I'm ready,' and then we said, 'Oh, I don't know ...'" He laughed. "The timing didn't click. [But] he's the only one who makes sense."

When asked if it had ever really been a serious concern, plugging a second guitarist into the equation, Andreas said, "It's something that comes and goes. Sometimes people talk about that, sometimes people forget. It's just something that we feel comfortable the way we are. There's a lot more room to play."

He added, "This thing about getting an extra guitar, it's not a technical thing. You have to put somebody in the band. You have to put another person. It's a lot more complicated. And even to put somebody there just to be there, playing ... I don't know ... it doesn't feel right. You really have to represent the songs the way they are *today*, you know. We're not trying to fool anybody. There are so many bands that use two guitars in the studio, and live they are … whatever they are. From Black Sabbath, Van Halen to Pantera, and so many bands. It's not only just because we had another guitar player before that we'd necessarily need another one. You have to feel very comfortable to have somebody there on stage and jam and represent something much bigger than the music itself. So … we never found that guy."

But a couple of months before the March 14 release of *Dante XXI*, which was universally hailed by critics as the strongest Sepultura album of the Green era, there were rumblings of dissent in the ranks. Rumors circulated that Igor wasn't happy, that he hadn't been enjoying himself on tour for a long time, even though he'd contributed quite a lot in studio while writing and recording the album.

In January of 2006, Borivoj Krgin reported through his Blabbermouth news site that Igor had decided to leave the band, and was being replaced, incidentally, by former Soulfly drummer Roy Mayorga.

Igor, writing to Sepultura's official website, refuted the report, asserting that he was merely taking a break. He'd recently been remarried after two years of separation from Monika, and had a child on the way. He wanted to spend a little time at home, recharge his batteries, enjoy some time off with his family. He confirmed that Roy was indeed hitting the skins for the upcoming European tour, but ensured fans that his own absence was only temporary.

As it turned out, most of the rumors, in this case, were true. Igor truly *hadn't* been happy touring since 2004. But he believed, initially anyway, that if the whole band went on hiatus for a while, it might help the situation. He had spoken with Andreas about seeking ways to inject fresh energy into Sepultura.

But with a strong new album tucked away in their collective pocket, Andreas, Paulo, and Derrick—and even Igor, to a point—understood that they couldn't just rest on their laurels. The first few weeks after an album's release were vital; the number of units sold immediately after the street date often determined tour budgets and the record company's level of financial support. For Sepultura's livelihood, they knew, they needed to hit the road and hit it hard.

They didn't have much time to find Igor's replacement, so Andreas, Paulo, and Derrick bandied about a list of drummers who had free time in their schedules. They initially wanted old friend Vinnie Paul to sit in, but the onstage murder of Vinnie's brother Darrell in 2004 was still too fresh. He wasn't ready to get back behind the kit yet. Instead, they settled on Mayorga, who was not only available, but having played with Soulfly recently, Roy also already knew a lot of the old material.

Before departing for Europe, Andreas met with Igor and they agreed to discuss their options again after Sepultura returned. Maybe Igor was right; maybe they just needed a rest. They'd been at it writing, recording, and touring for twenty years with very little time off. Even during the disenchanting months of 2002, the band stayed relatively busy.

They recalled the situation with Max all those years ago, how the difficulties had snowballed until no one was able to control them. With the clarity of growth and maturity, they considered the possibility that the problems with Max might've been solved if the band had simply gone on vacation for a year or two.

But once on the road, the trio accepted the reality of their predicament. In the current musical climate, a band like Sepultura could not survive without keeping its nose to the grindstone. In this changing era, illegal downloading was causing record sales to fall across the board. Sepultura's own sales were slowing even as their albums received increasingly fantastic critical praise. As professional musicians, they couldn't *afford* to take a hiatus. And further, they realized that they didn't really want to.

Shortly after the tour, Andreas tried to convince Igor to stick around a while longer, at least until the promotional cycle for *Dante XXI* was over. When Mayorga left to join Stone Sour as a fulltime member, the band brought in Mineiro Jean Dolabella to fill the drum slot, hoping that Igor would soon come back around.

But the Brazilian media was already referring to Dolabella as "Sepultura's new drummer," and on top of everything else, this was too much for Igor. On June 12, 2006, Igor Cavalera officially left the band, telling the press in Brazil, "I believe my mission in Sepultura has come to an end. I am very proud of everything we have done, but I feel that the group's current formation no longer lives up to my expectations as a musician and a person."

Monika also commented, "During a couple of years, I was always pushing Igor to continue with the band after Max left, and I think—even if he says 'I was done with the band, I don't want to play with them anymore'—I never felt that. I always felt like he wanted to fight and be playing and happy and on tour and all that."

Andreas, Paulo, and Derrick were disappointed by the statement, but not particularly surprised. Andreas, in particular, had felt the announcement coming, though he'd hoped Igor would wait at least until Sepultura were done promoting *Dante*. Then, he'd thought, perhaps they could all end it together, and on a high note. Since 1987, that first practice in Belo Horizonte, when everyone within earshot could sense the intense chemistry between him and Igor, they had been like musical soul mates. The guitarist couldn't imagine making another Sepultura album without him.

So they honored their contracts for those pre-confirmed shows, and made no plans beyond the last date. In a number of interviews, an unusually cryptic Andreas appeared to hint that the band might soon call it quits.

Once on the road, however, everything again fell back into place. Dolabella had the talent and the skills to do the job, but he was also full of excitement and all smiles on stage. He was *happy* to be there.

Igor had been right, months earlier, when he'd suggested Sepultura needed an injection of fresh energy.

Their decision to carry on brought backlash from a certain breed of "fan". Haters who had given up on the band after Max left, and even some of those who hadn't, demanded Sepultura either call it quits or change their name. But the facts remain; no one forced Max and Igor to leave. They left of their own volition.

In a number of post-split interviews, Max made his beliefs clear; Andreas, Igor, and Paulo should retire the name because it wasn't the same "tribe" anymore. Igor, when asked for an opinion after his own departure, originally stated that he chose to leave, and thus had no right to say one way or the other. He later changed his stance, siding with Max. No Cavaleras, they claimed, should mean no Sepultura.

A newspaper in Rio even quoted Igor as saying he and the other three had agreed to put the name Sepultura to rest after the *Dante xxi* tours ended, even though Paulo immediately disputed the claim.

In an interesting side note, Tuka Quinelli tells of a story Max once shared with her. When searching for a name for his new band back in 1997, he opened a Portuguese dictionary to a random page, and the first word he saw was Sepultura. In fact, the more vocal critics of the post-Cavalera lineup wondered precisely why Max and Igor didn't eventually take back the name. After all, they had started the band.

Nothing in the music business is that simple. In the 90s, Max, Igor, Andreas, and Paulo—in the eyes of trademark law—made up what was known as a general partnership and thus, all owned the name equally. This does not mean they each owned a piece of the name, a perfect 25%. It means they each owned 100% of the name, as mathematically confusing as that may sound. In theory, when Max quit, there was nothing stopping him from calling his new band Sepultura.

However, had that scenario played out, it would have been messy and expensive. In this alternate reality, with record labels and promoters wanting to invest in the "real" Sepultura, the case would likely have ended up in court, leaving the judge to decide. A verdict of this type usually relies upon a number of factors, such as who was the primary songwriter and who was most distinctly identified with the band.

Whatever the case, the legal partnership of Sepultura—consisting of Andreas Kisser, Paulo Xisto Pinto, Jr., Max Cavalera, and Igor Cavalera—dissolved in 1998 with the release of *Against*, and Max officially signed away his claim to the name shortly thereafter. In a proactive movement, Sepultura then trademarked the name as a corporation, protecting it in the case of any future disagreements.

But speaking to Nicolás Jara Miranda years later, Andreas explained, "We are not slaves, that is what I stress a lot: we are not slaves of a name, of an era, a year or a time. We recreate this everyday and we build this everyday so it can be alive. The fans that respect that fact stay together with us. Of course they do not have to like everything but they respect what Sepultura is doing. In a way, I can say that is what I expect: respect, even if they do not agree with what we are doing."

Jean Turrer Dolabella, another Mineiro, was—like his mates in Sepultura—blessed to be raised in a musical household. On May 14, 1978, he was born in Uberaba to parents who played everything from guitar and piano to (like Kisser's mother) the accordion. From a very young age, the boy only had aspirations to be a musician, playing drums and guitar and, perhaps not surprisingly, listening to Sepultura.

"I first listened to Sepultura when I was like 8 or 10 years old," he said, "and I developed so much respect for the band since they inspired me as a musician—as it occurred to a lot of people around the world—and beneath the music, they inspired me to do whatever I can, whatever I want. To consider that it is not easy for a kid in Brazil, like the people who started it then, to go out and play in a different country. They were the first band to do it, so they sort of opened all the doors. I was very influenced by this attitude; follow your dream, do what you really think is good. Life can be music, music can be life!"

Despite this influence, and the fact that the first "big" concert he attended was a Sepultura show in Uberlândia, 1991, on the *Arise* tour (where he was lucky enough to go backstage, fifteen years before he would *again* be backstage but as the band's drummer instead of just a fan), Jean grew to be a well-rounded musician, never wanting to feel locked into one particular musical genre or style. He took much inspiration from Van Halen, a group he listened to rather obsessively, as well as Led Zeppelin skinsman John Bonham and Faith No More's Mike Bordin.

At the age of fifteen, he was already playing drums professionally.

A few years later, Dolabella formed his first band, called Diesel, with his brother Ian. They recorded their self-titled debut album with Stanley Soares, a man who would later play a major role in Dolabella's fate.

Diesel had promise, quickly gaining traction in the Belo Horizonte underground scene with their heavy rock grooves and mainstream appeal—a drastically different sound than that of Sepultura. In the early 2000s, they fit right in with the likes of Silverchair and Red Hot Chili Peppers, and in fact, Diesel performed with both of those acts at Rock in Rio 3, after winning a Battle of the Bands competition.

Like their much heavier Mineiro cousins Sepultura, the band understood the professional limitations of trying to "make it" in Belo Horizonte, and relocated to Los Angeles, California, a hotbed of rock music. They renamed themselves Udora, after supposed legal disputes with the American blue jean company Diesel, and were quickly snatched up by a record label.

But the business is fickle. Shortly after Udora's *Liberty Square* album was released, the label dissolved into RCA, bought out by the industry giant. RCA wanted a single that Udora didn't have, and the band was dropped as quickly as they'd been signed. But Dolabella, at least, had a scholarship at L.A.'s prestigious Music Academy to fall back on. After graduating, he left Udora and returned to Belo Horizonte.

Andreas Kisser contacted him within months of his return home. Igor, Kisser said, was no longer interested in touring, and Sepultura didn't want to cancel a bunch of dates that had already been booked. Dolabella practiced a list of songs taken from recent live sets, auditioned, and a couple of days later, Paulo called him up and made it official.

As it turned out, when discussing their options after Roy Mayorga moved on, Stanley Soares had told Andreas about this amazing drummer he'd worked with named Jean Dolabella.

Though each of the Cavaleras exited Sepultura by choice, their own reunion in 2007 is worth mentioning because it impacts this story on a couple of different levels. After ten years of radio silence between the two, ten years their mother Vânia wished only that her boys would put the past aside and become brothers again, ten years of the drummer struggling with his decision to stay in Sepultura and not follow Max, Igor finally picked up the phone and called Gloria. They spoke for some time, and when Gloria handed the phone to her husband, Max nearly dropped dead in shock.

In short order, Max and Igor (the latter now spelling his name *Iggor* because he preferred the way it looked) formed a band called Cavalera Conspiracy, recording an album that featured members of Gojira, Soulfly, and Pantera. A handful of short tours preceded a second album, and when the band made their way down to Brazil, the brothers reunited with Jairo Guedz to perform "Troops of Doom." It was a special moment—three-quarters of the first real Sepultura lineup on stage, together again, and in the very same city where it had all started nearly thirty years before. Afterward, Max and Igor returned focus to their main interests—Max to Soulfly, Igor to Mixhell (a live percussion and dance fusion project begun with his wife Laima)—peaceful and content with their renewed relationship.

Cavalera Conspiracy, however, seemed to inspire in Max a certain nostalgia. Almost at once, after joining forces with Igor, Max began talking about a possible reunion with Andreas and Paulo, as well. Igor wasn't interested. The only reunion he cared about—the familial reunion with his brother—had already happened.

Sepultura, like Igor, had no interest in moving backward. In Jean Dolabella they found an enthusiastic new drummer whose background added a jazzy groove to the band's trademark metal riffery. Again, as it always had, their sound was evolving, changing.

Jean picked up on this tradition of evolution right away, and was, in fact, drawn to it. "Sepultura has never been the 'same' band," he said, offering the unique perspective of one who, like Derrick, had observed the music first from outside and then from within. "When you listen to *Beneath the Remains* and then *Arise*, or *Arise* and then *Chaos A.D.*, or *Chaos A.D.* and then *Roots*, you notice that Sepultura has always been changing—regardless of the members, the record company or anything else. The band is always looking for renovation, trying to do something new or cool. It is never going to be a band that keeps on doing and re-doing the same stuff, and it is weird that we still think this way regarding all the complaints and pressure we have had. For example, people who love *Arise* think the band should hold on to that style, a kind of thrash or whatever you call it. And then, people who like *Chaos A.D.* think we should stay in that period, and people who are keen on death metal want Sepultura to play it for the rest of their life.

"There are some bands that keep on doing the same thing and I respect it," Jean continued. "I think that is cool and I am not against that. I am just saying that Sepultura evolves and is always looking for the future, doing new stuff, bringing different elements, different cultures and different rhythms."

It had been almost ten years since their last member change. During that complicated year between Max's exit and Derrick's entry, Sepultura had to relearn how to write. And when they adopted Derrick, they were forced to do so again. Now, with Jean coming into the fold, it was much easier to adapt to a new musical personality because they had already done it once before.

Andreas explained the ease in transition, saying, "Everybody who came in brought something new and that is what we needed. I mean, Sepultura is not a band of hired musicians. If you are there, *you are there*. You have to contribute, to express your opinions, to put your style, of course respecting the past but not copying it, not trying to be somebody else, *but you*. So, all the rest is a consequence of that attitude. How much are you going to write? How much are you going to put in? That is another story. But, the spirit is there. If you are in, then you contribute. There is nobody to tell you what to do—that is not Sepultura. Everybody who came in took his time to adapt to a new situation, but we worked out great. You have to respect that time."

Unfortunately for Sepultura, like most other professional musicians, overall album sales had been on a steady decline since the proliferation of Napster in 2001. Even though fans and critics alike praised *Dante XXI* for its scope, courage, and quality, the record was Sepultura's poorest selling to date. File sharing and torrent sites made too it easy for anyone, anywhere, to download music whenever they wished. And for free. Without wading into the moral quagmire of intellectual property and the question of right and wrong, we can say without a doubt that the change in media presented both positives and negatives. On one hand, it gave musicians instantaneous access to a worldwide audience. On the other, it made it more difficult for bands—especially heavy metal bands—to survive.

Rather than embrace this technology early on and find a way to work with it, record labels tried to fight the loss of profits by raising CD prices. This, of course, had the opposite effect.

Paulo summed up a working musician's common frustrations, saying record companies "are all the same. They used to be like banks, now they all are fucked. It's good, at present, with the Internet and all that stuff; a person is able to search and find different types of music so easily. But, I think there should be a final recognition to the artist—that he/she gets paid a little bit for a download. Nowadays, basically, your music is for free. Few people buy your product. Most of them just download. I consider that we are in the middle of a big transition. Nobody knows what's really going on or what the direction to go is.

"As long as the touring does well and life goes on," he continued, "for me, that's the main thing. A record registers a moment of your life but the key moment is to be on stage. The power of Sepultura is being able to play live."

TWELVE

LIKE CLOCKWORK

The last ten years had been a back and forth struggle for the band, the sort defined by two steps forward and one step back. After all this time, though, it seemed things were steadily looking up. Many who'd previously had their doubts were beginning to accept that the band had long since stepped out of the shadow of its former incarnations. But the guys didn't disown those years or any in between. Rather, they embraced them, always balancing their live sets with a healthy mix of songs both old and new.

They respected the history of Sepultura, its roots and stages of infancy all the way through development, but they refused to become a nostalgia act.

In August of 2006, their music made the big screen in *Talladega Nights: The Ballad of Ricky Bobby*, starring former Saturday Night Live comedian Will Ferrell, with excerpts of both "Desperate Cry" and "Inner Self" featured in prominent spots in the film. The unexpected exposure caused an equally unexpected spike in record sales and downloads. A month later, they won two prizes at the Brazilian Video Music Awards for "Convicted in Life." The video, which had been filmed in February and was Igor's last appearance with the group he co-founded, took the awards both for Best Direction and Best Editing. With its graphic images of meat packing plants, animal slaughter, deforestation, and suicide, and digital manipulation that had the band members decaying limb by limb as they performed, "Convicted in Life" revisited Dante's message about the importance of choice, and how the wrong one in life can condemn us in death.

A US tour with Sworn Enemy, Diecast, and Suicide Silence, scheduled to begin in November of 2006, was unfortunately delayed by three dates as visa issues prevented Sepultura from making it to the States on time. If there was one thing they hated more than anything else, it was to cancel a show. But once there and in the groove of the road, it was again made apparent that they weren't planning to rest on past achievements. Of the nearly two-hour long set lists, almost half was represented by material from *Against* and onward. The staples, naturally, were tracks like "Territory," "Arise," and of course "Roots Bloody Roots."

A return to Europe at the beginning of 2007 saw Sepultura changing up their sets even more, rotating in different older songs, but never sacrificing the stage time to play less recent material. In fact, as the shows became longer, the balance of old songs and new became closer to equal. Deep cuts such as "Boycott" and "Activist" were dusted off and worked in. Audience turnout was consistently strong, even if album sales weren't as strong as they used to be.

The European tour was split into two legs, with Mexican and South American dates crammed in the middle of the two. Andreas stayed busy whenever near home, reprising his role as a *Bellini* composer, this time for *Bellini e o Demônio*, and working on a solo album, now accompanied by the talents of Jean Dolabella, that would take him five years to complete.

The second leg of 2007's Euro trek saw participation in the usual summer festivals, as well as the unusual. Always looking to expand their cultural horizons, Sepultura took part in the Lez'arts Schenique Festival in Sélestat, France, which integrated music and awareness of world causes. Each year, the theme was different; in 2007, it focused on the Tibetan independence movement. At this special event the band performed with Tibetan signer Loten Namling, who added traditional melodies and chants to the band's visceral music.

As well as hitting the standard locations across Europe, they continued on in their determination to play every and any place that would have them. The second half of the year saw concerts in out of the way areas as diverse as Latvia, Lithuania, Russia, and Estonia.

And even this far into their career, they were still hitting countries they'd never played before. In October, Sepultura descended upon India for the first time, scheduled to rock Delhi, Shillong, and Bangalore.

It is interesting to note that even highly experienced travelers such as they encountered culture shock from time to time, as Andreas explained in a Brazilian news report. India had no traffic laws to speak of, and cows, dogs, and chickens freely roamed the streets. Outside the Taj Mahal, snake charmers and children dancing with monkeys on leashes begged for spare change.

Though the shows rocked, the conditions weren't always ideal. In Shillong, for example, the band played on a stage that was tied together with twine and fabric, with exposed wires and cables haphazardly strewn about. They had to cut the set short not because of the shoddy construction, but because Jean was the unlucky recipient of food poisoning; all the condiments provided backstage were expired by years.

Bangalore, the third largest city in the country and the most modern of those on Sepultura's mini-tour, was no less chaotic, its traffic and congestion on par with São Paulo. But no matter the circumstances, the guys were ecstatic to be performing for such rabid fans in India. An emotional Green addressed them in each city, praising them, showering them with respect, and thankful for the memories he and the band would bring back home.

And 2008 brought another first, when Sepultura became one of the few international acts to hold a concert in Cuba since the establishment of Fidel Castro's communist regime in 1959.

Havana's José Martí Anti-Imperialist Tribune hosted the band in July, where they were also given the chance to pay their respects at the Che Guevara monument. For the Brazilians, performing in Cuba was one of those rare life-affirming events, considering the similarities between the nation's approach to censorship and that of the military dictatorship in Brazil. It was no small experience for Derrick Green, either; since the 1960 United States embargo against the country, Americans were forbidden to spend money in Cuba. Assuming that a visiting traveler would have to pay for something, be it a hotel or even just a meal, as much as a day trip was out of the question for Americans.

But the opportunity to play in Cuba came with a catch. They had to perform for free, as had Audioslave in 2005, and as would every visiting artist.

Over 50,000 Cubans witnessed the spectacle that is Sepultura in concert, and they loved every minute of it. The catch was worth it.

Still, the band didn't tour much that year. A worldwide economic crisis was in effect, and promoters were having difficulty booking shows because audiences were being more careful with their money. And though it would have been understandable to take that extended break after the *Dante XXI* tour cycle, as they'd originally planned with Igor, they instead chose to ride the momentum they'd gained in playing with Jean. They reconvened after a short vacation (during which Derrick had joined Musica Diablo, a viciously thrashy band spearheaded by Nitrominds' Andre Alves), and began sorting through the plethora of riffs and ideas they had developed during sound checks on the road.

"We record everything," Andreas said. "I mean, some songs of *A-Lex* came when we were touring—the first tour with Jean. We were sound checking, fooling around with riffs and we recorded every little part here and there. Then we listened to it [later] and we developed the songs. We are writing all the time, whatever we do, we keep the record for whatever situation we need it."

The *Dante* sessions had been such an enjoyable, challenging and inspiring experience that they again decided to write the soundtrack to a book, this time a literary classic they'd actually considered a few years earlier: *A Clockwork Orange* by Anthony Burgess.

When the band finally made it into the rehearsal studio, the album came to life in about three months. The spontaneity was a fitting metaphor for the immediacy of the book.

"In the very beginning," Derrick said, "the writing part is kind of jamming in the studio, just writing things. I bring my guitar, play certain riffs that I may have, and then Andreas takes it from there and elaborates it, and we talk if it must be faster or slower. It is very open. And also the vocal pattern appears at the time when we are writing. It is just what comes at the top of my head from hearing the song the first time."

While undertaking this next project, though not quite on the same magnitude as *Dante*, Derrick considered the songwriting in a similar fashion. Outside of simply analyzing *A Clockwork Orange*, he dug deeper into the story's themes by reading about Anthony Burgess, studying up on why the author developed the story the way he had. With Igor gone, Derrick and Andreas now handled all of the lyrics, so they would get together and break down their ideas, discuss the topics they were going to approach and how they were going to approach them. It was essential to ensure they didn't sing about the same subjects over and over again.

"It is much easier when you have a concept done," he explained, "because you can really divide it. This is how we did the book: it was divided in four different parts, so it was easier for us to get the lyrics, bass, drums, and certain other things. At the very beginning of the album, for example, we thought we should have more violent, more aggressive songs, since that was the state of mind of Alex—it was in this group setting. In the second part, going to a more restraining aspect of what the state is trying to give him, a

Making of A-Lex with conductor Alexey Kurkdjian.

certain treatment in order that he becomes a good person, and so diluting his free will. Then, the third part is primarily the revenge, all the bad things that Alex has done are coming back to haunt him. And the fourth being the reconciliation for regaining his free will again, and realizing this is not the way he wanted to live."

The goal was similar to that of *Dante*: mirror the book with modern-day events and situations. Like any good piece of literature, the story is timeless and can apply to every day and age.

And like most creative works of fiction, the idea for the book was born out of two unrelated ideas that were tied together to form something new and original.

Burgess had taken the old Cockney slang phrase, "as queer as a clockwork orange," and married it to the concept of aversion therapy. In 1961, when the author began writing the book, the British government was considering aversion therapy as a means to eliminate criminal impulse. The result of such brainwashing was what Burgess considered "a clockwork orange"—that is, a man that appears alive and organic on the outside, but is actually mechanical, like a clock or a machine, on the inside. The cover of *A-Lex*, a mesh of pieces from Kris Kuksi sculptures assembled by Ulisses Razaboni, Mário Níveo, Rodrigo Almeida, and Marco Piza, strengthens this idea by presenting an image of what seems

179

to be the inner workings of a clock, only constructed from bones and body parts instead of metal.

In the novella, the protagonist—who also functions as the antagonist, at times—is a juvenile named Alex. He and his friends—his *droogs*—are consumed with violent urges, speaking in their own slang, called Nadsat, based in Russian and English slang. Language is important within the general construct of the book, as it is in culture, uniting these droogs in their gang-like activities. Even the character's name is no accident; in Latin, the term *a-lex*, as titled on Sepultura's album, can mean "without law."

During one of their nightly rages, Alex and his droogs break into a countryside cottage, beating up the man who lives there and forcing him to watch as they brutally rape his wife. But Alex is caught by the police, and sentenced to fourteen years in prison. During this time, after killing another inmate, he is given aversion therapy—Ludovico's Technique—in an attempt to erase these impulses. The state's treatment has Alex watching sadistic movies while ingesting medications that make him violently ill. Their belief is that, over time, even the *thought* of violence will cause Alex to become physically ill.

But the impulses cannot be obliterated by this therapy, only buried. The state is treating the symptoms, not the cause.

And again, as with *Dante*, the lyrics told the character's story and the music reflected his state of mind. The loose and hasty jam session approach to songwriting and song structure served as a perfect metaphor for Alex's mental construct.

The construct of the album, though, was rather well organized, as Derrick had mentioned. Four strategically placed instrumental interludes separate the sections of *A-Lex* that deal with specific sections of the book, similar to the musical layout of *Dante XXI*. These interludes allow the listener to easily transition into the next "chapter" of the album, so to speak.

The slow, ascending chromatics of "A-Lex I" build into the feverishly paced "Moloko Mesto," one of the fastest tracks the band has done in years. With the first verse's lyrics written in the language of the droogs, the title—moloko meaning "milk" and mesto meaning "place"—refers to a hallucinogenic, milk-based drink that Alex and his friends imbibe in preparation for what they've termed the "ultraviolence." And ultraviolent is a fitting metaphor for the unyielding nature of the song. Derrick screams of the injustices of man, of drug abuse both illegal and prescribed, of how the fucked up system has bred violence in its people. Whether intentional or not, the statement draws a compelling parallel to the band's situation in Brazil during the late 80s and early 90s, when they defended the furious nature of their music against the media's criticisms.

"Filthy Rot," a stomping, addictive number that relies more on its rhythmic tendencies, revolves mostly around one riff—and only a few notes—throughout the song. It pounds, it pummels, and sounds just like the thrashing gang fight it is supposed to symbolize. The chanted, tribal chorus references the droogs and their anti-establishment lawlessness; when they heard a bum singing this old war anthem, they beat him half to death because they couldn't stand the state or anyone who supported it. Could this mirror the US or some other warmongering nation, the citizens of which spit upon and beat their own soldiers after they returned from yet another unpopular war?

The first single of the album, "We've Lost You!" received iconic video treatment from André Moraes, and a live debut at the 2008 Latin Grammy Awards where Sepultura preceded its performance by a rendition of Antônio Carlos Jobim's "The Girl from Ipanema." The classically picked intro bursts into a percussive riff that rattles teeth in the listener's head, a lumbering, depressing crunch. Alex appears to struggle balancing his intense appreciation for beauty with his unquenchable thirst for violence.

His thirst wins.

The video clip, on the other hand, deviates somewhat from the book, though adopting much of its imagery. We see a young Alex, his ultraviolent ways in development, drinking at the Milkbar,

Making of A-Lex.

Making of A-Lex.

witnessing a man attacking a woman. Alex beats the man to death, stomping him to a bloody pulp, before dragging him into the woods and setting his body on fire. The theme here is different from Burgess' novella, in which Alex is a complete sociopath who has no sense of moral right or wrong. In Sepultura's video, however, he is more of a young—though extreme—vigilante.

Returning to Burgess' message, "What I Do!" (which was later filmed for a "live" video clip) is the sound of Alex accepting the nature of his being, doing what he does simply for the primal pleasure of it. Though the lyrics address directly the character's state of being, they also serve as social commentary—as they did in the book, retaining a double meaning—attesting to an impetuous nature, a sense of entitlement that seems to run rampant in youth these days.

But Alex, in the early pages of *A Clockwork Orange*, does find moments of peace, moments of relief from his impulses if not remorse for his actions, when listening to his beloved Beethoven. Music is his savior. There's an interesting comparison to be made here, too, when we consider the commonality in adolescent heavy metal fans, not just in Brazil but across the world, who get their aggressions out through music.

"Alex II," the first interlude, begins with a psychedelic smattering of sounds. Alex has been captured by the police, sentenced by the state. One can imagine him being strapped to a table and rolled into a treatment center as the restrained, instrumental piece plays on.

Initially, he resists the treatment. On some level, Alex understands that the state has no moral right to rob him of choice. They are turning him into a machine, *a clockwork orange*, a man who functions in a peaceful manner only because he's been conditioned to. As mentioned earlier, they are treating the symptoms of his sickness, not the cause.

"The Treatment," as Sepultura delivers it, is a tense, wiry song playing inside Alex's mind as his system both rejects and accepts Ludovico's aversion therapy. Derrick absorbs the character's confusion, his psychosis, as he becomes distant—separated—from his sense of self.

The "Metamorphosis" has begun. With a slow, eerie introduction, Sepultura keeps the listener deep inside Alex's emotions as he mourns the loss of his humanity. The track is naturally more reserved than those before "The Treatment," and with "Sadistic Values," this pattern continues as Alex withdraws further into himself. He understands that, somewhere inside him, those ultraviolent tendencies still exist. Over clean guitars and snare drum rolls, Green's harmonized voice drips with defeat. In the second half of the song, the distortion and heavy guitars and double bass drums make a comeback, Derrick growling strongly as he laments those sadistic values that continue to haunt Alex.

During the next two short tracks, "Forceful Behavior" and "Conform" (the latter of which is built off of a riff that bring's Machine Head's "Take My Scars" to mind), we feel the anxiety rising as Alex desperately fights against an ideal the state is trying to force upon him. In under five minutes total, the two songs speak of the dangers of control, of grand scale conformity to some predefined, predetermined concept of what is right. With *A Clockwork Orange*, as *The New Yorker* noted, Burgess' message was that it is better to be "bad of one's free will than to be good through scientific brainwashing."

"Alex III" marks the character's release from prison after two years of serving. He is utterly harmless now after the treatment, like a child almost, unable to commit any type of violence even if it means defending himself from the violent acts of others. The lyrics of "The Experiment" are presented from third person point of view, an outsider's opinion of the state's therapy and how it has affected Alex and others like him. But it is also a warning. The velocity of "The Experiment" increases and Kisser manipulates his guitar into siren-like sounds as Alex learns two of his old droogs are now police officers, and seeking revenge for past experiences. The officers abduct him, drive him to the countryside, and beat the hell out of him.

With the opening, pounding bass lines of "Strike," the listener feels the character's fear and worry heightening as he runs to seek shelter in a nearby cottage. This is not just any cottage; it is the home of F. Alexander, the home Alex and his droogs had invaded earlier. The home of the woman they raped.

But the man doesn't recognize him. Upon hearing the story of Alex's aversion therapy, F. Alexander and his compatriots—a gang of political dissidents—seek to use the boy and his predicament as a tool to strike out against the state.

Alex refuses to take part. He verbally lashes out at the men, lapsing into his old

Making of A-Lex.

Nadsat speech, and only then does F. Alexander recognize him. Though "Enough Said" is only one-and-a-half minutes long, and contains only two lines, it roars with fury and vengeance.

The men lock Alex up in an attic. And F. Alexander knows just how to get back at him.

He'd learned that Ludovico's Technique had an unexpected effect on Alex. One of the movies Alex had been forced to watch during aversion therapy featured his beloved Beethoven on the soundtrack. As a result, he was even robbed the pleasure of listening to his favorite music.

The importance of this theme in the novella allowed Sepultura to experiment again with something they had never done before. Andreas and Jean collaborated with Alexey Kurkdjian, conductor of São Paulo's Sphaera Rock Orchestra, to arrange a metallic and orchestral version of Beethoven's 9th Symphony, which they called "Ludwig Van."

In *A Clockwork Orange*, after trapping Alex in the attic, F. Alexander plays classical music through the walls in hopes that Alex will commit suicide to relieve himself of the pain. He dives from a window instead, waking up in a hospital, where Ludovico's Technique is eventually reversed and Alex becomes his old self again.

"Alex ɪᴠ" is the beginning of the character's awakening. He realizes that aversion therapy represents a great paradox, especially if one willingly accepts it. To change who we are, we must first recognize that something needs to change. The difficulty lies in enforcing this. We must make a conscious effort, a choice, but Ludovico's "therapy" removes free will from the equation.

Through an old friend, Pete—as well as Pete's wife and child—

Making of A-Lex.

Alex finally wishes, for himself, to end his violent ways. This closing track, "Paradox," circles back around to the aggression of *A-Lex*'s earlier songs, but now Alex's anger is redirected toward our conditions of being brainwashed by television and the media and the state, being told what to think and what to believe and how to behave. Alex desires change for himself because *he* thinks he should change, not because anyone else thinks—or demands—that he should.

The inclusion of this final song was crucial. One thing Sepultura didn't want to do with *A-Lex* was plan their concept entirely around the film adaptation of *A Clockwork Orange*. Stanley Kubrick, the movie's director and writer, had based his vision on the American version of the book that omitted the final chapter in which Alex redeems himself of his violent ways. This twenty-first chapter was, for Anthony Burgess as well as Sepultura, an essential part of the story's appeal. Without it, the novella—and the film—ends on a note of despair, the depressing realization that Alex has succumbed to his demons.

Ending the album on a note of self-realization, and essentially hope, was a decision that revealed an ever more mature group of musicians. Though *Dante* closed on a similar note, it was the natural course of Alighieri's book. In the case of *A-Lex*, the choice to actively include the more uplifting of two outcomes said a lot about Sepultura.

The music itself, and the process of creating it, had also matured.

"I like to say it is a 'grown up' style due to the fact that we are not attached to anything," Jean said. "In a certain way, we do not care, meaning that when we were doing *A-Lex*, for example, there was not a structure to follow; it was jamming—a matter of doing whatever we thought was good. Specifically, if there is a course and that course sounds good, that is awesome. But if it is a song without a course, it is awesome too."

Delays during the mixing process pushed the original release date of October of 2008 back until January 23 of the following year. In the meantime, early in 2009, Andreas got together with some friends and formed an all-star cover band. The initial lineup was rounded out with Tim "Ripper" Owens on vocals, David Ellefson of Megadeth on bass, and former Megadeth drummer Jimmy DeGrasso. Intended solely as a way for them to indulge in some fun live jam sessions, Hail! never wrote—or considered writing—any original material. They announced their existence with a short tour of Chile, and would over the years tour such distant locations as Russia and Turkey with a rotating cast of members.

Dolabella also indulged in some side-project activity, working with Augusto Nogueira on the ongoing experimental and jazzy Indireto. Derrick befriended Sam Spiegel, brother of film director Spike Jonze, when Sam was in Brazil finishing off his electronic hip-hop infused project, N.A.S.A. Green and Spiegel began laying the foundation for a robo-funk, electronic R&B group called Maximum Hedrum.

A-Lex followed the trend of its recent predecessors, suffering from low first-week sales despite glowing reviews, and even landing on a number of charts worldwide. Since *Against*, as the public grew to accept the changes in the band—and the band continued to grow into themselves—critical reception of each release was successively greater, more positive. Sadly, online copyright laws—as well as record companies, for that matter—still hadn't caught up to the changes brought about by Internet file sharing and peer-to-peer networks. Once upon a time, musicians toured to promote their albums. Now, it was the other way around. Bands released albums so they would have a reason to go on tour.

If there's one recurring message in this story, it is that Sepultura not only adapts to change, they embrace it. Where they had once railed against the bootlegging of *Schizophrenia*, during a time when record sales could make or break a career, these days they understood that *no band* could rely on income from albums anymore.

"I think it is freer," Andreas said. "It is a transition phase. It is not very clear what is gonna happen. Internet is here and you can release an album in many different formats; pendrives, download, vinyl is coming back. So, you have to be more creative to deal with that. I think that in every transitional phase a lot of opportunities come up, and it is a very fertile time. You have to deal with that and create ideas to explore and go beyond the road. That is what we've always done. Being on the road with our merchandising."

Successful businesses can sometimes exist off of their brand alone, and to their benefit, Sepultura had one, while many of their peers didn't. Bozo's "S" logo had become an icon, appearing on everything from the obvious tour shirts and caps to sunglasses, board shorts, and havaiana flip flops. By 2012, it would even adorn the label of Sepultura's own Weizen beer.

But for a band like theirs, everything always came back to touring. "Just keep on the road," Andreas said. "There is no way to fight something that is changing. We have to adapt ourselves and create ideas to explore and present our music."

There was another side of the World Wide Web, too. Suddenly anyone with a computer and an internet connection could be a critic. The faceless, anonymous nature of the 'net allowed a certain type of person to say things they would never have the courage to say in a more personal environment. Some called the current lineup greedy, a "cover band," claiming they had no right to continue on as Sepultura without either of the Cavaleras. Suggesting they were riding on the notoriety of the band's name.

Of course the guys were aware of the critics. The loudest, harshest voices always have a way of standing out.

Paulo addressed this, saying, "We have been struggling a lot—especially with the new record—to show this new face, which is already old for us but not for most of the media people."

Much to the cynics' chagrin, this defiant attitude had enabled Sepultura to carry on as professional musicians, touring, doing what they love, despite the obstacles and member changes, for twenty-five years.

And in his usual unaffected manner, Paulo waved off the concern. "We are not scared of anything. We'll prove we can do it, once more. It's been proved a few times and if it needs to be proved again, we'll do it. And if it's my call, I'll be really happy to be in this band for another twenty-five years."

March saw them sharing the stage again with Iron Maiden, this time as direct support at the Quilmes Rock Festival in Buenos Aires, Argentina. And some members of each band recently played together in a different manner; Maiden bassist Steve Harris' Maidonians Football Club had met The Brazilians in a friendly soccer match in São Paulo the year before. The Brazilian side, featuring in its ranks Andreas Kisser and former Corinthian goalkeeper Ronaldo, lost 8 – 0 to the much more experienced and practiced Maidonians. (Later in 2009, Sepultura would stage a match against some of their fans in the Sepultribe. In this match, they fared much better.)

In August came the release of *Hubris I & II*, Kisser's solo album, finally seeing the light of day after so many years in progress, fittingly released the day after the guitarist's birthday. Featuring Jean Dolabella on drums and co-producing with Andreas himself, the two-disc album showcased Kisser's range of musical talents. The first disc, more rock-oriented with a focus on electric guitar, boasted Zé Ramalho as a guest vocalist on the track "Em Busca do Ouro." The second disc highlighted Andreas' love of the acoustic, nylon-stringed classical guitar.

But there was, as the saying goes, trouble in paradise. Jean was finding it hard adapting to the intensities of road life.

"I have been playing with Sepultura for three years now," he said. "The biggest tour lasted about two months in a row. Once the tour is over, we all come back home and stay, at least, a week or two a month. On the first tour, I thought, 'I am not able to do that. I cannot take it.' Then the second, the third and the fourth out of three hundred shows came and I got used to it."

But being away from home for so long was taking its toll. "It is not easy," he continued, "but I think nothing in life is. Sincerely, I do not think that we get a really good balance in life because we are always looking for something else. That is life! It is like, I'm playing in one of the biggest metal bands and I'm very happy with this, but I cannot stop playing other types of music. It is like that.

"You are never going to be extremely happy, like in the nirvana. I simply do not think that is possible."

It is a tough existence, no doubt. For many fans and young musicians-in-training, road life seems romantic. You travel from town to town like a nomad, seeing and experiencing new places, spreading your music to adoring crowds everywhere you go. But the reality is much more mundane; countless hours spent alternating between sleeping on tours buses and airplanes. You're on the move so much that you rarely have the opportunity to see the sights in any of the cities you play. The pay off of waiting and traveling for twenty-two hours every day is the two hours you spend on stage.

The road is littered with destroyed lives and dead musicians who couldn't take the monotony, the boredom. Who filled the empty hours with drugs and booze.

But for most veteran artists, the constant partying wears thin over time. People forget: for Sepultura, and other bands like them, touring is their job. It is how they put food on the table to feed their families. To survive for any extended period of time in this harsh business, they have to treat their work professionally.

"We keep focused," Andreas explained. "We have a show today, we know we have to play tonight, so we are not here drinking a lot or doing stupid shit that could affect our show. Of course, we did that many times when we were younger. Now, we are very focused on what we do. We know ourselves [enough] to know our limits. If I get a couple of beers, I know I'm gonna be fine to play."

Taking care of themselves on the road had become more and more of a priority over the years. Even Paulo, a notorious drinker who'd once imbibed thirteen bottles of wine over the course of a day or so, had toned down his partying. With a schedule as relentless as theirs, none of them could afford to get sick or injured.

Jean knew this firsthand. "I had some problems with my wrist," he said. "We were playing in Mexico for three days and at the first one I felt a little pain, at the second it got worse, and at the third it was impossible for me to play. I thought I was fucked. It was about a month or two before we went to the huge tour in Europe, so I had to do something.

"I went to the doctor and she told me I had to stretch. She taught me how, and how long to do it. The learning process lasted three weeks; I attended therapy twice a week. Nowadays, I have this routine before each show. Every night, I have forty to forty-five minutes of stretching and thirty minutes of warming up. I really have to do it! As a result, I feel so much better, there is no pain. I feel like I can [really] beat the drums."

January 2010 kicked off the year in a fantastic manner, with two more shows isupporting Metallica at São Paulo's Morumbi Stadium. Much of the globe would see Sepultura on tour that year, with one notable exception: the United States.

Also in January, SPV/Steamhammer announced they'd be rereleasing *A-Lex*, with two additional tracks. Confusing moves like these were indicative of the industry's failure to properly address shrinking sales in the face of free music online. And fans felt taken advantage of. Being forced to buy the whole album a second time—and barely a year after it had originally been released—for only two new tracks? What kind of incentive was that, especially when those two tracks would easily be found online?

Ultimately, the re-release never happened because Sepultura and SPV/Steamhammer parted ways a few months later.

This time, the band wouldn't be without a label for long.

THIRTEEN

A MOMENT IN TIME

Midway through 2010, Sepultura signed a deal with Nuclear Blast that held much greater promise for the band's future. Established in Germany in 1987, Nuclear Blast built its reputation on hard, honest work, and dedication that rivals fandom. This is primarily because those at the label—like Roadrunner had been—*are* fans of the bands they sign, and thus treat them accordingly. It is a trait that helps independent labels survive, and in some cases thrive, while the so-called "major" labels—whose concern for money and status more each year.

The band began writing properly while still on the road in 2010, something they'd never done in such depth before, not even when collecting riffs while sound checking during *Dante xxi*'s promotional treks. And back in São Paulo at the end of the year, they regularly leaked videos from rehearsal to show fans how the process was unfolding. Viewers witnessed an excited, happy, motivated band working through the songs together. Before finishing the writing, they'd already confirmed a number of tours, including one for early 2011 in North America. It would be their first extensive run there in about five years.

There was no doubt Nuclear Blast believed in Sepultura.

Still, even in the face of so much forward momentum, there was increasing chatter about a reunion of the "classic" lineup. As with any quality, long-running drama, certain characters impose their presence—either intentionally or out of circumstance—even long after they've exited the story. And for few other bands does the shadow of an ex-member linger as much as Sepultura.

The chatter was nothing new, even though there had never been any substance behind the rumors. A few years earlier, for example, there was talk that Sharon Osbourne had offered Max, Andreas, Paulo, and Igor one million dollars to reunite for a special headlining appearance at her husband's annual Ozzfest heavy metal festival. But as usual, it was all talk, none of it originating from any of the referenced parties.

But after Cavalera Conspiracy went on hiatus, Max's nostalgia seemed to grow, and he continued to speak about the possibilities of a return to Sepultura. For a time, he mentioned it in almost every interview he gave. In some, he would say the only person stopping it was Paulo. In others, Max would claim that he and Andreas were already in negotiations; that he'd offered to have Gloria manage him and Igor, so Paulo and Andreas could be managed by whomever they wished. Then he'd go on to say that tactic failed because Kisser didn't want Gloria involved at all.

Sepultura—still—weren't having it. They grew exhausted of refuting every new story, and Max's talk became so loud, so persistent, that it forced the band to release their own statement. There would be no reunion, they adamantly announced, and there had never been any consideration of one.

"Don't listen to fucking rumors anymore," Andreas said, clearly agitated. "We're tired of listening to this fucking bullshit that Max is saying all over the world, that there's going to be a reunion, and this and that. We're here to say there's no communication, no talks about any type of reunion, of any show, with the Cavaleras. Igor is doing his job, Max is *supposed to be* doing his job, and we are doing our job. We are Sepultura for twenty-six years and we are celebrating this with a new album, a new deal, and a new world tour. And I hope this is the end of fucking rumors and fucking... lies!"

With that final message out of the way, the following evening, Sepultura performed the *Arise* album—for the first time in its entirety—at a party in São Paulo celebrating Manifesto Bar's 16th year anniversary. It was an ironic and fitting way to close the book on all the reunion talk.

But all of this—the drama and the tension, and also twenty-six years of history and evolution—worked its way into the next album, which would be appropriately titled *Kairos*. The term, a Greek word that represents a special moment of indeterminate time, described perfectly the band's reflections on the past, their view of the present, and their outlook for the future.

To produce, they chose Roy Z, a man of many talents. Not only had he produced modern classics by Iron Maiden and Judas Priest vocalists Bruce Dickinson and Rob Halford, respectively, but he also served as each singer's lead guitarist, and was instrumental (no pun intended) in the writing of each disc. Roy's ear for music, and for guitar tones especially, would help Sepultura achieve the "live" sound they were seeking with *Kairos*.

An accomplished musician having spent many years honing chops with his own Latin Americanized rock band Tribe of

Gypsies, Roy was just the man Sepultura were looking for, and it was a wonder they hadn't worked together until now.

Though Green had already changed residence again by this point, trading São Paulo for Prague, Czech Republic, the move didn't disrupt Sepultura's plans in the slightest. They again retired to Trama Studios, this time with Roy in tow, and a bunch of video cameras courtesy of Jack Daniels Brazil, who sponsored a live stream of the sessions. For a few days every week, a couple of hours a day, fans stole a peek into the recordings as they happened. (On Thursdays, though, little work seemed to get done; the stream that day was mostly a promotion for Jack Daniels, with a bar table set up where the band and visitors hung out and had drinks.)

As opposed to the two previous albums, there was a conscious effort to not go overboard with the number of songs. They wanted to keep the disc short, focused on polishing each song, each part until it shined, rather than trying to fit as many tracks on the album as possible.

The streamlined-by-design "Spectrum" exemplifies this ideal nicely. Calling up their Ministry influences, Sepultura repeat the same riff almost all the way through to create a hypnotic, haunting vibe. The lyrics set the overall tone for *Kairos*, speaking of the struggles and the battles they've fought throughout the years, and the pride they feel for staying true to this fight they believe in. The title track expounds upon this theme, Derrick singing of how necessary it is—for them—to always move forward even while others are moving back, and creating this kairos moment over and over again.

This heavy, anthemic number eschews a typical guitar solo, instead employing a vaguely Indian-sounding melodic section in the middle. From this, it builds dynamically with a simple riff that leads to a sudden stop, and then locks in with the drums to forge a groove reminiscent of those classic breakdowns in "Desperate Cry" and "Dead Embryonic Cells."

"Relentless" is just as its title implies. Dolabella's unrelenting double bass drum rhythm and Paulo's equally thumping bass, married with Kisser's open E string chug and Derrick's distorted vocals—some of his most expressive ever—conjure up yet more industrial comparisons. With a two-part lead guitar solo that channels both signature Andreas and the trademark wails of Dimebag Darrell, listeners get their first evidence of Roy Z's (and

Derrick Green's) insistence that Kisser focus on creating more technical, masterful solos. On "Relentless," he does just that, writing one of his best leads ever, the type that will have even the most skilled guitarists drooling all over their fretboards.

If "Spectrum" weren't enough to convince fans of the debt Sepultura owed to industrial music, the band's version of "Just One Fix," from Ministry's legendary *Psalm 69: The Way to Succeed and the Way to Suck Eggs* removes all doubt. Originally planned as a bonus track, the song's inclusion in the *Kairos* sequence says much about its influence.

Slow, evil, and atmospheric, "Dialog" is an internal conversation, an admittance of imperfection and sometimes weakness, suggesting that even the most strong and persistent people have their moments of doubt. A very basic riff doubled by Paulo's low end, with an equally basic drumbeat laying the foundation, makes for one of the most crushing moments on the record. Again, Sepultura approaches with the strategy that the heaviest music doesn't always have to be complicated and difficult to play, though complication does make an appearance in another shining lead by Andreas.

As mentioned earlier, with the rise of the internet came the rise of the amateur critic. Derrick attacks these enemies directly, accusing them of only having the courage to say what they do because they're hiding behind a computer screen. No matter; all the shit talking, all the hatred and negativity only makes Sepultura work that much harder. And the detractors make them more grateful for the true fans, too. For those that believe in their music and continue to support them. With a psychotic dual lead at the beginning not too far removed from "Escape to the Void," "Mask" is a punch in the face. Over and over.

Originally written for *A-Lex*, and occasionally performed near the end of those tours, "Seethe" wasn't left off of the aforementioned album because it wasn't as good as the other tracks, but because it just didn't fit within the context of that album. It fits perfectly on *Kairos*, working off a fast, punkish beat and a progression guitarists will recognize as an acknowledgement to the verse riffs in "Dead Embryonic Cells." Featuring yet another jaw dropping lead, the tempo change halfway through the solo is again suggestive of earlier albums, and Derrick's absolutely furious vocals tell the tale of a man who, rather than succumbing to the demons of anger, uses the emotion to gain enlightenment.

The consistently brutal "Born Strong" reaches back musically to a not-so-distant past, sounding quite like a lost track from *Dante XXI*, even recalling some of the lyrics, though the majority of the message follows the theme of *Nation*. Continuing this feeling of *Dante*, "Embrace the Storm" at times comes across like a sequel to "Ostia." But the noticeably hardcore riff about halfway through sets it apart, exposing those influences of bands like Sick Of It All, Biohazard, and Agnostic Front, and the inspirational lyrics of such groups signing about drawing strength from the inevitability of change.

Derrick, up close and personal, in Albany, New York.

Revisiting the pure thrash days of *Beneath the Remains* and *Arise*, "No One Will Stand" would not have sounded out of place on either of those albums. By far the fastest song on *Kairos*, it speaks of unity, how the bullshit and the detractors brought the band closer together through the years. "No One Will Stand" attacks on all fronts, reiterating their belief that Sepultura as a whole is always greater than any of its individual parts.

Following in the tradition of collaboration with international percussion groups, "Structure Violence (Azzes)" sees the band working this time with the French Les Tambours du Bronx in another industrial nod. The two groups had met at a festival a few years prior and discussed the possibility of building something together in the future. For "Structure Violence," cultures collide, with lyrics in English, French, and Portuguese. But the bands never shared studio time; Les Tambours du Bronx worked out of France while Sepultura were recording in Brazil, the ease of the Internet allowing them to swap files back and forth to complete the song.

The digipack special edition included a pair of bonus tracks, one cover and one original. "Firestarter," originally by The Prodigy, was another idea born in the studio, out of the band's usual desire to not choose a typically metal song to record. A fun, upbeat track, "Firestarter" would later be slipped into live sets with immense crowd approval. And "Point of No Return," with its distinctive intro of muted accents and chords constructed of dissonant notes, sounds as if it could have just as easily been a bonus track for *Chaos A.D.*

With no doubt, *Kairos* achieves that "live" vibe Sepultura and Roy Z were seeking. More than half of the record was compiled of first takes, and having Derrick record his vocals in the control room, rather than an isolated vocal booth, helped create an organic, robust feel to the music. Completing this theme of the indefinable nature of time, *Kairos* contains four soundscape interludes: (2011), (1433), (5772), and (4648). Each represents the same time period, the year of *Kairos'* creation. 2011 on Gregorian calendars. 1433 on Islamic Hijri calendars. 5772 on Hebrew calendars. And 4648 on the Chinese lunar calendar. These interludes signify that time is, in essence, a made-up concept, and that our lives are a series of kairos moments. The sounds themselves are snippets of the band on the road, traversing from one place to another, passing the time in between time.

The cover, portraying a black and white winged creature both alive and decomposing, both human and not, presents the perfect visual representation of *Kairos*. The creature holds an hourglass, its sand either half emptied or half filled depending on one's perspective. Developed by Erich Sayers, a multi-talented artist who had introduced himself and his work to the band backstage at a show in Los Angeles, the *Kairos* artwork characterized Sepultura's outlook as much as it did the music contained within the package.

In April, the city of São Paulo held its annual Virada Cultural fest, a twenty-four hour party that praised and promoted cultural diversity. Sepultura landed on the bill for 2011's event. Vocally supporting the preservation of Brazilwood—without which many classical instruments such as violins, violas, and basses, could not be made—they arranged a special performance with São Paulo's Orquestra Experimental. The initiative was sparked by documentarian Otávio Juliano and Interface Films, who also happened to be compiling footage for a feature documentary spanning Sepultura's career.

The presentation opened with the orchestra alone, warming up the street crowd with Act I of Wagner's "Die Meistersinger von Nürnberg" and Sepultura's "Valtio." The band then entered the stage, in collaboration offering up rarely played (and in some cases, *never* before played) tracks like "Inquisition Symphony," "The Ways of Faith," "City of Dis," and "Ludwig Van."

Though the performance was filmed for an intended DVD release, the unpredictability of an open-air atmosphere—and in the street, no less—meant that the recording suffered from sound problems. Sepultura made loose plans to recreate the show, sometime in the future, and in a venue where they could control the acoustics a little bit better.

The North American tour rolled on a few days after Virada Cultural, the band headlining an unlikely package supported by Polish death metallers Hate and Austrian black metal monsters Belphegor. The tour, however, went over a storm, filling 1,000 and 2,000 seat arenas, the American fans happy to have Sepultura back on their shores. As *Kairos* wasn't scheduled to come out for a couple of months yet, they played only two new songs at these gigs: "Seethe," and the title track. Both received rabid receptions.

Andreas commented on the change in venue size over the years, saying, "We've been playing much smaller places and it was very hard, especially during *Against* times, to rebuild the confidence. It took a while, but we're much happier. We enjoy the music of Sepultura, the fans and everything, and we don't have to deal with any schizophrenic bullshit and baggage."

They were also taking their business as seriously as their music, working closely with Monika and Base 2 Productions as well as their agents and promoters overseas. Everything seemed to be on the up and up again, especially after *Kairos* was released in June. The disc charted in countries all over the world, received rave reviews from even the most doubtful listeners, and topped both *A-Lex* and *Dante xxi*'s numbers for first week sales. It was a well-earned reception in this day and age when few people bought records anymore.

Just after the release of *Kairos*, and just before an extensive European tour, Jean's tendonitis flared up again. As a result, the first show was rescheduled so the band would have time to find a suitable fill-in until Dolabella recovered. Luckily, their pals in Torture Squad, a thrash band from São Paulo, were in Europe touring for their *Hellbound* album. Torture Squad's drummer,

Amilcar Christófaro, had been weaned on Sepultura's music. He knew the songs inside and out, and was more than happy to sit in for the shows.

Some Sepultura devotees, however, wondered if something wasn't going on behind the scenes.

Though Dolabella's tendonitis was a real affliction, and did temporarily affect his ability to play, there was, in fact, something going on behind the scenes. But fans wouldn't learn about it until much later.

Meanwhile, Andreas was shuffling through Anthrax's catalogue and tightening his chops on those songs. Months earlier, he'd been contacted by Scott Ian, whose wife was scheduled to give birth in July, during which Anthrax would be on tour in Europe. This being Scott's first child, he wanted to be home for the delivery, but he didn't want his band to have to cancel any shows, some of which would be part of a monumental event.

The traditionally known "big four" thrash bands—Metallica, Megadeth, Anthrax, and Slayer—each with their own distinct, individual identities, were known for popularizing the metal genre in the early to mid eighties. Though Megadeth, Anthrax, and Slayer had joined forces before on a tour dubbed *Clash of the Titans*, Metallica was always a few steps above the others (and more than a few steps after the release of their eponymously titled album in 1991).

In 2010, thanks in part to renewed friendships between Megadeth leader Dave Mustaine and his former band Metallica (from which an uncontrollable and alcoholic Mustaine was unceremoniously booted in 1983), the "big four" united for the first time ever at the Sonisphere Festival in Warsaw, Poland. The one-off concert had Metallica headlining, naturally, with each of the other three groups performing nearly full-length sets for the massive, ecstatic and disbelieving audience.

Later that year, the four groups decided to extend this legacy by running *The Big 4* mini-tour the following summer. As Scott Ian would be unable to make the dates due to his impending fatherhood, he got his band's blessing to invite Andreas to fulfill the rhythm guitar duties.

Kisser joined Anthrax for a couple of their own headlining gigs, as well as four of *The Big 4* shows. Each night, at the end of Metallica's set, the members of all bands would take the stage to perform a song together.

Andreas was living the dream, high on emotion and adrenaline and *kairos*.

And while each member of Anthrax had his own shirt to perform in, showing on the back a circular representation of their logo in the dripping, spray-painted colors of the American flag, Andreas represented Brazil in his custom Anthrax shirt. His sported the same logo, but with the green, blue, and yellow of the Brazilian flag.

Immediately after the short run of dates, Kisser would get the logo tattooed on the inside of his forearm in remembrance, and to further honor his time in Anthrax, later slipped the "Madhouse" riff into live renditions of "Inner Self."

Sepultura weren't finished making their impression on 2011, either. After a string of shows in Europe, they returned to South America for a co-headlining stint with Machine Head, and in September, they became the first band to play the Rock In Rio festival four times. They brought Les Tambours du Bronx with them, integrating the French percussionists into their show, once again expanding the boundaries of what they could do.

And then they stunned their fans again.

FOURTEEN

THE HEAD, THE HEART, THE FUTURE

In early November of 2011, less than a month after Rock In Rio and with no other outward signs of trouble, the band announced the departure of Jean Dollabella. Though the news came as a shock to fans, Andreas explained that Jean's exit wasn't as sudden as it may have seemed at the time.

"Jean was leaving the band for a long time, actually," he said. "A year, year and a half before he actually left. He stayed until Rock In Rio because he wanted to do the big show, and of course, for us, it was more convenient to have him because he knew all the stuff. He knew the songs. So we knew for a year or something that he was leaving."

Though a consummate drummer, a musician's musician as it were, Jean wasn't cut from the same cloth as the other guys. The endless touring, weeks extending into months away from home and his family in São Paulo, had worn Dolabella down.

"Unfortunately," Andreas said, "he couldn't handle the road. He's not that type of musician. He's not a nomad. We did Rock In Rio, and then he left."

Known for his unfailing work ethic and an exceedingly technical, yet always creative approach to the drums, in five short years Jean had carved out a place in the hearts of fans. Though for Derrick, Andreas, and Paulo, the loss of another member was frustrating, the circumstances were understandable, and the split was amicable.

"Jean did a great job with us," Andreas said. "Great albums, really special albums, especially *Kairos*. He's here in São Paulo, building a studio."

But there were tours booked, more shows to play. *Kairos* wasn't even six months old, and the promotional cycle had only just begun. They'd experienced this before, with Igor, and the band knew they had to hit the road right away, as they had with *Dante XXI*, while the album was still fresh. They considered employing a drummer temporarily in order to finish the tours, tossing around names like former Slayer and Hail! drummer Paul Bostaph.

But fate had its own plan. While Sepultura had been suffering sound problems on the Sunset Stage at Rock In Rio, a Brazilian band called Glória was kicking off their set on the World Stage at the same time. That show would mark 20-year-old phenom drummer Eloy Casagrande's last with the band he had joined only six months earlier.

Of course the guys knew *of* Eloy; it seemed most musicians in the area did, Andreas included. "We knew he was a young wonder on drums from a very early age. He appeared on TV, he was from Santo André, which is the same region that Igor and Monika used to live. Igor's kids used to study at the same school that Eloy studied [at] for awhile. But he came after he knew we were looking for a drummer, and he was really not very satisfied with Glória, I guess. He was just doing the job. So he was more than happy to have the chance to work with us."

And a tough job it was at Rock In Rio. Glória's brand of metal was rather generic, more mainstream and geared toward teenagers and rebellious mallrats, compared to World Stage titans like Metallica and Motorhead, even Slipknot (who spurned much hatred from "true" metal fans, but had their roots deeply seated in the Florida death metal scene). Glória was greeted with boos and thrown bottles—quite like Lobão when he followed Sepultura back in 1991. At one point, Eloy recalled, a two-liter bottle filled with some unidentifiable liquid went flying past his head while he was playing, and he wondered if they would make it off the stage unscathed.

"Eloy came out of nowhere," Andreas said of his induction into Sepultura. "We were playing at the same time at Rock In Rio, with [Glória] on the World Stage—Palco Mundo—and we on the Sunset. And then a few weeks later, he came to a practice. Actually, he came to a show in São Paulo, with Angra, I think, and we met them backstage. We did an audition, but the first fucking hit on drums we knew he was the guy. He played so great, with such passion."

The groundwork was laid, the switch was made, even before anyone outside the band's inner circle knew anything was going on. On the same day—in the same press release, actually—that Sepultura revealed Jean's decision to move on, they introduced the world to their new drummer.

Born in Santo André on January 29, 1991, Eloy Casagrande Lopes was still fresh from the womb when Sepultura released their earth shattering *Arise*. At the age of six, he received his first drum set, a small, plastic toy kit, after drawing his parents' attention to the fact that he was constantly beating on things all over the house. By the age of seven, after taking some classes, he had shown such dedication to—and passion for—the instrument that they bought him a professional setup.

As with the other members of Sepultura, perhaps the greatest factor in Eloy's development as a musician was his family's unfailing support. With their assistance, he performed at church functions, trade fairs all over the country, and became known as a prodigy after appearing on television as a winner of numerous contests.

Two major competitions—and two victorious wins—gave notice of his talent. In 2004, Casagrande became champion at the Batuka International Drum Fest, held in São Paulo, exclusively for drummers under the age of thirteen. And the following year, he took first prize in the under-eighteen category of Modern Drummer's Undiscovered Drummer contest.

Known as the world's number one drum magazine, *Modern Drummer* launched Eloy into star status at just fourteen years old, in a competition that attracted hundreds of musicians from all over the globe.

After hearing of Igor Cavalera's departure in 2006, according to Paulo Jr., Eloy wanted to audition for Sepultura but was told by his parents that he was too young. Instead, he picked up several professional endorsements and joined Andre Matos' post-Angra solo band, where he continued to have a home until 2011, when called on to join Sepultura.

"I was in shock," Eloy said in the band's press release. "I'm a fan of the band for years; it'll be an honor to play with them."

Sepultura were never lacking in capable drummers. "I don't know how to put it, it's hard to explain," Andreas said, "but drums are a very natural thing here for [Brazilians]. Even myself or anybody can really beat on a bar table or something. We have that natural fucking feeling of *hit everything*."

But there was one big difference between Dolabella and Casagrande, as Andreas noted. "Jean's not really a metal guy. He has metal in his influences, but he's more of a ... like a jazz drummer. He can play anything. He's a great musician, but Eloy is more metal. Eloy is almost like a young Igor, a monster that has a lot of blood in his eyes," he said.

"Although Jean did a great job, you didn't feel that [metal influence]. He didn't know Judas Priest, for instance. He doesn't have that background—metal background—that every metal kid had. It was great, but he was not really going to last anyway on the road like that. But we're very lucky to have such musicians available for us when we need."

Eloy's initiation came swift. Less than two weeks after his public induction, this newest incarnation of Sepultura took off to Europe to co-headline a month's worth of *Thrashfest Classics* dates with Exodus. The theme of the tour had each band on the bill only performing songs from their most "classic" thrashiest albums, so Sepultura's set list consisted of tracks from *Beneath the Remains, Arise*, and *Chaos A.D.* (though the latter wasn't necessarily a thrash record, per se).

Their inclusion on the *Thrashfest Classics* lineup confused Sepultura at first, not because they didn't belong there—they most certainly did—but because they couldn't understand the point. They'd just released *Kairos*, an incredibly vital and strong album that preached the concept of paying tribute to the past without reliving it. To tour in support of *Kairos*, but not play any of it? It didn't exactly make sense.

But the more they'd considered the idea, the more exciting it became. It would be a fun way to revisit songs not performed live in years. And when it was over, that was it. They would move right back on to business as usual.

Those shows blew the doors off of every club that had the pleasure of hosting it. Exodus' Gary Holt frequently jammed with Sepultura, Andreas doing the same with Exodus. Tour mates Destruction and Heathen joined in for raucous versions of "Kaiowas." And night after night, Casagrande left audience members in shock, their teeth on the floor, with his precise and powerful skills, and his introductory drum solo to "Subtraction," especially. Already people began speculating about the *next* Sepultura album, wondering what this wunderkind was going to come up with in the studio.

The band wondered, too, feeling Eloy's hunger and talent lifting them to a new level.

Derrick, Paulo, and Andreas grew more in sync with Casagrande as the concerts went on. After a brief holiday rest, they dove right into Eastern Europe and the Baltics in 2012, and spent almost three weeks in Russia—the most extensive tour there yet—destroying the most obscure venues they could find. Mere days after the final show in Minsk, Belarus, Sepultura were again on American soil, their second North American jaunt in less than a year. The opening night, at the Yost Theater in Santa Ana, California, producer and guitarist extraordinaire, Roy Z, leant his talents to a rendition of Ministry's "Just One Fix" that saw Roy and Andreas trading extended guitar solos.

This tour, also including old-school thrashers Death Angel and new-school thrashers Havok, was special for another reason. For the first time ever, Sepultura toured *outside* of Brazil with another Brazilian band.

Krisiun's story wasn't so different from Sepultura's. They grew up on many of the same groups—Slayer, Morbid Angel, Kreator—and like Sepultura, Krisiun relocated to São Paulo in their early days for greater opportunity (though they came from Rio Grande do Sul, rather than Minas Gerais). Sepultura enjoyed giving something back to their local scene, since they were the band that opened this international door for other Brazilian groups.

And they'd had a long-established connection already. Krisiun's vocalist and bassist, Alex Camargo Kolesne had growled out verses of "Necromancer" with Derrick back in 2005 for the "Live in São Paulo" recordings.

A quick run through South America followed, and then yet another trek through Europe (which began with the reunion of Sepultura and Les Tambours du Bronx, this time at Rock In Rio, Lisbon). In June, the band flew back to the United States to take part in the first annual Orion Fest, hand picked by the host band, Metallica.

Returning to Europe to for the standard summer festivals, Sepultura decimated the stages at Germany's Wacken (once more with Les Tambours du Bronx) and Summer Breeze, England's Bloodstock, and Austria's RockInn Mountain Open Air, among others, as usual playing smaller, more intimate shows on the off days.

In November, after ten years away from one of their most rabid markets, Sepultura arrived in Indonesia to give fans a chance to see Derrick and Eloy in action. The turnout in Tenggarong, Jakarta, and Makassar was just as phenomenal as the cities they'd played for a decade earlier. In Tenggarong alone, they sold out a soccer stadium—some 40,000 people—with no other acts on the bill.

Indonesian fans were ecstatic to be seeing their Brazilian brothers again after so long, and the feeling was mutual.

Sepultura spent the year's end in style, on a cruise ship that ran a trip from Miami, Florida to the Bahamas and back. With over forty metal bands playing over the course of the journey, the so-called Barge To Hell was every headbanger's dream; a chance for fans to mingle with their favorite bands in a relaxing, vacation environment, where every night ended with alcohol and debauchery and devastating live performances.

Backstage at Orion Fest with Metallica's James Hetfield.

When 2012 came to a close the newly recharged band split off to enjoy some down time before writing the next disc. Derrick and Sam Spiegel finally released their long awaited Maximum Hedrum full-length album and set out on a short tour. Among the highlights was a hosted residency at Los Globos in Los Angeles, as well as performing at South by Southwest in Texas and appearing on former MTV host Carson Daly's late night television program.

Eloy, Andreas, and Yohan Kisser backstage at Metallica's Orion Festival.

Eloy lined up a batch of drum workshops across Brazil, and rejoined his Christian side band Iahweh for a few select shows. Even Paulo stayed busy this time, recording a guest spot for Belo Horizonte's Eminence (a band for which Jairo Guedz also used to play bass), and finally completing the debut album for his other band, The Unabomber Files, with Chakal vocalist and *Schizophrenia* contributor Vladimir Korg.

Andreas, ever consumed in work, began hosting "Pegadas de Andreas Kisser," a weekly radio show broadcast from Brazil to the world via the internet. The program was notable for its support of homegrown bands, always with an interest to turn non-Brazilian listeners on to groups they might not have heard otherwise. Kisser also took part in a new musical project, De La Tierra, a sort of Latin American super group featuring members of Maná, D-Mente, and Fabulosos Cadillacs.

Even though Derrick Green had, in his early days with Sepultura, slung on a guitar for a few live tracks, De La Tierra presented a new challenge for Andreas in the studio.

"It's the first time I'm playing with another guitarist after Max, after so long, and it's not easy to put two guitars together. You really have to know each other, and [me and Andrés Giminez] didn't play that much at all, but we're doing a pretty good job of putting together an arrangement and making it sound like a band," he said, laughing. "We practiced a little and he's a great musician, as well, and everybody's really connected."

Again, perhaps as a result of this project or because of Kisser's frequent jam sessions in Brazilian bars with his son Yohan on guitar, people started speculating about a possible vacancy in Sepultura's rhythm section.

"There are many people talking about Yohan, my son. Everybody's like, 'Oh, you're gonna put him in Sepultura?' Dude… he has a life to live," he said, laughing again, and shaking his head. "I don't want to do that to the kid, put him in the prison. He's more than welcome to jam, of course, but I think it would be too much for him. He's starting something of himself, he wants to do his own music and his own stuff.

"It would be a great experience, to be on the road. He actually did some shows on tour last year, in the summer, in Europe. He spent fifteen days of his vacation time with us on the road, and he jammed "Ratamahatta" with us and stuff. It was great. I don't have a problem doing that, but to officialize, you know, 'This is the guitar player…' It's too much for him. There's a lot at stake, if you go to a new place like that. And he deserves better, in the very best way of saying. He deserves better for his own life. He has to build something from himself, for himself."

Andreas went on, once more pondering this question of adding a second guitar and why some people felt it so important. "A different instrument there will make [the sound] bigger only if it is very tight. I mean, that's what I said: here [recording De La Tierra] we are finding ourselves now. This has a lot of room to get much better. Now we are knowing each other as guitar players ... me and Max, we were like, as one, pretty much. We played so much together. Since I joined the band, we used to practice every day, man. Every day. There was something very sacred for us about that. And very passionate. We loved to do that. And we'd go to the practice room every day and we'd play and play," he said, a touch of nostalgia entering his voice. "We'd play some covers, but we'd write ... we wrote a lot. And then we built that kind of style we had together, so ... it takes time."

Side projects notwithstanding, Sepultura remained everyone's number one priority, and the writing for album number thirteen progressed smoothly and quickly with the injection of Eloy's energy. The band's 30th anniversary loomed, and 2012 *did* bring a pair of reunions worth mentioning. After stepping down from his post at the dissolving Roadrunner Records, Monte Conner entered into a partnership to expand Nuclear Blast's US branch, bringing Monte and Sepultura back together on the same label. And at the end of the year, Ross Robinson leaked via Twitter that he had spoken to Andreas about producing the next record.

Thirty years into their career, the band were in a manner of speaking returning to their "roots." Some of the members had changed, the studio had changed (Richard Kaplan sold Indigo Ranch, and Robinson had set up shop with his own beachfront studio in Venice, California), but the spirit of Sepultura was still alive and kicking.

To everyone's relief, the vibe had changed from the last time they'd worked together, too. Even Ross mentioned that the atmosphere in the studio this time around was much less stressful, much more positive, and more conducive to creating something magical. Gone was the drama, gone were the arguments.

And looking back on their last collaboration, Ross realized they all had something to prove.

Partnering with Robinson was Steve Evetts, who Sepultura hadn't worked with since *Roorback*. It felt like a homecoming, long lost friends and family that hadn't seen each other in years, grown older and wiser and more grateful for such relationships.

Eloy tore through the drum tracks within a matter of days. As was Ross's way, while recording, he joined the whole band in a tiny jam room to *feel* the music and the spiritual connection between its creators. He absorbed the sounds, let them flow through him, physically responding in an infectious manner that filled the room—and everyone in it—with electricity.

In an exclusive partnership with Brazilian newspaper *Diario de Pernambuco* and journalist Emanuel Leite Jr., Andreas detailed the recording process in frequently written studio diaries. He explained that, due to certain circumstances, they were forced to do things a little differently this time around.

Typical sessions went like this: the whole band would jam the songs together, each instrument recorded onto its own isolated channel, allowing the drummer to put his parts down with the vigor of a live performance. Once the drums were completed, the guitars came next, built on top of the "scratch" tracks made while jamming the songs together. After the guitars, bass tracks were done the same way, with leads, vocals, and other assorted bits coming last.

This time, however, Derrick had to miss some of the sessions because of a previously confirmed mini-tour he'd committed to with Maximum Hedrum. So, rather than wait until the songs were finished before recording the vocals, Derrick sang his parts song by song as Andreas laid down the rhythm guitars.

As usual, they were always experimenting, always striving to do something different. The spontaneity of recording in such a way added to the live power of the record, as Andreas testified.

The studio received a couple of unexpected visitors in Dino Cazares and legendary Slayer skinsman Dave Lombardo. In the latter's case, Lombardo had sent Ross a text message saying he was in the area, out walking with his dog. The producer immediately wrote back, asking if the drummer would like to stop in and do something with Sepultura. Lombardo jumped at the opportunity.

It was yet another historical moment for Sepultura, and for Eloy especially, collaborating with the man who had developed a unique and instantly recognizable style of playing thrash metal. Even though the drum tracks were already completed, Ross and Evetts moved two kits into a parlor area, just in front of a large glass entryway that faced the sea. They quickly set up microphones, not wanting to waste the magic of the moment. With no cymbals or accoutrements, only drums, Eloy and Lombardo broke out an incredible tribal jam that was later inserted seamlessly into a song called "Obsessed."

The anticipation building behind the new album was intense. Palpable. Many believed the band was about to make a statement again, with Eloy, with Ross, with some of the most powerful music of their career. And in an innovative move, the title showed them again cracking their creative spine. Rather than a short, one or two word sentiment that would get the point across succinctly, they chose a phrase inspired by the classic silent film Metropolis. *The Mediator Between Head and Hands Must Be the Heart.* Some loved it, some hated it. But everyone was talking about it.

The title, as Andreas explained, was a reference to the modern day condition, how society in general is becoming more faceless, more robotized with the proliferation of social media and Internet relationships. But the heart lies at the root of our existence. It is what binds mankind together and keeps us human. It keeps us sympathetic. It keeps us alive and empathetic and real.

As of this writing, only the track list and the cover has been released to the public, song titles such as "The Age of the Atheist," "Impending Doom," "Trauma of War," and "The Bliss of Ignorants" revealing the theme, the necessity of heart, and how difficult it is to truly believe in anything these days. How difficult it is to remain hopeful.

In a timely move, when millions of fed up citizens took to the streets in Brazil to protest the rising costs of hosting 2014's World Cup—while hospital conditions suffered and children starved— Andreas sent his support to the people back home, insisting they keep hope alive, reminding them it is never a wasted effort.

But as hard as they tried, Sepultura could never escape drama. The same day *Diario de Pernambuco* revealed the image of Alexandre Wagner's charcoal drawing that graced *The Mediator*'s cover, Gloria Cavalera announced that Max's autobiography would be released, conveniently, in just four days. She promised the book would be controversial, and it would spill truths that had been buried for seventeen years. That it would finally tell the *real* story of why Max left the band.

This version purported that Gloria parted from Sepultura of her own free will, and had been planning to leave for some time before the end of 1996. The book also contained Cavalera's most scathing attacks on his former band mates and friends yet, with Paulo and Monika taking the brunt of the damage, leading one to wonder—for a man who was so vocal about wanting a "reunion"—what exactly he hoped to achieve.

"Let them do their things, we'll do our things," Monika said, resigned, but clearly a little agitated. "It's okay for us, we don't care. But why do they have to attack people? How many times I had to stop my car because [Gloria] was on the phone talking about the reunion, how good that could be, and we could get a lot of money, all the records, all the merchandise, all that. She said that she was going to split with me and then we'd be together on tour, she was really nice. But we've been very busy and I just want them to leave us alone. Do your thing, let us do our thing. The reunion is not going to happen because it's not supposed to happen. That's what I told Gloria the first time I spoke to her on the phone."

She continued, "But with all this situation, I never talked anything about anyone. But then [Max] decided to come after me for no reason … or maybe my work is so good that it's beginning to affect his."

The timing of the book's release, coupled with the supposed contentiousness of the text, may have been an attempt to steal some of Sepultura's thunder.

Because there was a lot of thunder being made by Sepultura.

Voices "in the know" murmured that *The Mediator* was by far the band's strongest work in years, rivaling even their earliest classics, that it would silence critics who insisted the band should have called it quits in 1996. With bonus cover songs from Death, as well as Chico Science and Nação Zumbi, the album again paid tribute to Sepultura's roots while not being defined by them.

And Monika had secured not just one night for the band at September's Rock In Rio, but two.

The first night had them sharing the stage again with Les Tambours du Bronx, this time for a DVD recording, and the second a special performance alongside Zé Ramalho. No other band—domestic or international—had played Rock In Rio as many times as Sepultura, and no other band had ever been graced the opportunity to play two complete sets on two different evenings.

What a change from 1991, when promoters placed them on the bill out of obligation, expecting them to disappear with no fanfare to speak of.

And 2014—Sepultura's 30th anniversary—held much in store, as well, with the career-spanning documentary finally planned

Soundchecking with Les Tambours Du Bronx on Rock In Rio's Palco Mundo.

for release, the usual rounds of relentless touring, and a number of other surprises.

As was their way, Andreas, Paulo, Derrick, and Eloy were marching forward, refusing to be distracted by the drama hurled at them by the media and former associates. In their every action, they showed that the name Sepultura had come to represent so much more than just music, so much more than just the people involved in its creation. Everything about the band's history—the good things and the bad things as well—had imbued the name with a deeper meaning, a spiritual meaning. *Sepultura* has become a symbol of struggle and persistence, of never giving in, of fighting onward even when times seem bleak. It stands for adaptation and evolution, and a refusal to stay complacent, as shown over and over again in this story.

It fact, it has come to mean the very opposite of its root origins; it's not about death, it's about life.

"The name is something that I have a lot of pride in and a lot of respect for," Derrick said. "Throughout the years, Sepultura has always had this. Truly, because it is always gonna be a struggle with the band. If you know anything about the band, from the beginning to where it is now, it has been a constant battle and nothing has ever really been easy for many different circumstances. Just the fact of being from a Third World country, to different people changing in the group, different management, different labels changing around ... just all the drama that involves dealing with the business aspect of it. But I feel that we have always been able to hold our heads up high with the name Sepultura. It is something that we truly believe in and respect."

Even today, Paulo still takes the bus.

Early morning check-in for the 4th Annual Bandas de Garage Festival in Brazil.

Though Green may not have been around for the creation of the name, he absolutely played a part in defining it.

"It is an incredible phenomena that the name is still relevant in conversations, even if you do not like what has happened in the past or what is happening now in Sepultura. It does not matter! It is still a topic of conversation just because there is so much mystery, legend, and myth behind it—along with things that are very real, very emotional, very passionate, and very strong. And I believe the name has always had different characters due to the incredible history that has happened."

"I think it means spirit," Andreas said. "The musical spirit. Let's say the word in the dictionary does not have any meaning; Sepultura means not grave, but the music we do, the style, the way we do our stuff, and that is what really keeps us together. To always try to find something new, find a challenge for us. That is why we are still here, despite all the changes. And of course, a lot of people have their own idea of what Sepultura should be or what Sepultura is.

"It is hard to define, but we know what Sepultura is all about and that is why we still enjoy working with each other, having this privilege to travel the world and represent Brazil everywhere, and going to new places—every year we visit a new place—where we have never been before. It's great! It is always to fulfill something. I think that is the spirit of the name."

Paulo agreed, adding, "Of course, I think there's been evolution; whoever is in the band—since day one up to now—really understands and knows how to represent the name. We could say we've created a monster and, even when very important pieces have left the band in the past, the name keeps strong and whoever comes in to fill up a place realizes and knows how to do it, in a way to not disappoint anyone. In these days, I think the name itself is stronger than any of the members."

But *Sepultura* also stands for passion and dedication, as Andreas affirms.

"If we did not have the passion, we would not be here. We are not slaves of ourselves," he said, restating an important theme that defines his personal beliefs. "We are not slaves of the name Sepultura. We recreate this name every day and that is because we love what we do, and all the rest is consequence. Being on stage is the best, but you have the consequence of traveling—planes, bus, snow and some shit just to get to that point. Loving what we do, we deal with the consequences of that."

Those consequences, however, can be hell if the people involved don't get along. It's one of the most common reasons why bands break up. But being in Sepultura now, without all the drama, without having to deal with the stress of certain interpersonal relationships, was more fun than ever.

"That's the way it's supposed to be," Andreas said. "You're already away from your family, and you don't want to live in hell. You wanna be with friends, and people you believe have the same point of view—not the same point of view, but the same objectives—and we are together in this battle. We gotta enjoy the ride. Always."

As he had mentioned earlier, why bother continuing if it only makes you miserable? This is a universal maxim, applying to every professional field outside of the music business. But it also applies to life in general, a testament to the value of change. We all strive to be happy and content. If circumstances are preventing you from achieving those successes, change the circumstances.

Many have wondered if the split in 1996 could've been avoided. For Sepultura, things *had* to change. And since then, they've all been unified in never going back to that place.

As Derrick explained, "I definitely see the future moving forward, never looking back. That is one thing that has made the band able to keep alive, actually moving forward and trying to recreate itself. For us, it is always important to keep very open and not put ourselves into a locked situation like, *this is the direction we have to go*. I think it better just to let things naturally happen and when we get to this certain point—where we need to go—it is definitely always going to be forward. As artists," he reasserted, "that is something extremely important for us."

Paulo summed it all up, reflecting on the life of a professional musician. "For most musicians," he said, "it's very hard. For me, I think, we've been very lucky to have such a special and strong thing going on. Most of the musicians play in a bar or have a second job and we have mostly dedicated our lives to Sepultura. We have had the chance to see places that could take more than a lifetime for a person.

"However, it's a very hard life. What we have chosen is a different type of job. In fact it's more than a job; it's more like a lifestyle to which you are devoted, which you can never stop. To consider that musicians, and artists in general, have no retirement plan—you retire when you die. So, if you are eighty-years-old and you can play, then you go and play.

"To artists, to musicians, there is not such a thing like retirement after forty years of service. You keep going until you're dead."

And for Sepultura, thirty years on, there is no grave in sight.

DISCOGRAPHY

STUDIO ALBUMS

Morbid Visions – Cogumelo Records, 1986
Schizophrenia – Cogumelo Records, 1987
Beneath the Remains – Roadracer Records, 1989
Arise – Roadrunner Records, 1991
Chaos A.D. – Epic/Roadrunner Records, 1993
Roots – Roadrunner Records, 1996
Against – Roadrunner Records, 1998
Nation – Roadrunner Records, 2001
Roorback (A 2–disc edition was packaged with the Revolusongs EP as a bonus) – SPV/Steamhammer, 2003
Dante XXI – SPV/ Steamhammer, 2006
A-Lex – SPV/Steamhammer, 2009
Kairos – Nuclear Blast, 2011
The Mediator Between Head and Hands Must Be the Heart – Nuclear Blast, 2013

EPS

Bestial Devastation (split with Overdose) – Cogumelo Records, 1985
Third World Posse – Roadracer Records, 1992
Refuse/Resist – Roadrunner Records, 1994
Natural Born Blasters – FM Records, 1996
Procreation of the Wicked – Roadrunner Records, 1997
Tribus – Roadrunner Records (Australia), 1999
Revolusongs (Only pressed in Brazil, Japan, Taiwan, and Argentina) – 2002

SINGLES

"Arise" – Roadrunner Records, 1991
"Dead Embryonic Cells" – Roadrunner Records, 1991
"Under Siege (Regnum Irae)" – Roadrunner Records, 1991
"Territory" – Roadrunner Records, 1993
"Refuse/Resist" – Roadrunner Records, 1994
"Slave New World" – Roadrunner Records, 1994
"Roots Bloody Roots" – Roadrunner Records, 1996
"Attitude" – Roadrunner Records, 1996
"Ratamahatta" – Roadrunner Records, 1996
"Choke" – Roadrunner Records, 1998

"Against" – Roadrunner Records, 1999
"Convicted in Life" – SPV/ Steamhammer, 2006
"Coquinho" (Promotional track written for a Brazilian Volkswagen commercial) – 2008
"Kairos" – Nuclear Blast, 2011
"The Age of the Atheist" – Nuclear Blast, 2013

LIVE ALBUMS

Under a Pale Grey Sky – Roadrunner Records, 2002
Live in São Paulo – SPV/ Steamhammer, 2005
Metal Veins – Alive at Rock in Rio (with Les Tambours Du Bronx) – MZA Music/Eagle Rock Entertainment, 2014

COMPILATIONS

Morbid Visions/Bestial Devastation (Featuring both recordings on one disc; notable as this was the first time *Bestial Devastation* was officially made available in the US) – Roadracer Records, 1991
The Roots of Sepultura (Collection of B-sides, demos, covers, live tracks, and selections from the "Rock in Rio" mix of *Arise*) – Roadrunner Records, 1996

Blood-Rooted – Roadrunner Records, 1997
B-Sides – Roadrunner Records (Brazil) – 1997
RDP + Sepultura – We Are a Fuckin' Shit! – 80's Jam Sessions – Rotthenness Records (Brazil), 2000

HOME VIDEOS

Under Siege (Live in Barcelona) – Roadrunner Records, 1992
Third World Chaos – Roadrunner Records, 1995
We Are What We Are – Roadrunner Records, 1997
Chaos DVD (Repackaging of *Under Siege, Third World Chaos,* and *We Are What We Are,* all of which had gone out of print) – Roadrunner Records, 2002
Live in São Paulo – SPV/ Steamhammer, 2005
Metal Veins – Alive at Rock in Rio (with Les Tambours Du Bronx) – MZA Music/Eagle Rock Entertainment, 2014

MUSIC VIDEOS

"Inner Self" – 1989
"Dead Embryonic Cells" – 1991
"Arise" – 1992
"Refuse/Resist" – 1993
"Territory" – 1993

"Slave New World" – 1994
"Roots Bloody Roots" – 1996
"Attitude" – 1996
"Ratamahatta" – 1996
"Choke" – 1998
"Bullet the Blue Sky" – 2003
"Mindwar" – 2004
"Refuse/Resist" (live version
from *Live in São Paulo*)
– 2005
"Convicted in Life" – 2006
"Ostia" – 2008
"We've Lost You" – 2009
"What I Do!" – 2009
"The Vatican" – 2013
"Da Lama ao Caos" – 2014
"Roots Bloody Roots" (live
version from *Metal Veins*)
– 2014
"Spectrum" (live version from
Metal Veins) – 2014

OTHER APPEARANCES

*Nativity in Black: A Tribute
to Black Sabbath*
(Contributed "Symptom of
the Universe") – Sony, 1994
*Sanguinho Novo... Arnaldo
Baptista Revisitado*
(Contributed a cover of
the Os Mutantes track, "A
Hora e a Vez do Cabelo
Nascer") – Eldorado, 1989
Virus 100 (A tribute to Dead
Kennedys, for which the
band contributed their
version of "Drug Me") –
Alternative Tentacles, 1992
*Tales from the Crypt: Demon
Knight – Soundtrack*
(Contributed their version
of the Titãs track "Policia")
– Atlantic Records, 1995
Instinto Coletivo ao Vivo
(Collaboration with
O Rappa on the track
"Niguém Regula a
América") – Warner Music,
2001
Freddy vs. Jason – Soundtrack
(Contributed "The Waste,"
an alternate version
of "Kamaitachi," with
Mike Patton on vocals) -
Roadrunner Records, 2003
Lisbela e o Prisoneiro
(Collaboration with Zé
Ramalho on the track "A
Dança das Borboletas") –
Natasha, 2003

ACKNOWLEDGMENTS

When I began this project a couple of years ago, I never imagined it would become the monster it has. From the beginning, it was simply intended as a passion project to celebrate a band I've adored since I stole my friend's *Under Siege: Live in Barcelona* videocassette way back in 1992. After all, I'd already written four books and knew everything there was to know about the band (or so I thought), so... it should be easy, right?

Hardly.

It may have been the most difficult undertaking yet. But it was—by far—the most rewarding. The lack of sleep, the stress of repeatedly missing self-imposed deadlines, the thousands of dollars spent on coffee and other assorted caffeinated beverages was all worth it. I am so grateful for the friends I have made and the people I've spoken to over the last year especially; fans, band members, family members. Nearly everyone I contacted was more than willing to help out in any way possible, and there just aren't enough words in any language to express my gratitude.

Above all, though, I have to thank Lourdinha Novo for her unfailing love and encouragement (even when I was grumpy or stressed out or tired or mentally absent or...), the countless hours she spent translating interviews or hunting down old Brazilian news articles, critiquing my work, patiently listening to me tell her the same story a hundred times, insisting I remain impartial even when I wanted so badly to spew my personal opinions. Without her, this book would not exist. Love you, babyzinha.

Digging into this story and the people involved in it, digging deeper into music I was already so familiar with, gave me an even greater appreciation and respect for what this band has done, and for what they continue to do. To Sepultura as a whole: thank you. You kick ass, and you're nothing short of an inspiration. As long as you keep making music, I'll keep headbanging at the front of the stage.

So many people helped turn this small idea—a biography spanning thirty years—from a dream into a reality, and to each of them I owe so much. My unofficial agent and manager Monika Bass Cavalera; Andreas, Patricia, and the Kisser family; Derrick Green; Jairo Guedz, Paulo Xisto, Jean Dolabella, Eloy Casagrande and the entire Sepulfamily for your support, openness, and approval from day one; The Great Antonio "Toninho" Coelho, Djalma "Thrashão" Agra, Tuka Quinelli, and Eric de Haas for the memories; Emanuel Leite Jr., for translation assistance and more help than I could ever possibly repay, and Diario de Pernambuco; Nicolás Jara Miranda for graciously providing a wealth of interview material, Silvio "Bibika" Gomes and André Barcinski, Joan KSK, Carlos Inciarte, Nick French, Milton Bratfisch Junior, Sami Saarela, Douglas Cirilo, Derek Novaes, Felipe Sanchez, Philipe Jacquemin, SOBFC, Sepularmy and Sepultribe friends worldwide for your help and passion; Rodrigo Bill Abecia; Alexey Kurkdjian; Phil Demmel; Johnny Kelly; Kymm Britton and Jason Newsted; Roy Z Ramirez; Nestor Junior; Rogério Alves, Déborah Guterman, Paula Carvalho, Renato Abramovicius and everyone at Editora Saraiva/Benvirá; Roberto Candido Francisco; Filip Karpow and all at In Rock, Poland; Borivoj Krgin and Blabbermouth.net; Marcelo Coleto at Rock Noize in Brazil; Nuno Costa at SoundZone Magazine in Portugal; RollingStone Indonesia; RollingStone Brasil; Nacho Belgrande and all at Whiplash.net; Manifesto Bar; my family, of course…

And to anyone I forgot, please forgive me. I'll add you to the revised edition that comes out when the band celebrates its semicentennial anniversary in twenty years.

THE ROLL OF HONOUR

Andrew Allison
Jose Augusto
 Nunes Vieira De
 Andrade
Heatsy Angel
Masafumi Arai
Kester Baird
Jeff Scott Brown
Benjamin Carette
Eric 'Viking'
 Chenoix
Jason Cichon
Victor Magalhaes
 Costa
Thomas Cotterill
Tony Cox
James Crone
Dorothy Davis
Mike Davis
Betty (Momz)
 Davis-Ricker
Andreas Eberhardt
Shannon Frye
Eduardo Garcia
Amer Garic
Leomar Pereira
 Gehling
Alex Gerlach
Steve Gray
Thomas Le Guenan
Jonas 'Gaston'
 Högberg
Matthew L. Heath
 (mhsepultura)
Kristjan B.
 Heidarsson
Ian Helps
Javier HkB

Darren Hollander
Oliver Holm
Philippe Jacquemin
Chris 'Johnno'
 Johnson
Justin Jowett
Sean Kernaghan
Bas Klomp
Piotr Kosc
Andreas Krispler
Markus Krispler
Kevin McDonald
Shane Meade
Sven Milewski
Clifton Igor Morris
Eric Nagel
Chuck Ninesling
Nicholas Nolan
Marius Evensen,
 Sepularmy
 Norway
Derek 'Sepulfreak'
 Novaes
Maria de Lourdes
 Peres Novo
Michal Xavantes
 Novoveský
Ethan O'Neill
Dan Pearsall
Marcus Vinicius
 Fonseca Popini
Partha Rathore
Stepultura Richards
Mark-Jan van Rijn
Gorka Rodrigo
John Ivar Roeste
Conroy Rowley
Sami Ruokangas

Sami Saarela
Rodrigo Salan
Felipe Sanchez
Thomas Sand
Christopher
 Santana
Andrew Sawtell
Nicolás sabotaje77
 Sepularmy
Nick Shortland
Trish Cat Shriver
Juan A. Simon
Soren Slaug
Melissa Slayman
Mike Sletten
Olaf & Thommy
 Sopakuwa
Igor Souza
Rebecca Stockman
Jean Taraud
Peter Van Tendeloo
Gabriel Teykal
Andy Thorn
Paolo Tiseo
Roman Tschopp
Florin Ungur
Carlos Veloso
Antti Vitikainen
Jeremy Wafford
Willem Wallinga
Jon (Muppet)
 Walton
Mariko Walton
Alexander
 Weiszhaupt
Gustav Ziolkowski
Marijn Zwart

PICTURE CREDITS

ABOUT THE AUTHOR

Jason Korolenko is a widely published writer of horror fiction and music journalism. *Relentless* has also been published in Brazil and Poland.

SPECIAL EDITIONS

BARRETT: THE DEFINITIVE VISUAL COMPANION TO THE LIFE OF SYD BARRETT
Russell Beecher and Will Shutes

"Beautifully packaged, eruditely written and full of insight (but, inevitably, tinged with sadness), Barrett feels like the ultimate work of art."
MOJO

ISBN (Classic Edition) 9781906615109
ISBN (Signature Edition) 9781906615116

FAIRPORT BY FAIRPORT
Fairport Convention with Nigel Schofield
ISBN (hardback) 9781906615482

DINOSAUR JR.
Dinosaur Jr.
ISBN (Classic Edition) 9781906615826
ISBN (Signature Edition) 9781906615420

VINTAGE BLACK GLAMOUR
Nichelle Gainer
ISBN (hardback) 9781906615895

MUSIC & CULTURE

THE CLASH
The Clash
ISBN (ePub & Kindle) 9781906615093

ESSENTIAL NEIL YOUNG
Steve Grant
ISBN (ePub) 9781906615505
ISBN (Kindle) 9781906615499

I WAS A TEENAGE SEX PISTOL
Glen Matlock with Peter Silverton
ISBN (hardback) 9781906615352
ISBN (paperback) 9781906615369
ISBN (ePub) 9781906615383
ISBN (Kindle) 9781906615376

LIFTING SHADOWS: THE AUTHORIZED BIOGRAPHY OF DREAM THEATER
Rich Wilson
ISBN (paperback) 9781906615581

PINK MOON – A STORY ABOUT NICK DRAKE
Gorm Henrik Rasmussen
ISBN (hardback) 9781906615284
ISBN (paperback) 9781906615291
ISBN (ePub) 9781906615246
ISBN (Kindle) 9781906615239

rocket88books.com

CPSIA information can be obtained at www.ICGtesting.com
Printed in the USA
BVOW03s0244070115

382276BV00011B/57/P